MTEL

English (07) Exam

SECRETS

Study Guide
Your Key to Exam Success

MTEL Test Review for the
Massachusetts Tests for Educator Licensure

Dear Future Exam Success Story:

Congratulations on your purchase of our study guide. Our goal in writing our study guide was to cover the content on the test, as well as provide insight into typical test taking mistakes and how to overcome them.

Standardized tests are a key component of being successful, which only increases the importance of doing well in the high-pressure high-stakes environment of test day. How well you do on this test will have a significant impact on your future, and we have the research and practical advice to help you execute on test day.

The product you're reading now is designed to exploit weaknesses in the test itself, and help you avoid the most common errors test takers frequently make.

How to use this study guide

We don't want to waste your time. Our study guide is fast-paced and fluff-free. We suggest going through it a number of times, as repetition is an important part of learning new information and concepts.

First, read through the study guide completely to get a feel for the content and organization. Read the general success strategies first, and then proceed to the content sections. Each tip has been carefully selected for its effectiveness.

Second, read through the study guide again, and take notes in the margins and highlight those sections where you may have a particular weakness.

Finally, bring the manual with you on test day and study it before the exam begins.

Your success is our success

We would be delighted to hear about your success. Send us an email and tell us your story. Thanks for your business and we wish you continued success.

Sincerely,

Mometrix Test Preparation Team

Need more help? Check out our flashcards at: http://MometrixFlashcards.com/MTEL

Copyright © 2016 by Mometrix Media LLC. All rights reserved.
Written and edited by the Mometrix Exam Secrets Test Prep Team
Printed in the United States of America

TABLE OF CONTENTS

Top 20 Test Taking Tips

1. Carefully follow all the test registration procedures
2. Know the test directions, duration, topics, question types, how many questions
3. Setup a flexible study schedule at least 3-4 weeks before test day
4. Study during the time of day you are most alert, relaxed, and stress free
5. Maximize your learning style; visual learner use visual study aids, auditory learner use auditory study aids
6. Focus on your weakest knowledge base
7. Find a study partner to review with and help clarify questions
8. Practice, practice, practice
9. Get a good night's sleep; don't try to cram the night before the test
10. Eat a well balanced meal
11. Know the exact physical location of the testing site; drive the route to the site prior to test day
12. Bring a set of ear plugs; the testing center could be noisy
13. Wear comfortable, loose fitting, layered clothing to the testing center; prepare for it to be either cold or hot during the test
14. Bring at least 2 current forms of ID to the testing center
15. Arrive to the test early; be prepared to wait and be patient
16. Eliminate the obviously wrong answer choices, then guess the first remaining choice
17. Pace yourself; don't rush, but keep working and move on if you get stuck
18. Maintain a positive attitude even if the test is going poorly
19. Keep your first answer unless you are positive it is wrong
20. Check your work, don't make a careless mistake

Copyright © Mometrix Media. You have been licensed one copy of this document for personal use only. Any other reproduction or redistribution is strictly prohibited. All rights reserved.

Literature and Language

William Faulkner

William Faulkner lived in the state of Mississippi in the United States of America from 1897-1962. He is known as one of the greatest authors of Southern literature in America, and of American literature in general. Faulkner wrote one play, poems, essays, screenplays, and especially novels and short stories. He based his writing on his experience living in Mississippi during the early 20th century. Many of his short stories and novels are set in a fictional Southern county modeled on the two counties where he lived. Faulkner was awarded the 1949 Nobel Prize for Literature and two Pulitzer Prizes for Fiction, both for novels: one for *A Fable* in 1954, and another for *The Reivers*, his final novel, in 1962. Titles of some of his best-known works include the novels *The Sound and the Fury; As I Lay Dying; Light in August; Absalom, Absalom!;* and the short story *A Rose for Emily.*

Geoffrey Chaucer

The Canterbury Tales
Medieval poet Geoffrey Chaucer (c. 1343-1400), called the "Father of English Literature," chiefly wrote long narrative poems, including *The Book of the Duchess, Anelida and Arcite, The House of Fame, The Parlement of Foules, The Legend of Good Women,* and *Troilus and Criseyde.* His most famous work is *The Canterbury Tales.* Its historical and cultural context is life during the Middle Ages, representing a cross-section of society—tradespeople, professionals, nobility, clergy, and housewives, among others, and religious pilgrimages, a common practice of the time. Its literary context is a frame-tale, that is, a story within a story. Chaucer described a varied group of pilgrims all on their way to Canterbury, taking turns telling stories to amuse the others. Tales encompass a broad range of subjects: bawdy comedy, chivalry, romance, and religion. These include *The Knight's Tale, The Miller's Tale, The Reeve's Tale, The Cook's Tale, The Man of Law's Tale, The Wife of Bath's Tale, The Friar's Tale, The Summoner's Tale, The Clerk's Tale, The Merchant's Tale, The Squire's Tale, The Franklin's Tale, The Physician's Tale, The Pardoner's Tale, The Nun's Priest's Tale,* and others.

The Parlement of Foules
In the brief preface to his poem "The Parlement of Foules," Geoffrey Chaucer refers to ancient Classical Roman author Cicero's "The Dream of Scipio." This was a philosophical dialogue Cicero wrote as a kind of epilogue to his famous longer book, *De re publica* ("*The Republic*"). It narrates that Roman senator and general Scipio the Younger dreams that his grandfather, the renowned general Scipio Africanus, visits him and escorts him to heaven. While viewing the spheres, he tells his grandson how the afterlife is the true life, earthly virtue earns the reward of Heaven, and earthly delights are less important. This reflects Stoic philosophy: Romans adapted Platonic ideals from the Greeks. Whereas "The Dream of Scipio" is a dream-vision on the nature of the universe as macrocosm, Chaucer's poem is a dream-vision on a smaller part of the universe as microcosm. He describes reading "The Dream of Scipio," then also dreaming of a visit from Scipio Africanus, who praises him and promises to reward him for reading Cicero's work.

Copyright © Mometrix Media. You have been licensed one copy of this document for personal use only. Any other reproduction or redistribution is strictly prohibited. All rights reserved.

In his dream-vision, Cicero views the universe with his famous grandfather, learning philosophical principles of virtue during earthly, illusory, and deathlike life, toward Heaven's rewards in the afterlife's true life. Geoffrey Chaucer uses less grand designs in his dream-vision: Hoping to learn something from Cicero's work and influenced by it, he also dreams of Scipio Africanus. However, instead of touring the universe and Stoic philosophy, Africanus takes Chaucer to the temple of Venus—connecting with Chaucer's preface statement that he writes about love. This poem is noteworthy for the first known reference to St. Valentine's Day as being for lovers. Leaving Venus's temple, Chaucer witnesses Nature's comic "parliament" wherein birds, symbolizing human suitors, select mates. He alludes to sexual maturity at two years for male predator birds contrasting with one year for females: Nature grants the female eagle's request to defer choice for another year, but lets other birds form couples. Chaucer's awakening by morning birdsong celebrates summer, and illustrates the phenomenon that dreams often retroactively incorporate real sounds heard just before waking.

Influence of Cicero's "Dream of Scipio": During Geoffrey Chaucer's lifetime (1300s), Cicero's philosophical dialogue "The Dream of Scipio," found at the end of his major work *De re publica* (*The* Republic) was a very popular, admired, and influential work. Medieval Christians appreciated Greek and Latin Stoic philosophies for their assigning more importance to spiritual virtues than materialism. They adapted these easily to Christianity for their similarity to Christian values, as they did with many other pagan traditions. Chaucer wrote several dream-vision poems influenced by the Classics, including "The House of Fame," influenced by Virgil's *Aeneid,* and "The Book of the Duchess," influenced by Ovid's *Metamorphoses.* He introduces *The Parlement of Foules* by recounting "The Dream of Scipio," and his own similar dream from the influence of reading this work, as homage to Cicero. He then segues to writing that though personally unsuccessful in love, he writes about love. He contrasts the brevity of life with the lengthiness of learning the poetic art. He concludes his preface asking help from Venus, Roman Goddess of Love.

William Shakespeare

William Shakespeare lived in England from 1564-1616. He was a poet and playwright of the Renaissance period in Western culture. He is generally considered the foremost dramatist in world literature, and the greatest author to write in the English language. He wrote many poems, particularly sonnets, of which 154 survive today, and approximately 38 plays. Though his sonnets were larger in number and are very famous, he is best known for his plays, including comedies, tragedies, tragicomedies and historical plays. His play titles include: *All's Well That Ends Well, As You Like It, The Comedy of Errors, Love's Labour's Lost, Measure for Measure, The Merchant of Venice, The Merry Wives of Windsor, A Midsummer Night's Dream, Much Ado About Nothing, The Taming of the Shrew, The Tempest, Twelfth Night, The Two Gentlemen of Verona, The Winter's Tale, King John, Richard II, Henry IV, Henry V, Richard III, Romeo and Juliet, Coriolanus, Titus Andronicus, Julius Caesar, Macbeth, Hamlet, Troilus and Cressida, King Lear, Othello, Antony and Cleopatra,* and *Cymbeline.*

Christopher Marlowe

Christopher Marlowe was born the same year as William Shakespeare (1564), but died at the age of 29. Some people have proposed Marlowe could have falsified his death and continued writing under Shakespeare's name. Most scholars reject this theory. In the 19th century, an anonymous author also suggested Shakespeare temporarily wrote under the

Copyright © Mometrix Media. You have been licensed one copy of this document for personal use only. Any other reproduction or redistribution is strictly prohibited. All rights reserved.

name Christopher Marlowe. In *As You Like It,* Shakespeare pays homage to Marlowe, quoting "Hero and Leander"; in Touchstone's dialogue, mentioning death over a "reckoning," thought to allude to Marlowe's presumed murder over money he owed; and including "in a little room," words from Marlowe's *Jew of Malta.* Shakespeare recycled Marlowe's themes from *Dido* in *Antony and Cleopatra,* from *Jew of Malta* in *The Merchant of Venice,* from *Edward II* in *Richard II,* and from *Dr. Faustus* in *Macbeth.* A speech in *Hamlet* echoes *Dido.* Shakespeare's character Marcadé in *Love's Labour's Lost* acknowledges the god Mercury in Marlowe's play *The Massacre at Paris,* with whom Marlowe identified himself in his poem "Hero and Leander."

Sir Thomas Browne

Sir Thomas Browne (1605-1682) was a British polymath, a practicing medical physician, scientist, religious philosopher, and author. His writing style was extraordinary and varied widely across his works. Browne was knighted in 1671 by King Charles II in recognition of his accomplishments. Among English-language writers, he has received widespread regard for his high originality. His thinking was paradoxical in that his interests embraced mysticism and other ancient esoteric disciplines, yet also a strong Christian religiosity and the nascent field of inductive scientific reasoning. His original mind produced many fresh ideas and perspectives, expressed with great complexity of both thought and language. Today he is less known and understood than many great authors, due not only to his advanced ideas and wording, but also to his many references to Biblical, Classical, and esoteric sources. The Oxford English Dictionary credits him with coining over 100 new English vocabulary words, most of which are commonly recognized today. Famous authors have consistently admired and cited him across all four centuries since his death.

Sir Thomas Browne's writing style influenced the literary world from his lifetime in the 17th century through the 21st century today. Eighteenth-century literary authority Dr. Samuel Johnson noted Browne's diverse linguistic sources, as well as his transfer of terminology among different artistic disciplines. He credited Browne with having "augmented our philosophical diction"; defended Browne's "uncommon words and expressions," observing that "he had uncommon sentiments"; and explained that Browne coined new vocabulary because he "was not content to express, in many words, that idea for which any language could supply a single term." The Oxford English Dictionary lists Browne as number 70 of top-cited sources; contains 803 Browne entries; quotes him in 3,636 entries; and credits him with originating over 100 English words, including the following 38: ambidextrous, analogous, approximate, ascetic, anomalous, carnivorous, coexistence, coma, compensate, computer, cryptography, cylindrical, disruption, electricity, exhaustion, ferocious, follicle, generator, gymnastic, herbaceous, insecurity, indigenous, jocularity, literary, locomotion, medical, migrant, mucous, prairie, prostate, polarity, precocious, pubescent, therapeutic, suicide, ulterior, ultimate, and veterinarian. (Hilton, OED, 8/12)

Metaphysical poets

Dr. Samuel Johnson, a famous 18th-century figure, who wrote philosophy, poetry, and authoritative essays on literature, coined the term "Metaphysical Poets" to describe a number of mainly 17th-century lyric poets who shared certain elements of content and style in common. The poets included John Donne (considered the founder of the Metaphysical Poets), George Herbert, Andrew Marvell, Abraham Cowley, John Cleveland, Richard Crashaw, Thomas Traherne, and Henry Vaughan. These poets encouraged readers to see the

- 4 -

Copyright © Mometrix Media. You have been licensed one copy of this document for personal use only. Any other reproduction or redistribution is strictly prohibited. All rights reserved.

world from new and unaccustomed perspectives by shocking and surprising them through their use of paradoxes; contradictory imagery; original syntax; combinations of religious, philosophical, and artistic images; subtle argumentation; and extended metaphors called conceits. Unlike their contemporaries, they did not allude to classical mythology or nature imagery in their poetry, but to current geographical and scientific discoveries. Some, like Donne, showed Neo-Platonist influences—like the idea that a lover's beauty reflected Eternity's perfect beauty. They were called metaphysical for their transcendence—Donne in particular—of typical 17th-century rationalism's hierarchical organization through their adventurous exploration of religion, ideas, emotions, and language.

William Blake

William Blake (1757-1827) is considered one of the major English Romantic poets. He was also an artist and printmaker. In addition to his brilliant poetry, he produced paintings, drawings, and notably, engravings and etchings, impressive for their technical expertise, artistic beauty, and spiritual subject matter. Because he held many idiosyncratic opinions, and moreover because he was subject to visions, reporting that he saw angels in the trees and other unusual claims, Blake was often thought crazy by others during his life, though others believed him angelic and/or blessed. His work's creative, expressive character, and its mystical and philosophical elements, led people to consider him both precursor to and member of Romanticism, and a singular, original, unclassifiable artist at the same time. Blake illustrated most of his poetry with his own hand-colored, illuminated printing. He also partially illustrated Dante's *Divine Comedy* a year before dying; the small portion he completed was highly praised. His best-known poetry includes *Songs of Innocence and of Experience*, *The Book of Thel*, *The Marriage of Heaven and Hell*, and *Jerusalem*.

William Wordsworth

William Wordsworth (1770-1850) was instrumental in establishing Romanticism when he and Samuel Taylor Coleridge, another major English Romantic poet, collaboratively published *Lyrical Ballads* (1798). Wordsworth's "Preface to Lyrical Ballads" is considered a manifesto of English Romantic literary theory and criticism. In it, Wordsworth described the elements of a new kind of poetry, which he characterized as using "real language of men" rather than traditional 18th-century poetic style. In this Preface he also defined poetry as "the spontaneous overflow of powerful feelings [which] takes its origin from emotion recollected in tranquility." *Lyrical Ballads* included the famous works "The Rime of the Ancient Mariner" by Coleridge, and "Tintern Abbey" by Wordsworth. His semi-autobiographical poem, known during his life as "the poem to Coleridge," was published posthumously, entitled *The Prelude* and regarded as his major work. Wordsworth was England's Poet Laureate from 1843-1850. Among many others, his poems included "Tintern Abbey," "I Wandered Lonely as a Cloud" (often called "Daffodils"), "Ode: Intimations of Immortality," "Westminster Bridge," and "The World Is Too Much with Us."

Samuel Taylor Coleridge

One of the six major Romantic English Poets, Samuel Taylor Coleridge (1772-1834) was also a philosopher and literary critic, and close friends fellow Romantic poet William Wordsworth, with whom he collaborated in publishing *Lyrical Ballads,* launching the Romantic movement. He wrote very influential literary criticism, including the major two-volume autobiographical, meditative discourse *Biographia Literaria* (1817). Coleridge

- 5 -

Copyright © Mometrix Media. You have been licensed one copy of this document for personal use only. Any other reproduction or redistribution is strictly prohibited. All rights reserved.

acquainted English-language intellectuals with the German idealist philosophy. He also coined many now familiar philosophical and literary terms, like "the willing suspension of disbelief," meaning that readers would voluntarily withhold judgment of implausible stories if their authors could impart "human interest and a semblance of truth" to them. He strongly influenced the American Transcendentalists, including Ralph Waldo Emerson. Coleridge's poem *Love,* a ballad (written to Sara Hutchinson), inspired John Keats' poem "La Belle Dame Sans Merci." He is credited with the origin of "Conversational Poetry" and Wordsworth's adoption of it. Some of his best-known works include "The Rime of the Ancient Mariner," "Christabel," "Kubla Khan," "The Nightingale," "Dejection: An Ode," and "To William Wordsworth."

John Keats

John Keats (1795-1821), despite his short life, was a major English Romantic poet. He is known for his six Odes: "Ode on a Grecian Urn," "Ode on Indolence," "Ode on Melancholy," "Ode to a Nightingale," "Ode to Psyche," and "To Autumn." Other notable works include the sonnet "O Solitude," "Endymion," "La Belle Dame Sans Merci," "Hyperion," and the collection *Lamia, Isabella, The Eve of St. Agnes and Other Poems*. The intensity and maturity he achieved in his poetry within a period of only around six years are often remarked since his death, though during life he felt he accomplished nothing lasting. He wrote a year before dying, "I have left no immortal work behind me—nothing to make my friends proud of my memory—but I have lov'd the principle of beauty in all things, and if I had had time I would have made myself remember'd." He was proven wrong. His verse from "Ode on a Grecian Urn" is renowned: "'Beauty is truth, truth beauty'—that is all / Ye know on earth, and all ye need to know."

George Gordon, Lord Byron

George Gordon Byron, commonly known as Lord Byron (1788-1824) was a major English Romantic poet. He is known for long narrative poems "Don Juan," "Childe Harold's Pilgrimage," and the shorter lyric poem "She Walks in Beauty." The aristocratic Byron travelled throughout Europe, living in Italy for seven years. He fought in the Greek War of Independence against the Ottoman Empire, making him a national hero in Greece, before dying a year later from a fever contracted there. He was the most notoriously profligate and flamboyant Romantic poet, with reckless behaviors including multiple bisexual love affairs, adultery, rumored incest, self-exile, and incurring enormous debts. He became friends with fellow Romantic writers Percy Bysshe Shelley, the future Mary Shelley, and John Polidori. Their shared fantasy writing at a Swiss villa the summer of 1816 resulted in Mary Shelley's *Frankenstein*, Byron's *Fragment of a Novel*, and was the inspiration for Polidori's *The Vampyre* establishing the romantic vampire genre. Byron also wrote linguistic volumes on American and Armenian grammars. He loved and kept many animals. His name is synonymous today with the mercurial Romantic.

Percy Bysshe Shelley

Percy Bysshe Shelley (1792-1822), a major English Romantic poet, was not famous during life but became so after death, particularly for his lyric poetry. His best-known works include "Ozymandias," "Ode to the West Wind," "To a Skylark," "Music," "When Soft Voices Die," "The Cloud," "The Masque of Anarchy"; longer poems "Queen Mab"/"The Daemon of the World" and "Adonaïs"; and the verse drama *Prometheus Unbound.* Shelley's second wife,

Copyright © Mometrix Media. You have been licensed one copy of this document for personal use only. Any other reproduction or redistribution is strictly prohibited. All rights reserved.

Mary Shelley, was the daughter of his mentor William Godwin and the famous feminist Mary Wollstonecraft (*A Vindication of the Rights of Woman*), and became famous for her Gothic novel *Frankenstein*. Early in his career Shelley was influenced by William Wordsworth's Romantic poetry, and wrote the long poem *Alastor, or the Spirit of Solitude*. Soon thereafter he met Lord Byron, and was inspired to write "Hymn to Intellectual Beauty". He composed "Mont Blanc," inspired by touring the French Alpine commune Chamonix-Mont-Blanc. Shelley also encouraged Byron to compose his epic poem *Don Juan*. Shelley inspired Henry David Thoreau, Mahatma Gandhi, and others to civil disobedience, nonviolent resistance, vegetarianism, and animal rights.

William Butler Yeats

William Butler Yeats (1865-1939) was among the greatest influences in 20th-century English literature. He was instrumental in the Celtic Revival/Irish Literary Revival, founding and initially running the Abbey Theatre, and was the first Irishman awarded the Nobel Prize for Literature (1923). An Irish Nationalist, he was passionately involved in politics. Yeats was believed transitional from Romanticism to Modernism. His earlier verses were lyrical, but later became realistic, symbolic, and apocalyptic. He was fascinated with Irish legend, occult subjects, and historical cycles—"gyres." He incorporated Irish folklore, mythology, and legends in "The Stolen Child," "The Wanderings of Oisin," "The Death of Cuchulain," "Who Goes with Fergus?" and "The Song of Wandering Aengus." Early collections included *The Secret Rose* and *The Wind Among the Reeds*. His later, most significant poetry collections include *The Green Helmet, Responsibilities, The Tower,* and *The Winding Stair.* Yeats's visionary, apocalyptic (1920) poem "The Second Coming" reflects his belief that his times were the anarchic end of the Christian cycle/gyre: "what rough beast, its hour come round at last, / Slouches toward Bethlehem to be born?"

Historical context of change between Middle Ages and Renaissance

The ancient Greek Athenian elite were a highly educated society, developing philosophies and writing about principles for creating poetry and drama. During the Roman Empire, the Romans assimilated and adapted the culture of the Greeks they conquered into their own society. For example, the gods of Roman mythology were essentially the same as in Greek myth, only renamed in Latin. However, after the fall of the Roman Empire, the many European countries formerly united under Roman rule became fragmented. There followed a 1,000-year period of general public ignorance and illiteracy—called the Dark Ages as well as the Middle Ages. Only the Church remained a bastion of literacy: monks and priests laboriously copied manuscripts one at a time by hand. Johannes Gutenberg's 1450 invention of the movable-type printing press changed everything: multiple copies of books could be printed much faster. This enabled a public return to literacy, leading to the Renaissance, or "rebirth"—reviving access and interest for Greek and Roman Classics, and generating a creative explosion in all arts.

Drama

Early development
Interestingly, early English drama originally developed from religious ritual. Early Christians established traditions of presenting pageants or mystery plays, each traveling on wagons and carts through the streets of its city, depicting events of the Judeo-Christian Old and New Testaments. Medieval tradition assigned responsibility for performing specific

Copyright © Mometrix Media. You have been licensed one copy of this document for personal use only. Any other reproduction or redistribution is strictly prohibited. All rights reserved.

plays to the different guilds. In Middle English, "mystery" meant both religious ritual/truth, and craft/trade. Historically, mystery plays were to be reproduced exactly the same every time as religious rituals. However, by human nature, some performers introduced individual interpretations of roles and/or even improvised. Thus drama was born. Narrative detail and nuanced acting were evident in mystery cycles by the Middle Ages. As individualized performance evolved, plays on other subjects also developed. Middle English mystery plays extant include the York Cycle, Coventry Cycle, Chester Mystery Plays, N-Town Plays, and Towneley/Wakefield Plays. Mystery plays have been revived in the 20th and 21st centuries. Dame Judi Dench (born in York) and other actors began their careers in mystery play revivals.

<u>Defining characteristics</u>
In the Middle Ages, it was common to compose plays in verse. Early Christian mystery plays were always written in verse. By the time of the Renaissance, Shakespeare and other dramatists wrote plays that mixed prose, rhymed verse, and blank verse. Shakespeare also often used rhyming couplets in his plays. The traditions of costumes and masks were seen in ancient Greek drama, medieval mystery plays, and Renaissance drama. Conventions like asides, wherein actors make comments directly to the audience unheard by other characters, and soliloquies, i.e., dramatic monologues, were also common during Shakespeare's Elizabethan dramatic period. Monologues dated back to ancient Greek drama. Elizabethan dialogue tended to use colloquial prose for lower-class characters' speech and stylized verse for upper-class characters. Another Elizabethan convention was the play-within-a-play, like in *Hamlet.* As drama moved toward realism, dialogue became less poetic and more conversational, as in most modern English-language plays. Contemporary drama, both onstage and onscreen, includes a convention of breaking the fourth wall, wherein actors directly face and address audiences.

Aristotle's criteria for tragedy in drama

In his *Poetics,* Aristotle defined five critical terms relative to tragedy. (1) *Anagnorisis:* Meaning tragic insight or recognition, this is a moment of realization by a tragic hero(ine) when s/he suddenly understands how s/he has enmeshed himself/herself in a "web of fate." (2) *Hamartia:* This is often called a "tragic flaw," but is better described as a tragic error. *Hamartia* is an archery term meaning a shot missing the bull's eye, used here as a metaphor for a mistake—often a simple one—which results in catastrophe. (3) *Hubris:* While often called "pride," this is actually translated as "violent transgression," and signifies an arrogant overstepping of moral or cultural bounds—the sin of the tragic hero who over-presumes or over-aspires. (4) *Nemesis:* translated as "retribution," this represents the cosmic punishment or payback that the tragic hero ultimately receives for committing hubristic acts. (5) *Peripateia:* Literally "turning," this is a plot reversal consisting of a tragic hero's pivotal action, which changes his/her status from safe to endangered.

Theory of tragedy proposed by Hegel

Georg Wilhelm Friedrich Hegel (1770-1831) proposed a different theory of tragedy than Aristotle (384-322 BCE) which was also very influential. Whereas Aristotle's criteria involved character and plot, Hegel defined tragedy as a dynamic conflict of opposite forces or rights. For example, if an individual believes in the moral philosophy of the conscientious objector, i.e., that fighting in wars is morally wrong, but is confronted with being drafted into military service, this conflict would fit Hegel's definition of a tragic plot premise. Hegel

- 8 -

Copyright © Mometrix Media. You have been licensed one copy of this document for personal use only. Any other reproduction or redistribution is strictly prohibited. All rights reserved.

theorized that a tragedy must involve some circumstance in which two values, or two rights, are fatally at odds with one another and conflict directly. Hegel did not view this as good triumphing over evil, or evil winning out over good, but rather as one good fighting against another good unto death. He saw this conflict of two goods as truly tragic. In ancient Greek author Sophocles' tragedy *Antigone,* the main character experiences this tragic conflict, between her public duties and her family and religious responsibilities.

Revenge tragedy

Along with Aristotelian definitions of comedy and tragedy, ancient Greece was the origin of the revenge tragedy. This genre became highly popular in Renaissance England, and is still popular today in contemporary movies. In a revenge tragedy, the protagonist has been done some serious wrong, such as the assault and murder of a family member. However, the wrongdoer has not been punished. In contemporary plots, this often occurs when some legal technicality has interfered with the miscreant's conviction and sentencing, or when authorities are unable to locate and apprehend the criminal. The protagonist then faces the conflict of suffering this injustice, or exacting his or her own justice by seeking revenge. Greek revenge tragedies include *Agamemnon* and *Medea.* Playwright Thomas Kyd's *The Spanish Tragedy* (1582-1592) is credited with beginning the Elizabethan genre of revenge tragedies. Shakespearean revenge tragedies include *Hamlet* (1599-1602) and *Titus Andronicus* (1588-1593). A Jacobean example is Thomas Middleton's *The Revenger's Tragedy* (1606, 1607). The 1974 movie *Death Wish* is a contemporary example.

Hamlet's "tragic flaw"

Despite virtually limitless interpretations, one way to view Hamlet's tragic error generally is as indecision: He suffers the classic revenge tragedy's conflict of whether to suffer with his knowledge of his mother's and uncle's assassination of his father, or to exact his own revenge and justice against Claudius, who has assumed the throne after his crime went unknown and unpunished. Hamlet's famous soliloquy, "To be or not to be" reflects this dilemma. Hamlet muses "Whether 'tis nobler in the mind to suffer the slings and arrows of outrageous fortune, / Or to take arms against a sea of troubles, / And by opposing end them?" He sees the final sleep of death as "the rub; / For in that sleep of death what dreams may come... Must give us pause... that the dread of something after death... makes us rather bear those ills we have / Than fly to others that we know not of? / Thus conscience does make cowards of us all." Hamlet's excessive conscience leads to paralyzing indecision, at least temporarily.

For much of William Shakespeare's tragedy, Hamlet suffers anxiety over what to do about his uncle Claudius's murdering his (Hamlet's) father, Hamlet. During this time, Hamlet's tragic error might be considered a lack of action, as he seems paralyzed by his quandary. But making matters worse, Hamlet attempts to kill Claudius surreptitiously by stabbing him through a tapestry, accidentally killing Polonius instead. However, he eventually becomes inspired with a solution to avoid direct confrontation: "The play's the thing / Wherein I'll catch the conscience of the king." He presents a play depicting a similar murder. By observing his reaction, Hamlet can confirm or deny Claudius's guilt (reported by the late King Hamlet's ghost, which Hamlet was unsure was a true ghost or the devil) to inform his decision. During the presentation, Gertrude fatally drinks wine that Claudius poisoned and intended for Hamlet. Then Laertes kills Hamlet, to avenge Hamlet's accidental murder of Laertes' father Polonius, and his sister Ophelia's madness and eventual suicide in reaction

- 9 -

Copyright © Mometrix Media. You have been licensed one copy of this document for personal use only. Any other reproduction or redistribution is strictly prohibited. All rights reserved.

to Hamlet's behavior. Hamlet's indecision delays action, but his actions have more tragic outcomes.

Dramatic comedies

Three types of dramas classified as comedy include the farce, the romantic comedy, and the satirical comedy. The farce is a zany, goofy type of comedy that includes pratfalls and other forms of slapstick humor. The characters appearing in a farce tend to be ridiculous or fantastical in nature, markedly more so than characters in other types of comedies. Another aspect of farce is inclusion in the plot of situations so improbable as to be unbelievable— albeit still highly entertaining. Farcical plots frequently feature complications and twists that can go on almost indefinitely. They also often include wildly incredible coincidences that rarely if ever would occur in real life. Mistaken identity, deceptions, and disguises are common devices used in farcical comedies. Shakespeare's play *The Comedy of Errors,* with its cases of accidental mistaken identity and slapstick, is an example of farce. Contemporary examples of farce include the Marx Brothers' movies, the Three Stooges movies and TV episodes, and the *Pink Panther* movie series.

Romantic comedy
Romantic comedies are probably the most popular of the types of comedy, in both live theater performances and movies. They include not only humor and a happy ending, but also love. In the typical plot of a romantic comedy, two people well suited to one another are either brought together for the first time, or reconciled after being separated. They are usually both sympathetic characters, and seem destined to be together yet separated by some intervening complication—such as an ex-lover(s), interfering parents or friends, or differences in social class. The happy ending is achieved through the lovers' overcoming all these obstacles. William Shakespeare's *Much Ado About Nothing;* Walt Disney's version of *Cinderella* (1950); Broadway musical *Guys and Dolls* (1955); and movies *When Harry Met Sally* (1989), starring Billy Crystal and Meg Ryan, written by Nora Ephron; *Sleepless in Seattle* (1993) and *You've Got Mail* (1998), both directed by Nora Ephron and starring Tom Hanks and Meg Ryan; and *Forget Paris* (1995), co-written, produced, directed by and starring Billy Crystal, are examples of romantic comedies.

Satirical comedy and black comedy
Satires generally mock and lampoon human foolishness and vices. Satirical comedies fit the classical definition of comedy by depicting a main character's rise in fortune, but they also fit the definition of satire by making that main character either a fool, morally corrupt, or cynical in attitude. All or most of the other characters in the satirical comedy display similar foibles. These include cuckolded spouses, dupes, and other gullible types; tricksters, con artists, and criminals; hypocrites; fortune seekers; and other deceptive types who prey on the latter, who are their willing and unwitting victims. Some classical examples of satirical comedies include *The Birds* by ancient Greek comedic playwright Aristophanes, and *Volpone* by 17th-century poet and playwright Ben Jonson, who made the comedy of humors popular. When satirical comedy is extended to extremes, it becomes black comedy, wherein the comedic occurrences are grotesque or terrible. Contemporary movie examples include Quentin Tarantino's *Pulp Fiction* (1994) and the Coen brothers' *Fargo* (1996).

Copyright © Mometrix Media. You have been licensed one copy of this document for personal use only. Any other reproduction or redistribution is strictly prohibited. All rights reserved.

Shakespearean comedy

Aristotle defined comedy not as a humorous drama, but as one in which the protagonist experiences a rise in fortune, and which has a happy ending. Such Classical definitions of drama were very popular during the Renaissance and the Elizabethan period within it, when William Shakespeare was writing. All of Shakespeare's comedies, as opposed to his tragedies, had happy endings. Not all of them are equally funny, although many are. His play *A Comedy of Errors* fits the comedic genre of the farce. Based and expanding on a Classical Roman comedy, it includes slapstick humor and mistaken identity—not deliberate, but accidental, and is generally light and "fluffy," with disturbing topics only hinted at but soon dissolved in laughter and love. Shakespeare's *Much Ado About Nothing* is a romantic comedy. It incorporates some more serious themes, including social mores; perceived infidelity; marriage's duality as both trap and ideal; and honor and its loss, public shame, and deception, but also much witty dialogue and a happy ending.

Comedy

Today, most people equate the idea of comedy with something funny, and of tragedy with something sad. However, the ancient Greeks defined these differently. Comedy needed not be humorous or amusing: it needed only a happy ending. The Classical definition of comedy, as included in Aristotle's works, is any work that tells the story of a sympathetic main character's rise in fortune. According to Aristotle, protagonists needed not be heroic or exemplary: he described them as not evil or worthless, but as ordinary people—"average to below average" morally. Comic figures who were sympathetic were usually of humble origins, proving their "natural nobility" through their actions as their characters were tested, rather than characters born into nobility—who were often satirized as self-important or pompous. Comedy's mirror-image was tragedy, portraying a hero's fall in fortune. While by Classical definitions, tragedies could be sad, Aristotle went further, requiring their depicting suffering and pain to cause "terror and pity" in audiences; that tragic heroes be basically good, admirable, and/or noble; and that their downfalls be through personal action, choice, or error, not by bad luck or accident.

Poetry

Unlike prose, which traditionally (except in forms like stream of consciousness) consists of complete sentences connected into paragraphs, poetry is written in verses. These may form complete sentences, clauses, or phrases. Poetry may be written in rhyming verses or unrhymed verse. It can be metered, i.e., following a particular rhythmic pattern, such as iambic, dactylic, spondaic, trochaic, or anapestic, or without regular meter. The terms iamb and trochee, among others, identify stressed and unstressed syllables in each verse. Meter is also described by the number of beats or stressed syllables per verse: dimeter (2), trimeter (3), tetrameter (4), pentameter (5), and so forth. With $\cup$ = unstressed, $/$= stressed, iambic = $\cup/$; trochaic = $/\cup$; spondaic =$//$; dactylic =$/\cup\cup$; anapestic =$\cup\cup/$. Poetry with neither rhyme nor meter is called free verse. Poems may be in free verse, metered but unrhymed, rhymed but without meter, or using both rhyme and meter. In English, the most common meter is iambic pentameter. Unrhymed iambic pentameter is called blank verse. Rhyme schemes identify which lines rhyme, such as ABAB, ABCA, AABA, and so on.

The ballad is a form historically and currently used in both musical songs and poems. The *ballade* was very popular in 14th- and 15th-century France; ballads were also common in

Copyright © Mometrix Media. You have been licensed one copy of this document for personal use only. Any other reproduction or redistribution is strictly prohibited. All rights reserved.

traditional English and American folk songs and poems. Poetry ballads often are rhymed and metered and cover subjects like love, death, murder, or religious topics. In dramatic monologue poems, the poet speaks in the voice of a character/persona. Elegies are mourning poems, traditionally with three parts: a lament, praise of the deceased, and solace for loss. Epic poems are long, recount heroic deeds and adventures, use very stylized language, and combine dramatic and lyrical conventions. Epigrams are memorable, one- or two-line rhymes. Epistolary poems are written and read as letters. Odes evolved from early poems with music and dance to Romantic poems expressing strong feelings and contemplative thoughts. Pastoral poems (and novels) idealize nature and country living. Limericks typically are two lines of iambic trimeter, two lines of iambic dimeter, and one line of iambic trimeter, usually humorous and/or bawdy.

Haiku was originally a Japanese poetry form. In the 13th century, haiku was the opening phrase of renga, a 100-stanza oral poem. By the 16th century, haiku diverged into a separate short poem. When Western writers discovered haiku, the form became popular in English and other languages. A haiku has 17 syllables, traditionally distributed across three verses as 5/7/5, with a pause after the first or second line. Haiku are syllabic and unrhymed. Haiku philosophy and technique are that brevity's compression forces writers to express images concisely, depict a moment in time, and evoke illumination and enlightenment. An example is 17th-century haiku master Matsuo Basho's classic: "Oh, old pond! / A frog jumps in— / the sound of water." Modern American poet Ezra Pound revealed the influence of haiku in his two-line poem "In a Station of the Metro"—line 1 has 5+7 syllables, line 2 has 7, but it still preserves haiku's philosophy and imagistic technique: "The apparition of these faces in the crowd; / Petals on a wet, black bough."

The sonnet traditionally has 14 lines of iambic pentameter, tightly organized around a theme. The Petrarchan sonnet, named for 14th-century Italian poet Petrarch, has an eight-line stanza, the octave, and a six-line stanza, the sestet. There is a change or turn, known as the volta, between the eighth and ninth verses setting up the sestet's answer or summary. The rhyme scheme is ABBA/ABBA/CDECDE or CDCDCD. The Petrarchan sonnet was introduced to 16th-century England by Sir Thomas Wyatt. The English or Shakespearean sonnet has three quatrains and one couplet, with the rhyme scheme ABAB/CDCD/EFEF/GG. This format better suits English, which has fewer rhymes than Italian. The final couplet often contrasts sharply with the preceding quatrains, as in Shakespeare's sonnets—for example, Sonnet 130, "My mistress' eyes are nothing like the sun." Variations on these two forms include 16th-century Edmund Spenser's Spenserian sonnet; 17th-century John Milton's Miltonic sonnet; and sonnet sequences, as used by 17th-century poet John Donne in *La Corona*, 19th-century poet Elizabeth Barrett Browning in *Sonnets from the Portuguese*, 19th-20th-century poet Rainer Maria Rilke, and 20th-century poets Robert Lowell and John Berryman.

Couplets and meter to enhance meaning in poetry

When a poet uses a couplet—a stanza of two lines, rhymed or unrhymed—it can function as the answer to a question asked earlier in the poem, or the solution to a problem or riddle. Couplets can also enhance the establishment of a poem's mood, or clarify the development of a poem's theme. Another device to enhance thematic development is irony, which also communicates the poet's tone and draws the reader's attention to a point the poet is making. The use of meter gives a poem a rhythmic context, contributes to the poem's flow, makes it more appealing to the reader, can represent natural speech rhythms, and produces

Copyright © Mometrix Media. You have been licensed one copy of this document for personal use only. Any other reproduction or redistribution is strictly prohibited. All rights reserved.

specific effects. For example, in "The Song of Hiawatha," Henry Wadsworth Longfellow uses trochaic (/ ◡) tetrameter (four beats per line) to evoke for readers the rhythms of Native American chanting: "*By* the *shores* of *Gitche Gumee*, / *By* the *shining Big*-Sea-*Water* / *Stood* the *wig*wam of No*ko*mis." (Italicized syllables are stressed; non-italicized syllables are unstressed.)

Reflection of content through structure

Wallace Stevens' short yet profound poem "The Snow Man" is reductionist: the snow man is a figure without human biases or emotions. Stevens begins, "One must have a mind of winter," the criterion for realizing nature and life does not inherently possess subjective qualities; we only invest it with these. Things are not as we see them; they simply are. The entire poem is one long sentence of clauses connected by conjunctions and commas, and modified by relative clauses and phrases. The successive clauses and phrases lead readers continually to reconsider as they read. Stevens' construction of the poem mirrors the meaning he conveys. With a mind of winter, the snow man, Stevens concludes, "nothing himself, beholds nothing that is not there, and the nothing that is" (ultimate reductionism). Linguist and poetics expert Jay Keyser once remarked (NPR, 2005) that he wrote all the words of "The Snow Man" on white cards and made them into a mobile; it was "perfectly balanced, like an Alexander Calder creation." He said the mobile visually represented the poem's content.

Contrast of content and structure

Robert Frost's poem "Stopping by Woods on a Snowy Evening" (1923) is deceptively short and simple, with only four stanzas, each of only four lines, and short and simple words. Reinforcing this is Frost's use of regular rhyme and meter. The rhythm is iambic tetrameter throughout; the rhyme scheme is AABA in the first three stanzas and AAAA in the fourth. In an additional internal subtlety, B ending "here" in the first stanza is rhymed with A endings "queer," "near," and "year" of the second; B ending "lake" in the second is rhymed in A endings "shake", "mistake," and "flake" of the third. The final stanza's AAAA endings reinforce the ultimate darker theme. Though the first three stanzas seem to describe quietly watching snow fill the woods, the last stanza evokes the seductive pull of mysterious death: "The woods are lovely, dark and deep," countered by the obligations of living life: "But I have promises to keep, / And miles to go before I sleep, / And miles to go before I sleep." The last line's repetition strengthens Frost's message that despite death's temptation, life's course must precede it.

Aspects that combine to total effect in Theodore Roethke's "The Waking"

"The Waking" is a villanelle, with five tercets, one quatrain, and only two rhymes. Roethke alternately repeats two main lines: "I wake to sleep, and take my waking slow," and "I learn by going where I have to go" throughout, gradually revealing meaning. Continuous overall rhythm and revolving sound patterns of interconnected rhyming and assonance create perpetual motion, reflecting the life cycle. Roethke's use of villanelle form perfectly suits this cyclical effect: repetition, becoming hypnotically chant-like, reinforces the poem's mystical quality. Waking to sleep, learning by going, and "think[ing] by feeling" represent paradoxes: meaning, like form, becomes circular. These symbolize abandoning conscious rationalism to embrace spiritual vision. We wake from the vision to "Great Nature," and "take the lively air" in life's dance. "This shaking keeps me steady"—another paradox—

- 13 -

Copyright © Mometrix Media. You have been licensed one copy of this document for personal use only. Any other reproduction or redistribution is strictly prohibited. All rights reserved.

juxtaposes and balances fear of mortality with ecstasy in embracing experience. The transcendent vision of all life's interrelationship demonstrates, "What falls away is always. And is near." Readers experience the poem holistically, like music, through Roethke's integration of theme, motion, and sound.

Sylvia Plath's use of villanelle form to convey meaning in "Mad Girl's Love Song"

Sylvia Plath wrote the poem "Mad Girl's Love Song" in college to exemplify young love. The two repeated lines, "I shut my eyes and all the world drops dead" and "(I think I made you up inside my head.)" reflect the existential viewpoint that nothing exists in any absolute reality outside of our own perceptions. In the first stanza, the middle line, "I lift my lids and all is born again," in its recreating the world, bridges between the repeated refrain statements—one of obliterating reality, the other of having constructed her lover's existence. Unlike other villanelles wherein key lines are subtly altered in their repetitions, Plath repeats these exactly each time. This reflects the young woman's love, also not changing throughout the poem. The final quatrain expresses some regret: "I should have loved a thunderbird instead; / At least when spring comes they roar back again." Plath contrasts the thunderbirds' rebirth with the unchanging love she depicts, and reinforces it. The unchanging repeated lines mirror the lack of progress in her love.

Ted Hughes' animal metaphors

Hughes frequently used animal metaphors, as in "Crow" and collected poems about the mythic creature-character Crow. In "The Thought Fox," a model of concise, structured beauty, Hughes characterizes the poet's creative process with succinct, striking imagery of an idea as a fox entering his head. Repeating "loneliness" in the first two stanzas emphasizes the poet's lonely work: "Something else is alive / Beside the clock's loneliness." He treats an idea's arrival as separate from himself. Three stanzas detail in vivid images a fox's approach from the outside winter forest at starless midnight —its nose, "Cold, delicately" touching twigs and leaves; "neat" paw prints in snow; "bold" body; wide, deep, brilliant green eyes; and self-contained, focused progress—"Till, with a sudden sharp hot stink of fox," he metaphorically depicts poetic inspiration as the fox's physical entry into "the dark hole of the head." Hughes ends by summarizing his vision of poet as an interior, passive idea recipient, with the outside world unchanged: "The window is starless still; the clock ticks, / The page is printed."

Effects of figurative devices on meaning in poetry

Through exaggeration, hyperbole communicates the strength of a poet's or persona's feelings and enhances the mood of the poem. Imagery appeals to the reader's senses, creating vivid mental pictures, evoking reader emotions and responses, and helping to develop themes. Irony also aids thematic development by drawing the reader's attention to the poet's point and communicating the poem's tone. Thematic development is additionally supported by the comparisons of metaphors and similes, which emphasize similarities among things compared, affect readers' perceptions of images and enhance the imagery, and are more creative than writing in only literal terms. The use of mood communicates the atmosphere of a poem, can build a sense of tension, and evokes the reader's emotions. Onomatopoeia appeals to the reader's auditory sense and enhances sound imagery even when the poem is visual (read silently) rather than auditory (read aloud). Rhyme connects and unites verses, gives the rhyming words emphasis, and makes poems more fluent.

Copyright © Mometrix Media. You have been licensed one copy of this document for personal use only. Any other reproduction or redistribution is strictly prohibited. All rights reserved.

Symbolism communicates themes, develops imagery, and evokes readers' emotional and other responses.

Poetic structure to enhance meaning in poetry

The opening stanza of Romantic English poet, artist and printmaker William Blake's famous poem "The Tyger" demonstrates how a poet can enhance the meaning of the work through creating tension by using line length and punctuation independently of one another: "Tyger! Tyger! burning bright / In the forests of the night, / What immortal hand or eye / Could frame thy fearful symmetry?" The first three lines of this stanza are trochaic (/ᴗ), with "masculine" endings—that is, strongly stressed syllables at the ends of each of the lines. But Blake's punctuation contradicts this rhythmic regularity by not providing any divisions between the words "bright" and "In" or between "eye" and "Could." This irregular punctuation foreshadows how Blake disrupts the meter at the end of this first stanza by using a contrasting dactyl (/ᴗᴗ), with a "feminine" (unstressed) ending syllable in the last word, "symmetry." Thus Blake uses structural contrasts to heighten the intrigue of his work.

In enjambment, one sentence or clause in a poem does not end at the end of its line or verse, but runs over into the next line or verse. Clause endings coinciding with line endings give readers a feeling of completion, but enjambment influences readers to hurry to the next line to finish and understand the sentence. In his blank-verse epic religious poem "Paradise Lost," John Milton wrote: "Anon out of the earth a fabric huge / Rose like an exhalation, with the sound / Of dulcet symphonies and voices sweet, / Built like a temple, where pilasters round / Were set, and Doric pillars overlaid / With golden architrave." Only the third line is end-stopped. Milton, describing the palace of Pandemonium bursting from Hell up through the ground, reinforced this idea through phrases and clauses bursting through the boundaries of the lines. A caesura is a pause in mid-verse. Milton's commas in the third and fourth lines signal caesuras. They interrupt flow, making the narration jerky to imply that Satan's glorious-seeming palace has a shaky and unsound foundation.

Novels

Historical novels set fiction in particular historical periods—including prehistoric and mythological—and contain historical, prehistoric, or mythological themes. Examples include Walter Scott's *Rob Roy* and *Ivanhoe*; Leo Tolstoy's *War and Peace*; Robert Graves' *I, Claudius*; Mary Renault's *The King Must Die* and *The Bull from the Sea* (an historical novel using Greek mythology); Virginia Woolf's *Orlando* and *Between the Acts*; and John Dos Passos's *U.S.A* trilogy. Picaresque novels recount episodic adventures of a rogue protagonist or *pícaro,* like Miguel de Cervantes' *Don Quixote* or Henry Fielding's *Tom Jones.* Gothic novels originated as a reaction against 18th-century Enlightenment rationalism, featuring horror, mystery, superstition, madness, supernatural elements, and revenge. Early examples include Horace Walpole's *Castle of Otranto,* Matthew Gregory Lewis' *Monk*, Mary Shelley's *Frankenstein*, and Bram Stoker's *Dracula.* In America, Edgar Allan Poe wrote many Gothic works. Contemporary novelist Anne Rice has penned many Gothic novels under the pseudonym A. N. Roquelaure. Psychological novels, originating in 17th-century France, explore characters' motivations. Examples include Abbé Prévost's *Manon Lescaut;* George Eliot's novels; Fyodor Dostoyevsky's *Crime and Punishment;* Tolstoy's *Anna Karenina;* Gustave Flaubert's *Madame Bovary;* and the novels of Henry James, James Joyce, and Vladimir Nabokov.

Copyright © Mometrix Media. You have been licensed one copy of this document for personal use only. Any other reproduction or redistribution is strictly prohibited. All rights reserved.

Novels of manners are fictional stories that observe, explore, and analyze the social behaviors of a specific time and place. While deep psychological themes are more universal across different historical periods and countries, the manners of a particular society are shorter-lived and more varied; the novel of manners captures these societal details. Novels of manners can also be regarded as symbolically representing, in artistic form, certain established and secure social orders. Characteristics of novels of manners include descriptions of a society with defined behavioral codes; the use of standardized, impersonal formulas in their language; and inhibition of emotional expression, as contrasted with the strong emotions expressed in romantic or sentimental novels. The novels of Jane Austen are examples of some of the finest novels of manners ever produced. In the 20th century, Evelyn Waugh's *Handful of Dust* is a novel of social manners, and his *Sword of Honour* trilogy is a novel of military manners. Another 20th-century example is *The Unbearable Bassington* by Saki (the pen name of writer H. H. Munro), focusing on Edwardian society.

Sentimental love novels originated in the movement of Romanticism. Eighteenth-century examples of novels that depict emotional rather than only physical love include Samuel Richardson's *Pamela* (1740) in English, and Jean-Jacques Rousseau's *Nouvelle Héloïse* (1761) in French. Also in the 18th century, Laurence Sterne's novel *Tristram Shandy* (1760-1767) is an example of a novel with elements of sentimentality. The Victorian era's rejection of emotionalism caused the term "sentimental" to have undesirable connotations. In the 19th century, William Makepeace Thackeray and Charles Dickens, while not considered sentimental novelists by any means, both included sentimental elements in some of their novels: for example, in Dickens' *A Christmas Carol*. A 19th-century author of genuinely sentimental novels was Mrs. Henry Wood (e.g., *East Lynne,* 1861). In the 20th century, Erich Segal's sentimental novel *Love Story* (1970) was a popular bestseller, staying on the New York Times Best Seller List for 41 weeks, and was adapted into a movie (also released in 1970) which was also well received by both movie audiences and film critics, receiving numerous award nominations.

Epistolary novels are told in the form of letters written by their characters rather than in narrative form. Samuel Richardson, the best-known author of epistolary novels like *Pamela* (1740) and *Clarissa* (1748), widely influenced early Romantic epistolary novels throughout Europe that freely expressed emotions. Richardson, a printer, published technical manuals on letter-writing for young gentlewomen; his epistolary novels were natural fictional extensions of those nonfictional instructional books. Nineteenth-century English author Wilkie Collins' *The Moonstone* (1868) was a mystery written in epistolary form. By the 20th century, the format of well-composed written letters came to be regarded as artificial and outmoded. English novelist Christopher Isherwood tried to revive the form in *Meeting by the River* (1967), but this was criticized for using chatty and informal letters to tell a story with a serious religious theme. A 20th-century evolution of letters was tape-recording transcripts in French playwright Samuel Beckett's drama *Krapp's Last Tape.* Though evoking modern alienation, Beckett still created a sense of fictional characters' direct communication without author intervention as Richardson had.

Pastoral novels and fiction (as well as poetry) lyrically idealize country life as idyllic and utopian, akin to the Garden of Eden. *Daphnis and Chloe*, written by Greek novelist Longus around the second or third century, was pastoral and influenced Elizabethan pastoral romances like Philip Sidney's *Arcadia* and Thomas Lodge's *Rosalynde* (both 1590). William Shakespeare based his play *As You Like It* on *Rosalynde.* Jacques-Henri Bernardin de St. Pierre's French work *Paul et Virginie* (1787) demonstrated the early Romantic view of the

Copyright © Mometrix Media. You have been licensed one copy of this document for personal use only. Any other reproduction or redistribution is strictly prohibited. All rights reserved.

innocence and goodness of nature. Later non-pastoral novels like *The Rainbow* (1915) and *Lady Chatterley's Lover* (1928), both by D. H. Lawrence, contain pastoral elements. Growing realism transformed pastoral writing into less ideal and more dystopian, distasteful and ironic depictions of country life in George Eliot's and Thomas Hardy's novels. Saul Bellow's novel *Herzog* (1964) may demonstrate how urban ills highlight an alternative pastoral ideal. Some scholars feel the pastoral satire *Cold Comfort Farm* (1932) by Stella Gibbons (also adapted into a movie) has made British novelists less able to take the pastoral tradition's lyricism seriously.

Bildungsroman is German, literally meaning "education novel." This term is also used in English to describe "apprenticeship" novels focusing on coming-of-age stories, including youth's struggles and searches for things such as identity, spiritual understanding, or the meaning in life. Johann Wolfgang von Goethe's *Wilhelm Meisters Lehrjahre* (1796) is credited as the origin. Charles Dickens' two novels *David Copperfield* (1850) and *Great Expectations* (1861) also fit this form. H. G. Wells wrote *bildungsromans* about questing for apprenticeships to address modern life's complications in *Joan and Peter* (1918), and from a Utopian perspective in *The Dream* (1924). School *bildungsromans* include Thomas Hughes' *Tom Brown's School Days* (1857) and Alain-Fournier's *Le Grand Meaulnes* (1913). Many Hermann Hesse novels, including *Demian, Steppenwolf, Siddhartha, Magister Ludi,* and *Under the Wheel* are *bildungsromans* about struggling/searching youth. Samuel Butler's *The Way of All Flesh* (written in 1885 and published in 1903) and James Joyce's *A Portrait of the Artist as a Young Man* (1916) are two outstanding modern examples. Variations include J. D. Salinger's *The Catcher in the Rye* (1951), set both within and beyond school, and William Golding's *Lord of the Flies* (1955), a novel not set in a school but one that is a coming-of-age story nonetheless.

Roman à clef, French for "novel with a key," means the story needs a real-life frame of reference, or key, for full comprehension. In Geoffrey Chaucer's *Canterbury Tales,* the Nun's Priest's Tale contains details that confuse readers unaware of history about the Earl of Bolingbroke's involvement in an assassination plot. Other literary works fitting this form include John Dryden's political satirical poem *Absalom and Achitophel* (1681), Jonathan Swift's satire *A Tale of a Tub* (1704), and George Orwell's political allegory *Animal Farm* (1945), all of which cannot be understood completely without knowing their camouflaged historical contents. *Roman à clefs* disguise truths too dangerous for authors to state directly. Readers must know about D. H. Lawrence's enemies to comprehend *Aaron's Rod* (1922). To appreciate Aldous Huxley's *Point Counter Point* (1928), readers must realize that the characters Mark Rampion and Denis Burlap respectively represent author Huxley and real-life critic John Middleton Murry. Marcel Proust's *Remembrance of Things Past (À la recherché du temps perdu,* 1871-1922) is informed by his social context. James Joyce's *Finnegans Wake* is an enormous *roman à clef* via multitudinous personal references.

Realism

Realism is a literary form whose goal is to represent reality as faithfully as possible. Its genesis in Western literature was a reaction against the sentimentality and extreme emotionalism of the works written in the literary movement of Romanticism, which championed feelings and their expression. Realists focused in great detail on immediacy of time and place, on specific actions of their characters, and the justifiable consequences of those actions. Some techniques of realism include writing in the vernacular, i.e., the characters' ordinary conversational language; writing in specific dialects used by some

Copyright © Mometrix Media. You have been licensed one copy of this document for personal use only. Any other reproduction or redistribution is strictly prohibited. All rights reserved.

characters; and emphasizing the analysis and development of characters more than the analysis and development of plots. Realistic literature often addresses various ethical issues. Historically, realistic works have often concentrated on the middle classes of the authors' societies. Realists eschew treatments that are too dramatic or sensationalistic as exaggerations of the reality that they strive to portray as closely as they are able.

Satire

Satire uses sarcasm, irony, and/or humor as social criticism to lampoon human folly. Unlike realism, which intends to depict reality as it exists without exaggeration, satire often involves creating situations or ideas deliberately exaggerating reality to be ridiculous to illuminate flawed behaviors. Ancient Roman satirists included Horace and Juvenal. Alexander Pope's poem "The Rape of the Lock" satirized the values of fashionable members of the 18th-century upper-middle class, which Pope found shallow and trivial. The theft of a lock of hair from a young woman is blown out of proportion: the poem's characters regard it as seriously as they would a rape. Irishman Jonathan Swift satirized British society, politics, and religion in works like *A Tale of a Tub.* In *A Modest Proposal,* Swift used essay form and mock-serious tone, satirically "proposing" cannibalism of babies and children as a solution to poverty and overpopulation. He satirized petty political disputes in *Gulliver's Travels.* Swift was known as a master of the ancient Roman Horatian and Juvenalian satirical styles.

Literary terminology

In works of prose such as novels, a group of connected sentences covering one main topic is termed a paragraph. In works of poetry, a group of verses similarly connected is called a stanza. In drama, when early works used verse, these were also divided into stanzas or couplets. Drama evolved to use predominantly prose. Overall, whether prose or verse, the conversation in a play is called dialogue. Large sections of dialogue spoken by one actor are called soliloquies or monologues. Dialogue that informs audiences but is unheard by other characters is called an aside. Novels and plays share certain common elements, such as characters—the people in the story; plot—the action of the story; a climax—when action and/or dramatic tension reaches its highest point; and denouement—the resolution following the climax. Sections dividing novels are called chapters, while sections of plays are called acts. Subsections of plays' acts are called scenes. Novels' chapters are usually not subdivided, although some novels have larger sections divided into groups of chapters.

Romanticism

The height of the Romantic movement occurred in the first half of the 19th century. It identified with and gained momentum from the French Revolution (1789) against the political and social standards of the aristocracy and its overthrowing of them. Romanticism was also part of the Counter-Enlightenment, a reaction of backlash against the Enlightenment's insistence on rationalism, scientific treatment of nature, and denial of emotionalism. Though expressed most overtly in the creative arts, Romanticism also affected politics, historiography, natural sciences, and education. Though often associated with radical, progressive, and liberal politics, it also included conservatism, especially in its influences on increased nationalism in many countries. The Romantics championed individual heroes, artists, and pioneers; freedom of expression; the exotic; and the power of the individual imagination. American authors Edgar Allan Poe and Nathaniel Hawthorne, Laurence Sterne in England, and Johann Wolfgang von Goethe in Germany were included

Copyright © Mometrix Media. You have been licensed one copy of this document for personal use only. Any other reproduction or redistribution is strictly prohibited. All rights reserved.

among well-known Romantic authors. The six major English Romantic poets were William Blake, William Wordsworth, Samuel Taylor Coleridge, Lord Byron, Percy Bysshe Shelley, and John Keats.

Rhetorical devices vs. figures of speech

Although figures of speech and rhetorical devices are very similar and overlap in many aspects of their definitions, one difference is that a figure of speech uses the effect of altering word meanings to express an idea more colorfully or vividly. For example, instead of saying a woman is strong-willed; free-spirited; feisty; attractive, yet unpredictable; and maybe dangerous, some people use the figure of speech, "She's a pistol." When the main purpose of a figure of speech becomes that of convincing or persuading the audience—the writer's readers or the speaker's listeners—of the writer's point or argument, then the figure of speech can be said to become a rhetorical device. One type of rhetorical device is anaphora: the repetition at regular intervals of the same word or phrase, used to create an effect. Walt Whitman used anaphora in his poems *Crossing Brooklyn Ferry:* "Flood-tide below me! I watch you, face to face; / Clouds of the west! sun there half an hour high! I see you also face to face." and *Song of Myself* (Part 51): "Do I contradict myself? / Very well then I contradict myself, / (I am large, I contain multitudes.)"

Both figures of speech and rhetorical devices are used to create calculated effects and communicate specific emphases. One main difference is that figures of speech change the meanings of words. For example, instead of writing, "She is brave", one writes "She is a tiger": this figure of speech employs a metaphor, conveying the same meaning but using a different word than the original. By contrast, an example of a rhetorical device used by some sources (Literary Devices.net 2014, Quizlet.com 2014) uses repetition to create emphasis without changing word meanings: "I am never ever going to rob anyone for you and never, never ever give in to your sinful wish." In Book V of *Paradise Lost,* the great poet John Milton uses rhetoric: "...advise him of his happy state—/ Happiness in his power left free to will, / Left to his own free will, his will though free / Yet mutable..." Describing Adam, Milton emphasized humanity's free will by repeating the words "free" and "will". But he also created ambiguity by writing "though free / Yet mutable", i.e. free will was changeable: Adam could lose freedom by sinning/erring.

Alliteration is both a literary and rhetorical device, using several words in sequence with the same initial sound. An example as literary device is in Wallace Stevens' (1922) poem "The Emperor of Ice Cream": "And bid him whip in kitchen cups concupiscent curds." Two examples of alliteration as rhetorical devices used by speakers for effect are Julius Caesar's "Veni, vidi, vici" ("I came, I saw, I conquered"), and John F. Kennedy's 1961 Inaugural Address: "Let us go forth to lead the land we love." Both repeated word-initial sounds to make their speeches more memorable. Hyperbole is extreme exaggeration for emphasis or effect. An example is in Andrew Marvell's famous (1650~1652) *carpe diem*-tradition poem "To His Coy Mistress": "My vegetable love should grow / Vaster than empires, and more slow; / An hundred years should go to praise / Thine eyes and on thine forehead gaze; / Two hundred to adore each breast, / But thirty thousand to the rest." Marvell exaggerates his love "Had we but world enough and time" as potentially growing longer than empires, hundreds and thousands of years.

Irony is the literary and rhetorical device of expressing one meaning by stating it using words that have the opposite meaning. In everyday speech it is also called sarcasm. An

Copyright © Mometrix Media. You have been licensed one copy of this document for personal use only. Any other reproduction or redistribution is strictly prohibited. All rights reserved.

example of irony in literature in Shakespeare's tragedy *Julius Caesar* is in Act 3, Scene 2, in Marc Antony's famous eulogy speech at Caesar's funeral: "He was my friend, faithful and just to me. / But Brutus says he was ambitious, / And Brutus is an honorable man." Antony is using irony when he calls Brutus "honorable" to mean he is not. Four lines earlier, he also says "For Brutus is an honorable man; / So are they all, all honorable men..." ironically and indirectly indicting the many dishonorable men involved. Oxymoron juxtaposes apparently contradictory words; some everyday speech examples include "jumbo shrimp", "deafening silence", "conspicuous absence", etc. A literary example is in Shakespeare's *Hamlet*, Act 3, Scene 4: "I must be cruel only to be kind." Shakespeare's phrasing was so popular it has since been adopted into everyday expressions.

Use of rhetoric in poetry

In Holy Sonnet 10 – "Death, be not proud" – the great Metaphysical poet John Donne rhetorically berates Death. In the final sestet, Donne writes: "Thou art slave to fate, chance, kings, and desperate men, / And dost with poison, war, and sickness dwell, / And poppy or charms can make us sleep as well / And better than thy stroke; why swell'st thou then?" This illustrates the message stated in the first quatrain: "Death, be not proud, though some have called thee / Mighty and dreadful, for thou art not so; / For those whom thou think'st dost overthrow / Die not, poor Death, nor yet canst thou kill me." Donne opens denying Death is as powerful or horrible as some say, then adding that some whom Death thinks it kills do not die, and neither can Death kill him. He supports this argument by subsequently diminishing Death's reputed power, characterizing Death as a "slave"; associating it with the poor company of "poison, war, and sickness"; and ultimately asks the rhetorical question, "why swell'st thou then?" meaning Death has no reason to swell with pride—deflating Death's value and strength.

Literary irony

In literature, irony demonstrates the opposite of what is said or done. Three types are verbal irony, situational irony, and dramatic irony. Verbal irony uses words opposite to the meaning. Sarcasm may use verbal irony. An everyday example is describing something confusing as "clear as mud." In his 1986 movie *Hannah and Her Sisters,* author/director/actor Woody Allen says to his character's date, "I had a great evening; it was like the Nuremburg Trials." Notice these employ similes. In situational irony, what happens contrasts with what was expected. In dramatic irony, narrative informs audiences of more than its characters know. O. Henry's short story *The Gift of the Magi* uses situational irony: a husband and wife each sacrifice their most prized possession to buy each other a Christmas present. The irony is that she sells her long hair to buy him a watch fob, while he sells his heirloom pocket-watch to buy her the jeweled combs for her hair she had long wanted; in the end, neither of them can use their gifts.

Literal and figurative meaning

When language is used literally, the words mean exactly what they say and nothing more. When language is used figuratively, the words mean something more and/or other than what they say. For example, "The weeping willow tree has long, trailing branches and leaves" is a literal description. But "The weeping willow tree looks as if it is bending over and crying" is a figurative description—specifically, a simile or stated comparison. Another figurative language form is metaphor, or an implied comparison. A good example is the

Copyright © Mometrix Media. You have been licensed one copy of this document for personal use only. Any other reproduction or redistribution is strictly prohibited. All rights reserved.

metaphor of a city, state, or city-state as a ship, and its governance as sailing that ship. Ancient Greek lyrical poet Alcaeus is credited with first using this metaphor, and ancient Greek tragedian Aeschylus then used it in *Seven Against Thebes,* and then Plato used it in the *Republic.* Henry Wadsworth Longfellow later famously referred to it in his poem, "O Ship of State" (1850), which has an extended metaphor with numerous nautical references throughout.

Figurative language

Figurative language is any language that extends past the literal meanings of the words. It serves the function of offering readers new insight into the people, things, events, and subjects covered in a work of literature. Figurative language also enables readers to feel they are sharing the authors' experiences. It can stimulate the reader's senses, make comparisons that readers find intriguing or even startling, and enable readers to view the world in different ways. Seven specific types of figurative language include: imagery, similes, metaphors, alliteration, personification, onomatopoeia, and hyperbole. Imagery is descriptive language that accesses the senses. Imagery can describe people, animals, or things. For example, the images T. S. Eliot uses in his poem "The Waste Land" of towers crumbling, wells dried up, and tombstones toppled over create mental images for the reader of the decay of a civilization.

Alliteration, personification, imagery, and simile
Alliteration is using a series of words containing the same sounds—assonance with vowels, and consonance with consonants. Personification is describing a thing or animal as a person. Imagery is description using sensory terms that create mental images for the reader of how people, animals, or things look, sound, feel, taste, and/or smell. This verse from Alfred Tennyson's poem "The Eagle" uses all of these types of figurative language: "He clasps the crag with crooked hands." Tennyson used alliteration, repeating /k/ and /kr/ sounds. These hard-sounding consonants reinforce the imagery giving visual and tactile impressions of the eagle. Tennyson also used personification, describing a bird as "he" and calling its talons "hands." Similes are stated comparisons using "like" or "as." William Wordsworth's poem about "Daffodils" begins, "I wandered lonely as a cloud." This simile compares his loneliness to that of a cloud. It is also personification, giving a cloud the human quality loneliness.

Metaphor and onomatopoeia
Metaphor is an implied comparison that does not use "like" or "as" the way a simile does. Henry Wadsworth Longfellow echoes the ancient Greeks in "O Ship of State": the metaphor compares the state and its government to a nautical ship and its sailing. Onomatopoeia uses words imitating the sounds of things they name/describe. For example, in his poem "Come Down, O Maid," Alfred Tennyson writes of "The moan of doves in immemorial elms, / And murmuring of innumerable bees." The word "moan" sounds like some sounds doves make, "murmuring" represents the sounds of bees buzzing, and "buzzing" is also an onomatopoetic word. And in his play *The Tempest,* in scene 2 of Act One, William Shakespeare's character Ariel says, "Hark, hark! / Bow-wow. / The watch-dogs bark! / Bow-wow. / Hark, hark! I hear/ The strain of strutting chanticleer / Cry, 'cock-a-diddle-dow!'" Onomatopoetic words represent the sounds of a dog barking and a rooster crowing, respectively. ("Strain" is also imagery describing a rooster's crow as song; "strain" paired with "strutting" is alliteration.)

Copyright © Mometrix Media. You have been licensed one copy of this document for personal use only. Any other reproduction or redistribution is strictly prohibited. All rights reserved.

Hyperbole

Hyperbole is excessive exaggeration used for humor or emphasis rather than for literal meaning. For example, in *To Kill a Mockingbird*, Harper Lee narrated, "People moved slowly then. There was no hurry, for there was nowhere to go, nothing to buy and no money to buy it with, nothing to see outside the boundaries of Maycomb County." This was not literally true; Lee exaggerates the scarcity of these things for emphasis. In "Old Times on the Mississippi," Mark Twain wrote, "I... could have hung my hat on my eyes, they stuck out so far." This is not literal, but makes his description vivid and funny. In his poem "As I Walked Out One Evening", W. H. Auden wrote, "I'll love you, dear, I'll love you / Till China and Africa meet, / And the river jumps over the mountain / And the salmon sing in the street." He used things not literally possible to emphasize his meaning that he will love the person addressed forever.

Literary examples of metaphor

A metaphor is an implied comparison, i.e. it compares something to something else without using "like", "as", or other comparative words. For example, in "The Tyger" (1794), William Blake writes, "Tyger Tyger, burning bright, / In the forests of the night;" this is a metaphor as Blake compares the tiger to a flame not by saying it is like a fire, but by simply describing it as "burning." Henry Wadsworth Longfellow's poem "O Ship of State" (1850) uses an extended metaphor by referring consistently throughout the entire poem to the state, union, or republic as a seagoing vessel, referring to its keel, mast, sail, rope, anchors, and to its braving waves, rocks, gale, tempest, and "false lights on the shore". Within the extended metaphor, Wordsworth uses a specific metaphor: "...the anchors of thy hope!" This is a metaphor because, like Blake (above), Wordsworth does not say the state's hope is like a ship's anchors; he equates them without using comparative words.

Literary examples of similes

A simile is a directly stated comparison of one thing to another thing, often using "like" or "as". In his novel *Lord Jim* (1900), Joseph Conrad writes in Chapter 33, "I would have given anything for the power to soothe her frail soul, tormenting itself in its invincible ignorance like a small bird beating about the cruel wires of a cage." Conrad uses the word "like" to compare the girl's soul to a small bird. His description of the bird beating at the cage shows the similar helplessness of the girl's soul to gain freedom. In his poetic Scots song "A Red, Red Rose" (1794), Robert Burns writes, "O my Luve's like a red, red rose, / That's newly sprung in June: / O my Luve's like the melodie, / That's sweetly play'd in tune." Burns uses "like" to compare his beloved to a beautiful, freshly blooming flower. In a second simile, he compares her to a beautiful musical melody. In the poem *The Daffodils* (1888), Wordsworth writes, "I wandered lonely as a cloud / that floats on high o'er vales and hills," comparing his persona's loneliness to that of a single cloud in the sky.

When an author uses similes to compare one thing to another, this gets readers' attention; stimulates readers' imaginations; and appeals to readers' senses by describing sensations of sight, sound, touch, smell, and/or taste. Similes lend more lifelike characteristics to fictional and poetic characters. Readers can more easily relate emotions expressed by authors to their own personal experiences when they read similes authors use. Consequently, readers can better understand literary subject matter when authors compare things to other things using similes. Additionally, similes offer readers ways to introduce more variety into the way they think, and show them different/new perspectives for perceiving reality. In his

Copyright © Mometrix Media. You have been licensed one copy of this document for personal use only. Any other reproduction or redistribution is strictly prohibited. All rights reserved.

"Sonnet 18" (1609), Shakespeare writes, "Shall I compare thee to a summer's day? / Thou art more lovely and more temperate". This simile does not use "like" or "as" the way many similes do, yet it does directly state a comparison by using the verb "compare".

Literary examples of personification

Personification is the device of attributing human qualities and/or behaviors/actions to something that is not human. While personification is the literary term for this, a synonym used in the social sciences is anthropomorphism. In his romantic tragedy *Romeo and Juliet* (1597), Shakespeare writes dialogue spoken by Capulet (Act 1, Scene 2): "When well-appareled April on the heel / Of limping winter treads..." This contains three instances of personification: (1) April is a month, not a lady, yet he describes April as being well-dressed and as (2) treading (walking); (3) winter is a season, does not have a physical heel, and cannot limp. In his poem "Loveliest of Trees" (1896), A. E. Housman describes the cherry tree as "Wearing white for Eastertide." He personifies the tree's white flowers as white clothing, as a human would wear for Easter. In her short story, "How Pearl Button Was Kidnapped" (1912), Katherine Mansfield describes "...little winds playing hide-and-seek..." She personifies breezes as playing children.

Personification, i.e. attributing human qualities and actions to inanimate objects, non-human living things, or abstract concepts, imbues text with more profound meanings. We humans tend to be anthrocentric; i.e., we view the world from our human perspective, seeing non-human entities in a human light as well. When authors and poets use personification, they bring inanimate objects to life and characterize plants, animals, and ideas with human traits. Readers can better understand the nature and behaviors of non-human things/creatures by reading about them through the lens of personification. We can more easily relate to human beings, qualities, traits, and behaviors than non-human ones. Moreover, author use of personification opens up new, divergent, varied, and creative perspectives for readers. As an example, in his poem "Ode: Intimations of Immortality from Recollections of Early Childhood" (1807), William Wordsworth writes, "The Moon doth with delight / Look round her when the heavens are bare". He personifies the inanimate object of the moon as a human female looking around "her", creating a vivid visual image and investing the scene with emotional mood and tone.

First-person narration

First-person narratives let narrators express inner feelings and thoughts, especially when the narrator is the protagonist as Lemuel Gulliver is in Jonathan Swift's *Gulliver's Travels.* The narrator may be a close friend of the protagonist, like Dr. Watson in Arthur Conan Doyle's *Sherlock Holmes.* Or the narrator can be less involved with the main characters and plot, like Nick Carraway in F. Scott Fitzgerald's *The Great Gatsby.* When a narrator reports others' narratives secondhand or more, s/he is a "frame narrator," like the nameless narrator of Joseph Conrad's *Heart of Darkness* or Mr. Lockwood in Emily Brontë's *Wuthering Heights.* First-person plural is unusual but can be effective, as in Isaac Asimov's *I, Robot;* William Faulkner's *A Rose for Emily;* Maxim Gorky's *Twenty-Six Men and a Girl;* or Jeffrey Eugenides' *The Virgin Suicides.* Author Kurt Vonnegut is the first-person narrator in his semi-autobiographical novel *Timequake.* Also unusual but effective is a first-person omniscient (rather than the more common third-person omniscient) narrator, like Death in Markus Zusak's *The Book Thief* and the dead girl's ghost in Alice Sebold's *The Lovely Bones.*

Copyright © Mometrix Media. You have been licensed one copy of this document for personal use only. Any other reproduction or redistribution is strictly prohibited. All rights reserved.

Second-person narration

While second-person address is very commonplace in popular song lyrics, it is the least used form of narrative voice in literary works. Popular serial books of the 1980s like *Fighting Fantasy* or *Choose Your Own Adventure* employed second-person narratives. In some cases, a narrative combines both second-person and first-person voices, speaking of "you" and "I." This can draw readers into the story, and it can also enable the authors to compare directly "your" and "my" feelings, thoughts, and actions. When the narrator is also a character in the story, as in Edgar Allan Poe's short story "The Tell-Tale Heart" or Jay McInerney's novel *Bright Lights, Big City*, the narrative is better defined as first-person despite its also addressing "you."

Third-person narration

Narration in the third person is the most often-used type, as it allows authors the most flexibility. It is so common that readers simply assume without needing to be informed that the narrator is not a character in, or involved in the story. Third-person singular is used more frequently than third-person plural, though some authors have also effectively used plural. However, both singular and plural are most often included in stories according to which character(s) is/are being described. The third-person narrator may be either objective or subjective, and either omniscient or limited. Objective third-person narration does not include what the characters described are thinking or feeling, while subjective third-person narration does. The third-person omniscient narrator knows everything about all characters, including their thoughts and emotions, and all related places, times, and events, whereas the third-person limited narrator may know everything about a particular character of focus, but is limited to that character; in other words, the narrator cannot speak about anything that character does not know.

Alternating-person narration

Although authors more commonly write stories from one point of view, there are also instances wherein they alternate the narrative voice within the same book. For example, they may sometimes use an omniscient third-person narrator and a more intimate first-person narrator at other times. In J. K. Rowling's series of *Harry Potter* novels, she often writes in a third-person limited narrative, but sometimes changes to narration by characters other than protagonist Harry Potter. George R. R. Martin's series *A Song of Ice and Fire* (the basis for the popular HBO TV series *Game of Thrones*) changes the point of view to coincide with divisions between chapters. The same technique is used by Erin Hunter (a pseudonym for several authors of the *Warriors, Seekers,* and *Survivors* book series). Authors using first-person narrative sometimes switch to third-person to describe significant action scenes, especially those where the narrator was absent or uninvolved, as Barbara Kingsolver does in her novel *The Poisonwood Bible.*

Classic analysis of plot structure

In *Poetics,* Aristotle defined plot as "the arrangement of the incidents." He meant not the story, but how it is structured for presentation. In tragedies, Aristotle found results driven by chains of cause-and-effect preferable to those driven by the protagonist's personality/character. He identified "unity of action" as necessary for a plot's wholeness; its events must be internally connected, not episodic or relying on *deus ex machina* or other

Copyright © Mometrix Media. You have been licensed one copy of this document for personal use only. Any other reproduction or redistribution is strictly prohibited. All rights reserved.

external intervention. A plot must have a beginning, middle, and end. Gustav Freytag adapted Aristotle's ideas into his Triangle/Pyramid (1863). The beginning, today called the exposition/incentive/inciting moment, emphasizes causes and de-emphasizes effects. Aristotle called the ensuing cause-and-effect *desis*, or tying up, today called complication(s) which occur during the rising action. These culminate in a crisis/climax/reversal/turning point, Aristotle's *peripateia*. This occurs at the plot's middle, where cause and effect are both emphasized. The falling action, which Aristotle called the *lusis* or unraveling, is today called the dénouement. The resolution comes at the catastrophe/outcome or end, when causes are emphasized and effects de-emphasized.

Story vs. discourse

In terms of plot, "story" is the characters, places, and events originating in the author's mind, while "discourse" is how the author arranges and sequences events—which may be chronological or not. Story is imaginary; discourse is words on the page. Discourse allows story to be told in different ways. One element of plot structure is relating events differently from the order in which they occurred. This is easily done with cause-and-effect; for example, in the sentence, "He died following a long illness," we know the illness preceded the death, but the death precedes the illness in words. In Kate Chopin's short story "The Story of an Hour" (1894), she tells some of the events out of chronological order, which has the effect of amplifying the surprise of the ending for the reader. Another element of plot structure is selection. Chopin omits some details, such as Mr. Mallard's trip home; this allows readers to be as surprised at his arrival as Mrs. Mallard is.

Analysis of plot structures through recurring patterns in actions or events

Authors of fiction select characters, places, and events from their imaginations and arrange them in ways that will affect their readers. One way to analyze plot structure is to compare and contrast different events in a story. For example, in Kate Chopin's "The Story of an Hour," a very simple but key pattern of repetition is the husband's leaving and then returning. Such patterns fulfill the symmetrical aspect that Aristotle said was required of sound plot structure. In James Baldwin's short story, "Sonny's Blues," the narrator is Sonny's brother. In an encounter with one of Sonny's old friends early in the story, the brother initially disregards his communication. In a subsequent flashback, Baldwin informs us that this was the same way he had treated Sonny. In Nathaniel Hawthorne's "Young Goodman Brown," a pattern is created by the protagonist's recurrent efforts not to go farther into the wood; in Herman Melville's "Bartleby the Scrivener," by Bartleby's repeated refusals; and in William Faulkner's "Barn Burning," by the history of barn-burning episodes.

Conflict

A conflict is a problem to be solved. Literary plots typically include one conflict or more. Characters' attempts to resolve conflicts drive the narrative's forward movement. Conflict resolution is often the protagonist's primary occupation. Physical conflicts like exploring, wars, and/or escapes tend to make plots most suspenseful and exciting. Emotional, mental, and/or moral conflicts tend to make stories more personally gratifying or rewarding for many audiences. Conflicts can be external or internal. A major type of internal conflict is some inner personal battle, or "man against himself." Major types of external conflicts include "man against nature," "man against man," and "man against society." Readers can identify conflicts in literary plots by asking themselves who the protagonist is, who or what

Copyright © Mometrix Media. You have been licensed one copy of this document for personal use only. Any other reproduction or redistribution is strictly prohibited. All rights reserved.

the antagonist is, why the antagonist is an antagonist, why the protagonist and antagonist conflict, what events develop the conflict, which event is the climax, what the outcome tells them about the protagonist, and whether they sympathized or identified with the protagonist or antagonist and why.

Mood and tone

Mood is a story's atmosphere, or the feelings the reader gets from reading it. The way authors set the mood in writing is comparable to the way filmmakers use music to set the mood in movies. Instead of music, though, writers judiciously select evocative or descriptive words to evoke certain moods. The mood of a work may convey joy, anger, bitterness, hope, gloom, fear, an ominous feeling, or any other emotion the author wants the reader to feel. In addition to vocabulary choices, authors also use figurative expressions, particular sentence structures, and choices of diction that project and reinforce the moods they want to create. Whereas mood is the reader's emotions evoked by reading what is written, tone is the emotions and attitudes of the writer that s/he expresses in the writing. Authors use the same literary techniques to establish tone as they do to establish mood. An author may use a humorous tone, an angry or sad tone, a sentimental or unsentimental tone, or something else entirely.

Purposes of good dialogue

In literary fiction, effectively written dialogue serves at least one but usually several purposes. It advances the story and moves the plot. It develops the characters. It sheds light on the work's theme(s) or meaning(s). It can, often subtly, account for the passage of time not otherwise indicated. It can alter the direction that the plot is taking, typically by introducing some new conflict(s) or changing (an) existing one(s). Dialogue can establish a work's narrative voice and/or the characters' voices and set the tone of the story or of particular characters. When fictional characters display enlightenment or realization, dialogue can give readers an understanding of what those characters have discovered, and how. Dialogue can illuminate the motivations and wishes of the story's characters for its readers. By using consistent thoughts and syntax, dialogue can support character development. Skillfully created, it can also represent real-life speech rhythms in written form. Via conflicts and ensuing action, dialogue also provides drama.

In fictional literary works, effectively written dialogue should not have only the effect of breaking up or interrupting sections of narrative. Well-written dialogue does not reproduce verbatim things said in an author's real-life experiences. While dialogue may supply exposition for readers, it must nonetheless be believable. Dialogue should be dynamic, not static, and it should not resemble regular prose not representing conversation. Authors should not use dialogue as prose contexts for self-consciously "clever" similes or metaphors, which is unnatural and awkward. Dialogue should not slow down the movement of the plot or the story. When narrative would better establish a story's setting, authors should not substitute dialogue, which would be inappropriate. Authors should not express their own opinions in characters' dialogue. They should not try to imitate what real-life characters would say; dialogue must seem and sound natural, rather than actually duplicating natural speech. Dialogue should also not simply consist of conversations enclosed in quotation marks that do not serve the purpose of the story.

Copyright © Mometrix Media. You have been licensed one copy of this document for personal use only. Any other reproduction or redistribution is strictly prohibited. All rights reserved.

Literary theme

When we read parables, their themes are the lessons they aim to teach. When we read fables, the moral of each story is its theme. When we read fictional works, the authors' perspectives regarding life and human behavior are their themes. Unlike in parables and fables, themes in literary fiction are not meant to preach or teach the readers a lesson. Hence themes in fiction are not as explicit as they are in parables or fables. Instead they are implicit, and the reader only infers them. By analyzing the fictional characters through thinking about their actions and behavior, and understanding the setting of the story and reflecting on how its plot develops, the reader comes to infer the main theme(s) of the work. When writers succeed, they communicate with their readers such that some common ground is established between author and audience. While a reader's individual experience may differ in its details from the author's written story, both may share universal underlying truths which allow author and audience to connect.

Determining theme

In well-crafted literature, theme, structure, and plot are interdependent and inextricable: each element informs and reflects the others. The structure of a work is how it is organized. The theme is the central idea or meaning found in it. The plot is what happens in the story. (Plots can be physical actions or mental processes—e.g., Marcel Proust.) Titles can also inform us of a work's theme. For instance, Edgar Allan Poe's title "The Tell-Tale Heart" informs us of its theme of guilt before we even read about the repeated heartbeat the protagonist begins hearing immediately before and constantly after committing and hiding a murder. Repetitive patterns of events or behaviors also give clues to themes. The same is true of symbols: in F. Scott Fitzgerald's *The Great Gatsby,* for Jay Gatsby the green light at the end of the dock symbolizes Daisy Buchanan and his own dreams for the future. More generally, it symbolizes the American Dream, and narrator Nick Carraway explicitly compares it to early settlers' sight of America rising from the ocean.

Thematic development

In *The Great Gatsby*, F. Scott Fitzgerald portrayed 1920s America as greedy, cynical, and rife with moral decay. Jay Gatsby's lavish weekly parties symbolize the reckless excesses of the Jazz Age. The growth of bootlegging and organized crime in reaction to Prohibition is symbolized by the character of Meyer Wolfsheim and by Gatsby's own ill-gotten wealth. Fitzgerald symbolized social divisions using geography: the "old money" aristocrats like the Buchanans lived on East Egg, while the "new money" bourgeois like Gatsby lived on West Egg. Fitzgerald also used weather, as many authors have, to reinforce narrative and emotional tones in the novel. Just as in *Romeo and Juliet*, William Shakespeare set the confrontation of Tybalt and Mercutio and its deadly consequences on the hottest summer day under a burning sun, in *The Great Gatsby*, Fitzgerald did the same with Tom Wilson's deadly confrontation with Gatsby. Both works are ostensible love stories carrying socially critical themes about the destructiveness of pointless and misguided behaviors—family feuds in the former, pursuit of money in the latter.

In Victor Hugo's novel *Les Misérables*, the overall metamorphosis of protagonist Jean Valjean from a cynical ex-convict into a noble benefactor demonstrates Hugo's theme of the importance of love and compassion for others. Hugo also reflects this in more specific plot events. For example, Valjean's love for Cosette sustains him through many difficult periods

Copyright © Mometrix Media. You have been licensed one copy of this document for personal use only. Any other reproduction or redistribution is strictly prohibited. All rights reserved.

and trying events. Hugo illustrates how love and compassion for others beget the same in them: Bishop Myriel's kindness to Valjean eventually inspires him to become honest. Years later, Valjean, as M. Madeleine, has rescued Fauchelevent from under a fallen carriage, Fauchelevent returns the compassionate act by giving Valjean sanctuary in the convent. M. Myriel's kindness also ultimately enables Valjean to rescue Cosette from the Thénardiers. Receiving Valjean's father-like love enables Cosette to fall in love with and marry Marius. And the love between Cosette and Marius enables the couple to forgive Valjean for his past crimes when they are revealed.

In one of his shortest stories, Poe used economy of language to emphasize the murderer-narrator's obsessive focus on bare details like the victim's cataract-milky eye, the sound of a heartbeat, and insistence he is sane. The narrator begins by denying he is crazy, even citing his extreme agitation as proof of sanity. Contradiction is then extended: the narrator loves the old man, yet kills him. His motives are irrational—not greed or revenge, but to relieve the victim of his "evil eye." Because "eye" and "I" are homonyms, readers may infer that eye/I symbolizes the old man's identity, contradicting the killer's delusion that he can separate them. The narrator distances himself from the old man by perceiving his eye as separate, and dismembering his dead body. This backfires in another body part when he imagines the victim's heartbeat, which is really his own. Guilty and paranoid, he gives himself away. Poe predated Freud in exploring the paradox of killing those we love and the concept of projecting our own processes onto others.

William Faulkner contrasts the traditions of the antebellum South with the rapid changes of post-Civil War industrialization in his short story *A Rose for Emily*. The central character, Emily Grierson, denies the reality of modern progress, living inside the isolated world of her house. Contradictorily, she is both a testament to time-honored history and a mysterious, eccentric, unfathomable burden. Faulkner portrays her with deathlike imagery even in life, comparing her to a drowned woman and referring to her skeleton. Emily symbolizes the Old South; as her social status is degraded, so is the antebellum social order. Like Miss Havisham in Charles Dickens' *Great Expectations*, Emily preserves her bridal bedroom, denying change and time's passage. Emily tries to control death through denial, shown in her necrophilia with her father's corpse and her killing Homer Barron to stop him from leaving her, then also denying his death. Faulkner uses the motif of dust throughout to represent not only the decay of Emily, her house, and Old Southern traditions, but also how her secrets are obscured from others.

The great White Whale in *Moby-Dick* plays various roles to different characters. In Captain Ahab's obsessive, monomaniacal quest to kill it, the whale represents all evil, and Ahab believes it his duty and destiny to rid the world of it. Ishmael attempts through multiple scientific disciplines to understand the whale objectively, but fails—it is hidden underwater and mysterious to humans—reinforcing Melville's theme that humans can never know everything; here the whale represents the unknowable and may be interpreted as symbolizing God. Melville reverses white's usual connotation of purity in Ishmael's dread of white, associated with crashing waves, polar animals, albinos—all frightening and unnatural. White is often viewed as an absence of color, yet white light is the sum total of all colors in the spectrum. In the same way, white can signify both absence of meaning, and totality of meaning incomprehensible to humans. As a creature of nature, the whale also symbolizes how 19th-century white men's exploitative expansionistic actions were destroying the natural environment.

Copyright © Mometrix Media. You have been licensed one copy of this document for personal use only. Any other reproduction or redistribution is strictly prohibited. All rights reserved.

Because of the old fisherman Santiago's struggle to capture a giant marlin, some people characterize Ernest Hemingway's story as telling of man against nature. However, it can more properly be interpreted as telling of man's role as part of nature. Both man and fish are portrayed as brave, proud, and honorable. In Hemingway's world, all creatures, including humans, must either kill or be killed. Santiago reflects, "man can be destroyed but not defeated," following this principle in his life. As heroes are often created through their own deaths, Hemingway seems to believe that while being destroyed is inevitable, destruction enables living beings to transcend it by fighting bravely with honor and dignity. Hemingway echoes Romantic poet John Keats' contention that only immediately before death can we understand beauty as it is about to be destroyed. He also echoes ancient Greek and Roman myths and the Old Testament with the tragic flaw of overweening pride/overreaching. Like Icarus, Prometheus, and Adam and Eve, the old man "went out too far."

Universal theme in ancient religious texts

The Old Testament book Genesis, the Quran, and the Epic of Gilgamesh all contain flood stories. Versions differ somewhat: Genesis describes a worldwide flood, attributing it to God's decision that mankind, his creation, had become incontrovertibly wicked in spirit and must be destroyed for the world to start anew. The Quran describes the flood as regional, caused by Allah after sending Nuh (notice the similarity in name to Noah) as a messenger to his people to cease their evil. The Quran stipulates Allah only destroys those who deny or ignore messages from his messengers. Marked similarities also exist: in the Gilgamesh poems Utnapishtim, like Noah, is instructed to build a ship to survive the flood. Both men send out birds afterward as tests, and both include doves and a raven, though with different outcomes. Historians and archeologists believe a Middle Eastern tidal wave was a real basis for these stories. However, their universal themes remain the same: the flood was seen as God's way of wiping out humans whose behavior had become ungodly.

Theme of overreaching

A popular theme throughout literature is the human trait of reaching too far or presuming too much. In Greek mythology, Daedalus constructed wings of feathers and wax that men might fly like birds. He permitted his son Icarus to try them, but cautioned the boy not to fly too close to the sun. The impetuous youth (in what psychologist David Elkind later named adolescence's myth of invincibility) ignored this, flying too close to the sun: the wax melted, the wings disintegrated, and Icarus fell into the sea and perished. In the Old Testament, God warned Adam and Eve not to eat fruit from the tree of knowledge of good and evil, that they might remain pure and innocent. Ignoring this banished them from Eden's eternal perfection, condemning them to mortality and suffering. The Romans were themselves examples of over-reachers in their conquest and assimilation of most of the then-known world and ultimate demise. In Christopher Marlowe's *Dr. Faustus* and Johann Wolfgang von Goethe's *Faust,* the protagonist sells his soul to the Devil for unlimited knowledge and success.

Carpe diem tradition in poetry

Carpe diem is Latin for "seize the day." A long poetic tradition, it advocates making the most of time because it passes swiftly and life is short. It is found in multiple languages, including Latin, Torquato Tasso's Italian, Pierre de Ronsard's French, and Edmund Spenser's English,

Copyright © Mometrix Media. You have been licensed one copy of this document for personal use only. Any other reproduction or redistribution is strictly prohibited. All rights reserved.

and is often used in seduction to argue for indulging in earthly pleasures. Roman poet Horace's Ode 1.11 tells younger woman Leuconoe to enjoy the present, not worrying about inevitable aging. Two Renaissance Metaphysical Poets, Andrew Marvell and Robert Herrick, treated *carpe diem* more as a call to action. In "To His Coy Mistress," Marvell points out that time is fleeting, arguing for love, and concluding that because they cannot stop time, they may as well defy it, getting the most out of the short time they have. In "To the Virgins, to Make Much of Time," Herrick advises young women to take advantage of their good fortune in being young by getting married before they become too old to attract men and have babies.

"To His Coy Mistress" begins, "Had we but world enough, and time, / This coyness, lady, were no crime." Using imagery, Andrew Marvell describes leisure they could enjoy if time were unlimited. Arguing for seduction, he continues famously, "But at my back I always hear/Time's winged chariot hurrying near; / And yonder all before us lie / Deserts of vast eternity." He depicts time as turning beauty to death and decay. Contradictory images in "amorous birds of prey" and "tear our pleasures with rough strife / Thorough the iron gates of life" overshadow romance with impending death, linking present pleasure with mortality and spiritual values with moral considerations. Marvell's concluding couplet summarizes *carpe diem*: "Thus, though we cannot make our sun / Stand still, yet we will make him run." "To the Virgins, to Make Much of Time" begins with the famous "Gather ye rosebuds while ye may." Rather than seduction to live for the present, Robert Herrick's experienced persona advises young women's future planning: "Old time is still a-flying / And this same flower that smiles today, / Tomorrow will be dying."

Making predictions

When we read literature, making predictions about what will happen in the writing reinforces our purpose(s) for reading and prepares us mentally for beginning to read, and for continuing to read further. We can make predictions before we begin reading and during our reading. As we read on, we can test the accuracy of our predictions, revise them in light of additional reading, and confirm or refute our predictions. Some things that can help readers to make predictions about literary works include: thinking about the title of the book, poem, or play; looking at the illustrations when there are any; considering the structure of the text as we read; making use of our existing knowledge relative to the subject of the text; asking ourselves questions about the story, characters, and subject matter, particularly "why" and "who" questions; and then answering these questions for ourselves by referring to the text.

Textual evidence

Textual evidence to evaluate reader predictions about literature includes specific synopses of the work, paraphrases of the work or parts of it, and direct quotations from it. The best literary analysis shows special insight into a theme, character trait, or change. The best textual evidence supporting analysis is strong, relevant, and accurate. Analysis that is not best, but enough, shows reasonable understanding of theme, character trait, or change; contains supporting textual evidence that is relevant and accurate, if not strong; and shows a specific and clear response. Analysis that partially meets criteria also shows reasonable understanding, but the textual evidence is generalized, incomplete, only partly relevant or accurate, or connected only weakly. Or there may be only relevant, accurate textual evidence, but no analysis and a vague or unclear response. Analysis that is vague, too general or incorrect, with an unclear response and irrelevant or incomplete textual

Copyright © Mometrix Media. You have been licensed one copy of this document for personal use only. Any other reproduction or redistribution is strictly prohibited. All rights reserved.

evidence; that only summarizes the plot; and/or that answers the wrong question, or answers no question, is not enough to be adequate.

Making connections to enhance reading comprehension

Reading involves thinking. For good comprehension, readers make text-to-self, text-to-text, and text-to-world connections. Making connections helps readers understand text better and predict what might occur next based on what they already know, such as how characters in the story feel or what happened in another text. Text-to-self connections with the reader's life and experiences make literature more personally relevant and meaningful to readers. Readers can make connections before, during, and after reading—including whenever the text reminds them of something similar they have encountered in life or other texts. Knowing a work's genre (mystery, fantasy, or whatever it may be); common practices of a certain author; a story's geographical, historical, and social setting; characters that remind us of other people; familiar plot elements; literary structure and devices (such as flashbacks); themes encountered in other works; and similar use of language and tone to other works are all means for connections. Venn diagrams and other graphic organizers help visualize connections. Readers can also make double-entry notes: key content, ideas, events, words, and quotations on one side, and the connections with these on the other.

Summarizing literature to support comprehension

When reading literature, especially demanding works, summarizing helps readers identify important information and organize it in their minds; briefly monitor understanding; identify the main theme(s), problems and solutions; and sequence the story. Readers can summarize before, during, and after they read. They can refer to examples of other occasions in life for summarizing: giving others directions, generally describing our weekends or summers in limited time, and explaining news items/articles we read, to name a few. To summarize literary content, readers should use their own words. Previewing a text's organization before reading by examining the book cover, table of contents, and illustrations also aids summarizing. So does making notes of key words and ideas in a graphic organizer while reading. Graphic organizers can also be used after reading: readers skim the text, pick out the most important parts of three to five sentences, and determine what can be omitted with the aid of the organizer. Unimportant details should be omitted in summaries. Summaries of nonfiction can include description, problem-solution, comparison-contrast, sequence, main ideas, and cause-and-effect.

Evaluation of summaries of literary passages

A summary of a literary passage is a condensation in the reader's own words of the passage's main points. Some guidelines for evaluating a summary of a literary passage include: The summary should be complete yet concise. It should be accurate, balanced, fair, neutral, and objective, excluding the reader's own opinions or reactions. It should reflect in similar proportion how much each point summarized was covered in the original passage. Summary writers should include tags of attribution, like "Macaulay argues that" to reference the original author whose ideas are represented in the summary. Summary writers should not overuse quotations: they should only quote central concepts or phrases they cannot precisely convey in words other than those of the original author. Another aspect in evaluating a summary is whether it can stand alone as a coherent, unified composition, albeit a brief one. In addition, evaluation of a summary should include whether

Copyright © Mometrix Media. You have been licensed one copy of this document for personal use only. Any other reproduction or redistribution is strictly prohibited. All rights reserved.

its writer has cited the original source of the passage so that readers of the summary can find it.

Literary theories and criticism and interpretation

Literary theory gives a rationale for the literary subject matter of criticism, and also for the process of interpreting literature. For example, Aristotle's *Poetics'* requirement of unity underlies any discussion of unity in Sophocles' *Oedipus Rex.* Postcolonial theory, assuming historical racism and exploitation, informs Nigerian novelist and critic Chinua Achebe's contention that in *Heart of Darkness,* Joseph Conrad does not portray Africans with complete humanity. Gender and feminist theories support critics' interpretation of Edna Pontellier's drowning at the climax of Kate Chopin's novel *The Awakening* (1899) as suicide. Until the 19th century, critics largely believed literature referenced objective reality, holding "a mirror up to nature" as William Shakespeare wrote. Twentieth-century Structuralism and New Historicism were predated and influenced by radical, non-traditional, historicized, cross-cultural comparative interpretations of biblical text in 19th-century German "higher criticism." Literary critic Charles Augustin Saint-Beuve maintained that biography could completely explain literature; contrarily, Marcel Proust demonstrated in narrative that art completely transformed biography. A profound 19th-century influence on literary theory was Friedrich Nietzsche's idea that facts must be interpreted to become facts.

Drawing inferences

Inferences about literary text are logical conclusions that readers make based on their observations and previous knowledge. By inferring, readers construct meanings from text relevant to them personally. By combining their own schemas or concepts and their background information pertinent to the text with what they read, readers interpret it according to both what the author has conveyed and their own unique perspectives. Authors do not always explicitly spell out every meaning in what they write; many meanings are implicit. Through inference, readers can comprehend implied meanings in the text, and also derive personal significance from it, making the text meaningful and memorable to them. Inference is a natural process in everyday life. When readers infer, they can draw conclusions about what the author is saying, predict what may reasonably follow, amend these predictions as they continue to read, interpret the import of themes, and analyze the characters' feelings and motivations through their actions, and much more.

Textual evidence to analyze literature

Knowing about the historical background and social context of a literary work, as well as the identity of that work's author, can help to inform the reader about the author's concerns and intended meanings. For example, George Orwell published his novel *1984* in the year 1949, soon after the end of World War II. At that time, following the defeat of the Nazis, the Cold War began between the Western Allied nations and the Eastern Soviet Communists. People were therefore concerned about the conflict between the freedoms afforded by Western democracies versus the oppression represented by Communism. Author Orwell had also previously fought in the Spanish Civil War against a Spanish regime that he and his fellows viewed as oppressive. From this information, readers can infer that Orwell was concerned about oppression by totalitarian governments. This informs *1984*'s story of Winston Smith's rebellion against the oppressive "Big Brother" government of the fictional

Copyright © Mometrix Media. You have been licensed one copy of this document for personal use only. Any other reproduction or redistribution is strictly prohibited. All rights reserved.

dictatorial state of Oceania and his capture, torture, and ultimate conversion by that government.

Effects of story events on works' meanings

Novelist E. M. Forster has made the distinction between story as relating a series of events, such as a king dying and then his queen dying, versus plot as establishing motivations for actions and causes for events, such as a king dying and then his queen dying from grief over his death. Thus plot fulfills the function of helping readers understand cause-and-effect in events and underlying motivations in characters' actions, which in turn helps them understand life. This affects a work's meaning by supporting its ability to explain why things happen, why people do things, and ultimately explain some of the meaning in life. Some authors find that while story events convey meaning, they do not tell readers there is any one meaning in life or way of living, but rather are mental experiments with various meanings and ways of life enabling readers to explore. Hence stories may not necessarily be constructed to impose one definitive meaning, but rather to find some shape, direction, and meaning within otherwise random events.

Analysis of character development

To understand the characters in a literary text, we can consider what kinds of observations the author makes about each character. We can look for contradictions in what a character thinks, says, and does. We can notice whether the author's observations about a character differ from what other characters in the story say about that character. We can note how the author describes each character. A character may be dynamic in that s/he changes in some significant way(s) during the story, or static in that s/he remains the same from the beginning of the story to the end. Characters may be perceived as "flat" or, in other words, not fully developed and/or without salient personality traits, or "round," as in more well developed, with characteristics that stand out vividly. Another thing to consider is whether characters in a story symbolize any universal properties. In addition, as readers we can think about whether we could compare and/or contrast the attributes of two characters in the same story to analyze how authors develop characters.

Explanations of Medieval/Renaissance Christian allegory

The student should explain that in literature, authors of allegory use all of the literal plot elements of their writing as symbols to represent more abstract subjects. For example, in *The Divine Comedy*, Dante symbolizes the human soul's efforts to achieve moral beliefs and behaviors and become united with God by narrating his persona's literal adventures as he travels through the kingdoms of Hell, Purgatory, and Heaven (*Inferno, Purgatorio,* and *Paradiso*). What appear literal stories of fantasy experiences are allegorical references to the human spiritual quest. The student should provide textual evidence, for example, quoting the *Inferno*'s opening: "Midway on our life's journey, I found myself / In dark woods, the right road lost". The student could then explain that by the plural first-person possessive in "*our* life's journey", Dante connects his persona's story to all of humanity's universal experience, reinforcing this by referring to "the right road" of which he has lost track. The student should explain the "dark woods" as an allegorical symbol of a human being's sinful, unenlightened Earthly existence and the "right road" symbolizing the life of virtue that unites people with God.

Copyright © Mometrix Media. You have been licensed one copy of this document for personal use only. Any other reproduction or redistribution is strictly prohibited. All rights reserved.

Example student explanation of poet's use of quote from earlier poet's work

In "The Love Song of J. Alfred Prufrock", Eliot's six-line epigraph is from Canto 27 of Dante's *Inferno.* Eliot quotes Dante's original Italian, spoken by Guido da Montefeltro: *"S'io credesse che mia risposta fosse / A persona che mai tornasse al mondo, / Questa fiamma staria senza piu scosse. /Ma perciocche giammai di questo fondo/Non torno vivo alcun, s'i'odo il vero, / Senza tema d'infamia ti rispondo."* Eliot omits translation: "If I believed my answer would be to a person who could return to the world, this flame would stay without more motion; but because nobody has ever come back alive from this abyss, if what I hear is true, without fear of infamy I can reply." Guido, fearing worldly ill repute for evil Earthly deeds, believed he could confide these to Dante—also trapped in Hell, hence unable to repeat them. Guido's "flame" represents his disembodied form in Hell: if he believed Dante could return to Earth (which he ultimately did), he/it would move/speak no more. "Prufrock" echoes the hellish setting, depicting hypocrites pretending goodness. Prufrock's concern for his reputation echoes Guido's: *Prufrock*'s dramatic monologue is best safely addressed to nobody who would repeat it.

Interpretation of quotes and references in first section of T. S. Eliot's *The Waste Land*

In *The Waste Land*'s first section, "The Burial of the Dead", Eliot refers to Chaucer's *Canterbury* Tales opening about April—but twisting it from Chaucer's happy depiction of its "sweet showers" to "...the cruelest month, breeding / Lilacs out of the dead land, mixing / memory and desire..." He quotes Wagner's opera *Tristan and Isolde* retelling the Arthurian story of adulterous lovers and the loss experienced through their actions. Eliot used his extensive knowledge of literature to reinforce his depiction of the fragmented, decayed "waste land" of post-World War I twentieth-century society. Two major influences Eliot took were *From Ritual to Romance* by Jessie Weston and *The Golden Bough* by Sir James Frazier—both British contemporaries of Eliot (born in America but resettled in England). Both authors described ancient fertility rites reflected Arthurian legend and modern religion and thought—prominently, the Fisher King legend. His wounds, causing impotence, made his country a "waste land." The land's fertility could be reclaimed by healing the Fisher King. Eliot incorporates the Fisher King theme in *The Waste Land*—yet without healing potential, reinforcing the modern world's lack of mythological or religious narrative to unify it.

Example student explanation of extended metaphor of mechanical object as an animal

In her poem "I like to see it lap the Miles", Emily Dickinson describes a railroad train, a new invention during her time, via extended metaphor comparing it to a horse. She writes of seeing the train "lap the miles—/And lick the Valleys up—/And/...feed itself at Tanks..." She describes seeing it "...prodigious step / Around a Pile of Mountains...And then a Quarry pare / To fit its Ribs..." She describes the train's whistle as "...horrid—hooting stanza" and further characterizes it as a "neigh". She concludes the poem by describing how the train, like a horse, will "...punctual as a Star / Stop—docile and omnipotent / At its own stable door—", representing the train depot/station as a horse's "stable". Juxtaposing the opposites of docility and omnipotence, Dickinson alludes to the way horses are physically powerful, yet often gentle and obedient to much smaller, physically weaker humans. Through the extended metaphor, she moreover likens the train to a horse, for its great power harnessed and controlled by humans.

Copyright © Mometrix Media. You have been licensed one copy of this document for personal use only. Any other reproduction or redistribution is strictly prohibited. All rights reserved.

Student interpretation of imagery

In Act I, Scene V of *Romeo and Juliet*, Shakespeare writes dialogue wherein Romeo describes how beautiful Juliet is using visual imagery: "O, she doth teach the torches to burn bright! / It seems she hangs upon the cheek of night / Like a rich jewel in an Ethiope's ear..." By saying she "teaches" torches to burn brightly, Shakespeare makes the point that Juliet's radiance surpasses that of the flames, contrasting it with the darkness of night. Then, he compares night's darkness to an Ethiopian's skin, and Juliet's contrasting brilliance to a gem's glow in an earring against the dark skin. In "Ode to Autumn", Keats uses auditory imagery to bring the season's "music" alive: "...in a wailful choir the small gnats mourn /...Or sinking as the light wind lives or dies; / And full-grown lambs loud bleat from hilly bourn; / Hedge-crickets sing; and now with treble soft / The redbreast whistles from a garden-croft, / And gathering swallows twitter in the skies." He appeals to readers' hearing, describing intermittent wind; gnats mourning in a "wailful choir"; lambs bleating; crickets singing; a robin's soft treble whistling; and swallows twittering.

Copyright © Mometrix Media. You have been licensed one copy of this document for personal use only. Any other reproduction or redistribution is strictly prohibited. All rights reserved.

Rhetoric and Composition

Evaluating information sources in various media forms

With the wealth of media in different formats available today, users are more likely to take media on their face value with less questioning. However, to understand the content of media, consumers must act as educated consumers by critically evaluating each source. Users should ask themselves about media sources: Who is delivering this message, and why? What methods do a media source's publishers employ to gain and maintain users' attention? Which points of view is the media source representing? What are the various ways in which a reader of a media source could interpret the message that the source is delivering? And what information is missing from the message conveyed by a media source? Is the source scholarly, i.e., peer-reviewed? Does it include author names and their credentials pertinent to the information? Who publishes it, and why? Who is the target audience? Is the language technically specific or non-technical/public? Are sources cited, research claims documented, conclusions based on furnished evidence, and references provided? Is the publication current? All of these questions and more can and should be asked of media sources.

For books, consider whether information is up-to-date, and whether historical perspectives apply. Content is more likely to be scholarly if publishers are universities, government, or professional organizations. Looking for book reviews also informs users. For articles, look for biographical author information; publisher name; frequency of periodical publication; and whether advertising is included and, if so, whether for certain occupations/disciplines. For web pages, check their domain names, publishers or sponsors (strip back URLs to uncover), look for author/publisher contact information, check dates of most recent page updates, and be alert to biases and verify information's validity. Quality and accuracy of web pages located through search engines rather than library databases ranges widely, indicating careful user inspection. Web page recommendations from reliable sources like university faculties can help indicate quality and accuracy. Citations of websites by credible or scholarly sources also show reliability, as do links from other reputable sites. Authors' names, relevant credentials, affiliations, and contact information support their authority. Site functionality, such as ease of navigation, ability to search, site maps and/or indexes, are also criteria to consider.

Persuasive media

Some media using persuasion are advertising, public relations, and advocacy. Advertisers use persuasion to get consumers to purchase goods and services. The public relations field uses persuasion to give consumers good impressions of companies, governments, or organizations. Advocacy groups use persuasion to garner support or votes. Sources use commercials, public service announcements, speeches, websites, and newsletters, among others. Activists, lobbyists, government officials, and politicians use political rhetoric involving persuasive techniques. Basic techniques include using celebrity spokespersons, whom consumers admire or aspire to resemble; or, conversely, "everyday people" (albeit often portrayed by actors) with whom consumers identify. Using expert testimonials lends credibility. Explicit claims of content, effectiveness, quality, and reliability—which often

Copyright © Mometrix Media. You have been licensed one copy of this document for personal use only. Any other reproduction or redistribution is strictly prohibited. All rights reserved.

cannot be proven or disproven—are used to persuade. While news and advocacy messages mostly eschew humor for credibility's sake (except in political satire), advertising often persuades via humor, which gets consumer attention and associates its pleasure with advertised products and services. "Weasel words," such as qualifiers, are often combined with exaggerated claims. Intensifiers—hyperbole, superlatives, and repetition—within and of messages, and sentimental appeals are also persuasive.

Intermediate techniques

Dangerous propagandist Adolf Hitler said people suspect little lies more than big ones; hence the "Big Lie" is a persuasion method requiring consumers' keen critical thinking to identify. A related method is charisma, which can induce people even to believe messages they would otherwise reject. Euphemism substitutes abstract, vague, or bland terms for more graphic, clear, and unpleasant ones. For example, the terms "layoffs" and "firing" are replaced by "downsizing," and "torture" is replaced with "intensive interrogation techniques." Extrapolation bases sweeping conclusions on small amounts of minor information to appeal to what consumers wish or hope to be so. Flattery appeals to consumer self-esteem needs, such as the McDonald's slogan, "You deserve a break today" or L'Oreal's "You're worth it." Flattery is sometimes accomplished through contrast, like ads showing stupid actions by others to make consumers feel superior and smarter. "Glittering generalities" are "virtue" concepts, such as beauty, love, health, democracy, freedom, and science. Persuaders hope these gain consumer acceptance without questioning what they mean, whether their use is applicable, or investigating evidence. The opposite is name-calling to persuade rejecting someone or something.

American citizens love new ideas and technology. Persuaders exploit this by emphasizing the newness of products, services, and candidates. Conversely, they also use nostalgia to evoke consumers' happy memories, which they often remember more than unhappy ones. Citing "scientific evidence" is an intermediate version of the basic technique of expert testimonials. Consumers may accept this as proof, but some advertisers, politicians, and other persuaders may present inaccurate or misleading "evidence." Another intermediate technique is the "simple solution." Although the natures of people and life are complex, when consumers feel overwhelmed by complexity, persuaders exploit this by offering policies, products, or services they claim will solve complicated problems with simple means. Persuaders also use symbols—images, words, and names we associate with more general, emotional concepts like lifestyle, country, family, religion, and gender. While symbols have power, their significance also varies across individuals: for example, some consumers regard the Hummer SUV as a prestigious status symbol, while others regard it as environmentally harmful and irresponsible.

Advanced techniques

Ad hominem, Latin for "against the man"—also called "shoot the messenger"—attacks someone delivering a message, not the message itself. It operates by association: problems with the messenger must indicate problems with the message. "Stacking the deck" misleads by presenting not complete information, but only selected information supporting persuader positions. Denial evades responsibility, either directly or indirectly, for controversial or unpopular subjects: A politician saying, "I won't mention my opponent's tax evasion issues" manages to mention them while seeming less accusatory. Persuaders use majority belief, such as "Four out of five dentists recommend this brand" or the ubiquitous "[insert number] people can't be wrong." In an intensified version, persuaders exploit group dynamics at rallies, speeches, and other live-audience events where people are vulnerable

Copyright © Mometrix Media. You have been licensed one copy of this document for personal use only. Any other reproduction or redistribution is strictly prohibited. All rights reserved.

to surrounding crowd influences. Scapegoating—blaming one person or group for complex problems, is a form of the intermediate "simple solution" technique, a practice common in politics. Timing also persuades, like advertising flowers and candy preceding Valentine's Day, ad campaigns preceding new technology rollouts, and politician speeches following big news events.

Rules and rationales for writing blogs

Expert web designer, copywriter, and blogger Annabel Cady (http://www.successfulblogging.com/) shares the following blog-posting rules: Format all posts considering page layout and for easy scanning. Column width should be a maximum of 80 characters, including spaces, for easier reading. Headings and subheadings separate text visually, enable scanning or skimming, and encourage continued reading. Bullet-pointed or numbered lists enable quick information location and scanning. Punctuation is critical, so beginners should use shorter sentences until confident. Blog paragraphs should be far shorter—two to six sentences each—than paragraphs written on paper to enable "chunking" because reading onscreen is more difficult. Sans serif fonts are usually clearer than serif fonts, and larger font sizes are better. Highlight important material and draw attention with **boldface**, but avoid overuse. Avoid hard-to-read *italics* and ALL CAPITALS. Include enough blank spaces: overly busy blogs tire eyes and brains. Images not only break up text, but also emphasize and enhance text, and can attract initial reader attention. Use background colors judiciously. Be consistent throughout posts: people read them in different orders. Tell a story with a beginning, middle, and end.

Educational benefits of digital media

Digital media are powerful by being flexible, versatile, and able to be transformed, marked, and networked. For example, printed ink on paper and paint on canvas are permanent. However, digital images of these—while they sacrifice physical texture and some visual depth, tone, and subtlety in the latter case—have the advantage that they can be displayed on anything from a giant public video screen, to a desktop or laptop monitor, to a palm device or smartphone screen in multiple global locations. Digital images can also be manipulated to sharpen, blur, darken, or lighten them, or remove, transpose, duplicate, recombine, and restore portions. Images, text, and voice can be saved exactly and reliably over time periods, and also adapted or changed to the benefit of teachers of diverse classrooms. Digital media are not limited to text and pictures as books are: they also include video and audio, and combine video and sound with text. Students can interact with multiple media at once, choose preferred formats, and compensate for or adapt to learning difficulties.

Unlike hard copies, digitally-saved materials can be linked to each other. Embedded hyperlinks afford many learning supports to students, such as dictionaries, thesauruses, encyclopedias; reading comprehension prompts; supplementary materials to build student background knowledge; visual graphic organizers; and electronic notepads for keeping running notes. Students can rapidly navigate between words in a text and their dictionary definitions; images and their descriptions; videos and their captions; or a passage of text by an author and an audio file of it being read aloud, or an audio file of related sounds. Another advantage for teachers and students is that websites and pages are often constantly updated in real time. Educators and learners can access information and opinions contributed by a wide variety of peers, experts, and mentors—not just locally, but globally.

Copyright © Mometrix Media. You have been licensed one copy of this document for personal use only. Any other reproduction or redistribution is strictly prohibited. All rights reserved.

Multimedia packages enable multisensory, multimodal experiences rather than simply reading print. Access is almost instantaneous. Networking affords teachers and students interconnected communication and information, plus formats and experiences more similar in their diversity to the diversity of individual learners.

Transforming and marking digital media

Students can use within-media transformations to change how website content is displayed by turning graphics or sound on or off, adjust volume, and change text and image appearance by using different computers, different browsers, adjusting browser settings, and so on. Cross-media transformations can convert speech to text or text to speech via software, and can do so automatically by embedding into other software and browsers. This helps students with vision and hearing problems, auditory processing deficits, and reading or learning disabilities. HTML (Hypertext Markup Language) and XML (Extensible Markup Language), both used in web design, enable text choices like certain fonts for certain parts of web pages. With minimal training, teachers and students can use these tools to change and mark online text to accommodate different learning needs. For example, students can underline all summary sentences in detailed texts, and teachers can italicize all English words in a text having Greek or Latin roots, or boldface all metaphors. Unlike highlighter pens, digital markups can be hidden, displayed, expanded, deleted, and changed as student needs change.

Instructional videos

Instructional videos have great two-way communication potential because whoever produces a video can build opportunities for questions and feedback into its format and presentation. Videos can be made to target particular audiences interested in their subject matter. Advantages include that videos can be paused for discussion, and replayed whenever needed to see or hear parts again. They also enable their producers to record processes, including "before," "during," and "after" phases. They can be played back immediately after recording. They are accessible, because most communities have at least one DVD player or computers. Even the video producer's own laptop can be used to play video files. Videos also have the advantage of high status. Moreover, video players and computers are continually becoming less expensive to buy and use. Disadvantages include needing editing software and equipment in some cases, needing support from other print materials, the danger of overuse if other media or methods could be more appropriate, and higher up-front costs. Producers must account for the costs of script development and hiring local performers as needed.

DVDs or CDs

DVDs and CDs are often passively received by audiences (except those designed to be interactive games), which gives viewers the potential to participate, and are becoming increasingly prevalent and popular. They are commonly used to target specific audiences; younger people are especially attracted to them. Compared to many other media formats, discs are comparatively inexpensive to make, and are easy to transport due to their small size and weight. They enjoy high status, and people tend to perceive them as "professional" in nature. They are more resistant to damage and aging than older videotape technology, making them more durable. Some disadvantages include needing computer access to produce and play, and certain software programs to produce, especially if the producer

Copyright © Mometrix Media. You have been licensed one copy of this document for personal use only. Any other reproduction or redistribution is strictly prohibited. All rights reserved.

wants to include video animation and audio commentary—as is common today on movie DVDs, for example. If a DVD includes video animation, this alone can cost at least a couple thousand dollars. Producers must also consider the time of paid staff, and production and labeling expenses.

Effectively delivering speeches

Speakers should deliver speeches in the natural manner of a conversation rather than being rigidly formal or theatrical. Effective delivery is also supported by speaker confidence. Speakers should be direct, building audience rapport through personal connection. Using vivid imagery activates listeners' feelings. Speakers should be mindful of the occasion, subject, and audience of their speeches and take care to use appropriate language for these. Good speakers learn vocal control, including loudness, speed, pitch, use of pauses, variety among vocal tones, pronunciation of words, and clear articulation. They employ their voices to express enthusiasm and emphasize important points. Nonverbal behaviors, such as eye contact with all listeners, facial expressions, gestures, and body movements clarify communication, stress important ideas, and influence listener perceptions that the speaker is trustworthy, competent, of good character, and hence credible. Nonverbal communications should seem as spontaneous and natural as vocal or verbal ones. Good posture is important. Speakers should know their speeches well and practice copiously. They should avoid tapping pencils or their feet, eye- or face-rubbing, pacing, hair-twirling, or other random or irrelevant movements.

Media and format choices

Experts consider effective communication strategies to combine two or three different media types. Media and format choices are influenced by the target audience; the presenters' budget; the best channels of communicating for specific audiences; the duration of the communication; and, with communication intended to promote social change, the relative importance of inducing meaningful audience participation. Two media types are TV and radio. Both are high-status mass media that reaches many people. TV reaches the general public but also can be customized for specialized target audiences, while radio reaches specific target audiences. TV has a broad reach, radio broad-to-medium. TV has the advantage of video plus audio, while audio only is one radio disadvantage. Both are useful for communicating simple slogans and messages, and both can generate awareness, interest, and excitement. A disadvantage is that TV is more expensive than radio, while radio is more expensive than other media. TV and radio audiences cannot interact directly except during call-in programs. Programming times may be inconvenient, but tape, digital sound, and digital video recording (DVR) can remedy this.

Newspapers

Except for the occasional community columns, news releases, and letters to the editor, newspaper pages and features afford little opportunity for audience input or participation. However, they reach and appeal to the literate public, though the general public is unlikely to read them. Cost is an advantage: those producing their own news releases and photographs can do so for free. Hiring a PR writer costs money, but not as much as radio or TV spots do. Additional advantages include that newspaper features are high-status, and that audiences can reread and review them as often as they like. Disadvantages include that they do not reach audiences in as much depth as TV and radio, that they require literacy of

Copyright © Mometrix Media. You have been licensed one copy of this document for personal use only. Any other reproduction or redistribution is strictly prohibited. All rights reserved.

audiences, and that their publication is subject to editors' whims and biases. Newspaper pieces combining advertising and editorial—"advertorials"—afford inclusion of paid material, but are viewed as medium-status. They share other disadvantages with newspaper features and pages, but they cost more.

Internet websites and blogs, and mobile phones and text messaging

Computer literacy is required for online material, but participation potential is high via websites, e-networking, list-serves, and blogging. Mobile phones and text messaging have potential for enormous direct, public, two-way and one-on-one communication, timely information and reminders. Web media need a literate public. They can be designed for specific audiences. Mobile and text media are ubiquitously popular, but also appeal especially to certain demographics like teens and young adults. Web media afford global information, are accessible by increasingly technology-literate populations, and are high-status. List-serves can be inexpensive. Links to related websites and pages within existing sites are also advantages. Mobile and text media are increasing in reach, especially in rural regions; are decreasing in cost; and are very popular. Web media disadvantages include requiring computers, people to design and manage them and supply content, and technical support. Mobile and text media disadvantages include required brevity in texts, provider messaging charges, and working best when connected to other communications.

Public presentations and PowerPoint presentations

Public presentations allow great potential for audience participation and interaction. Feedback can also be incorporated in PowerPoint presentations. Public presentations can directly target various audiences. PowerPoint presentations are best for sophisticated audiences like professionals, civil servants, and service organizations. Public presentations can encourage the establishment of partnerships and groups, stimulate local ownership of issues and projects, and make information public. Well-designed PowerPoint presentations are good for stimulating audience interest, selling ideas, and marketing purposes. Also, they are accessible online by many more computer users in addition to the in-person presentations' audiences. Public presentations' drawbacks include only being useful for moments in a process rather than throughout; being limited to nights, weekends, or when audiences are available; and not always attracting the intended audiences. PowerPoint disadvantages include requiring projectors and equipment, electricity, and computer skills to show them, and being limited to communicating more general points, outlines, and summaries rather than conveying a lot of information in more detail.

Evaluating speeches for concise information

To convince or persuade listeners and/or reinforce a message, speeches must be succinct. Audiences become confused if speakers include excessive anecdotes and details. If a speaker takes three minutes or more to get to the point when making a statement and/or answering a question, audience attention will flag, and will only get worse when details get off the subject. With answers, the asker and speaker may both even forget what the question was. Speakers should practice not only rehearsing written speeches, but also to develop skill for spontaneous question-and-answer sessions after speeches. Speakers should differentiate necessary from simply interesting information because audience members' brains stop processing input beyond their limits to prevent overload. Speakers should know what point(s) they wish to make. They should not fear pausing before

- 41 -

Copyright © Mometrix Media. You have been licensed one copy of this document for personal use only. Any other reproduction or redistribution is strictly prohibited. All rights reserved.

responding to questions, which indicates thoughtfulness and control. Restating questions increases comprehension, appropriate responses, and allows time to form answers mentally.

Clearly written prose and speeches

To achieve clarity, a writer or speaker must first define his or her purpose carefully. The speech or piece must be organized logically, so that sentences make sense and follow each other in an understandable order. Sentences must also be constructed well, and the writer should choose the words used with precision. Organizing a speech in advance using an outline provides the writer/speaker with a blueprint, directing and focusing the composition to meet its intended purpose. Organized speeches enable audiences to comprehend and retain the presented information more easily. Humans naturally seek to impose order on the world by seeking patterns. Hence, when ideas in a speech are well-organized and adhere to a consistent pattern, the speaker communicates better with listeners. Speechwriters can use chronological patterns to organize events, sequential patterns to organize processes by their steps, and spatial patterns to help audiences visualize geographical locations and movements or physical scenarios. Comparison-contrast patterns give audiences insight about similarities and differences between and among topics, especially when listeners are more familiar with one than the other.

Attributes and benefits of certain organizational patterns

When a speechwriter uses an advantages-disadvantages pattern of organization, s/he presents audiences with the pros and cons of a topic. This aids writers in discussing two sides of an issue objectively without an argumentative position, enabling listeners also to weigh both aspects. When a speechwriter uses a cause-and-effect pattern, it can help to persuade audiences to agree with an action or solution the speaker advocates by showing significant relationships between and among factors. Writers may separate an outline into two main "cause" and "effect" sections, or separate it into sections, one for each cause, that includes its effect(s). Persuasive writing also benefits from problem-solution patterns: by establishing the existence of a problem, writers induce audiences to realize a need for change. By supplying a solution and supporting its superiority above other solutions, the writer convinces audiences of the value of that solution. When none of these patterns—or chronological, sequential, spatial, or comparison-contrast patterns—applies, writers often use topical patterns. These organize information by various subtopics and types within the main topic or category.

Techniques to ensure active listening and productive participation

When assigning students to participate in cooperative learning projects and/or discussions, teachers should consider their cognitive, emotional, behavioral, and social developmental levels. If a teacher assigns a topic for age levels younger than the class, students will be bored and unengaged. If the topic assigned is for age levels older than the students, they will be confused, overwhelmed, or lost. Before initiating class or group discussions, teachers should model and explain appropriate behaviors for discussions—particularly for students unfamiliar or inexperienced with these. For example, teachers can model by demonstrating active listening, including eye contact, affirming or confirming the speaker's message, and restating the speaker's message for confirmation or correction. Teachers should establish clear ground rules, such as not interrupting others when they are speaking; not

- 42 -

Copyright © Mometrix Media. You have been licensed one copy of this document for personal use only. Any other reproduction or redistribution is strictly prohibited. All rights reserved.

monopolizing the conversation; not engaging in cross-talk; not insulting classmates verbally; taking turns; waiting for appropriate openings in the conversation to make comments; and, for young children and students with behavioral issues, not engaging in physical contact like hitting, kicking, and biting.

Posters and brochures

Both posters and brochures share in common the lack of potential feedback—unless they have been broadly tested, or if their publication is accompanied by workshops and other participatory events at the community level or higher. Both can target audiences of the general public and more specific public sectors. Posters are better for communicating simple slogans and messages, while brochures can include more detail and are better for printing instructional information. Both can be inexpensive to produce. Posters particularly can often be printed in-house without using outside printing companies. Disadvantages of posters include the simplicity required of their messages, and the requirement of literacy in written language and visual elements to understand them. Disadvantages of brochures include their limitations of distribution to specific groups or areas and, like posters, also requiring literacy to read and understand them. Because of their size, a given number of posters costs more than the same number of brochures. Moreover, if brochures are printed only as needed and in-house, they can cost even less.

Flyers and fact sheets

Flyers and fact sheets have one-way communication potential because readers cannot give feedback. Their target audiences are general. Some advantages of using this form of media include flexibility: people can distribute them following various community meetings; put them on car windshields in parking lots or in supermarkets and other stores; on bulletin boards at community agencies and organizations, public and private elementary and secondary schools, colleges, and universities; hand them out at community events and from convention booths and other displays; and also mail them out to recipients. When printed on colored paper using black ink, they can be very inexpensive. They afford recipients the convenience of being able to review them at their leisure. Organizations and individuals can produce flyers and fact sheets in-house, or even at home with desktop publishing software. Disadvantages include their limitation to single facts or tips, and specific information on specified topics. They cost the same as printing brochures, but fact sheets printed in black and white cost half what full-color brochures do.

Informative/explanatory writing

Instructional methods to guide student writing
Teachers can use mentor texts, which they can find from multiple everyday sources, and align them with the writing standards for their students' grade levels. Teachers can compose informative and/or explanatory text in front of their classes to model composition for them. They can use the "thinking out loud" technique for additional modeling. By doing this, they demonstrate for students the process of defining and expressing ideas clearly in writing and supporting those ideas using details like explanations, descriptions, definitions, examples, anecdotes, and/or processes. Teachers should employ scaffolding with students: They begin with explicit instruction, proceed to modeling, and then provide students with activities to allow them to practice. These activities can include guided writing exercises; shared writing experiences; cooperative practice, wherein they collaborate with classmates

- 43 -

Copyright © Mometrix Media. You have been licensed one copy of this document for personal use only. Any other reproduction or redistribution is strictly prohibited. All rights reserved.

to write; regular, descriptive feedback that refers to the learning objectives that the teachers have established; peer conferences; and teacher conferences about how students can extend their thinking and refine their writing skills.

Guidelines for grades K-5 and expectations for elementary grade students
Teachers can pose questions related to the content area subjects they are teaching for students to answer, and they can invite and make use of interesting elementary-grade student questions like, "Why did immigrants come to America?" "Why does my face turn red in cold weather?" "Why does my dog drool?" or "Why does my cat knead with his/her paws?" In lower elementary grades, students may choose or be assigned topics, give some definitions and facts about the topics, and write concluding statements. Students in upper elementary grades should be able to introduce topics, focus them, group information logically, develop topics with enough details, connect ideas, use specific academic vocabulary, and write conclusions. To develop these skills, students must have many opportunities for researching information and writing informative/explanatory text. Experts on writing standards recommend roughly one-third of elementary student writing be informative/explanatory text. Children must read informational texts with depth and breadth, and use writing as a learning tool, to fulfill the objective of building knowledge through reading and writing.

Expectations and recommendations for grades 6-12
Standards expect high school students to use informative/explanatory text to communicate and investigate complex concepts, information, and ideas; effectively choose, analyze, and organize content; and write accurately and clearly. Informative/explanatory text is recommended to comprise approximately 40 percent of high school students' writing across curriculum content subjects. Teachers can present brief mentor texts that use informative writing in creative, engaging form to students as illustrative demonstrations. Using mentor texts as templates, teachers can model for students composing similar texts about other topics. Teachers then have students apply this format to write about topics the students select, giving them support and/or scaffolding. Thereafter, teachers can have students write short texts on various topics that necessitate them using their prior knowledge and doing some research. "Thinking aloud" to model the cognitive writing process, and modeling composition for students, are important. Some experts also recommend that teachers assign frequent short research instead of traditional longer library-research term papers. Authentic writing tasks include conducting and reporting survey/interview research, producing newspaper front pages, and composing web pages.

Evaluating arguments made by informational text writers

First, identify an argument's conclusion. Then identify premises the author states supporting the conclusion. How readers word conclusions they identify can affect their identification of premises; they may want to reword or even redefine the conclusion. Try to paraphrase premises for clarification and make the conclusion and premises fit. List all premises first, sequentially numbered, then finish with the conclusion. Identify any premises or assumptions not stated by the author but required for stated premises to support the conclusion. Read word assumptions sympathetically, as the author might. Evaluate whether premises reasonably support the conclusion: For inductive reasoning, the reader should ask if the premises are true, and if they support the conclusion. If so, how strongly? For deductive reasoning, the reader should ask if the argument valid or invalid. If all premises are true, the argument is valid if the conclusion cannot be false. But if it can,

Copyright © Mometrix Media. You have been licensed one copy of this document for personal use only. Any other reproduction or redistribution is strictly prohibited. All rights reserved.

then the argument is invalid. Alter an invalid argument to become valid, adding any premises needed. Are premises true, false, or questionable? How might the author defend them? Optional recursion: Start again, this time using significant premises as conclusions, and find and evaluate more supporting arguments.

Determining an informational author's purpose

Informational authors' purposes are why they wrote texts. Readers must determine authors' motivations and goals. Readers gain greater insight into text by considering what motivated the author. This develops critical reading skills. Readers perceive writing as a person's voice, not simply printed words. Uncovering author motivations and purposes empowers readers to know what to expect from text, read for relevant details, evaluate authors and their work critically, and respond effectively to the motivations and persuasions of the text. The main idea of a text is what the reader is supposed to understand from reading it; the purpose of the text is why the author has written it and what the author wants readers to do with its information. Authors state some purposes clearly, while others may be unstated but equally significant. When purposes stated contradict other parts of text, authors may have hidden agendas. Readers can better evaluate a text's effectiveness, whether they agree or disagree with it, and why they agree or disagree through identifying unstated author purposes.

Technical material for non-technical readers

Writing about technical subjects for non-technical readers differs from writing for colleagues in that authors begin with a different goal: it may be more important to deliver a critical message than to impart the maximum technical content possible. Technical authors also must assume that non-technical audiences do not have the expertise to comprehend extremely scientific or technical messages, concepts, and terminology. They must resist the temptation to impress audiences with their scientific knowledge and expertise, and remember that their primary purpose is to communicate a message that non-technical readers will understand, feel the impact of, and respond to by changing their attitudes and/or taking appropriate actions. Similarities in non-technical and technical styles include: both should formally cite references when used, and acknowledge other authors' work utilized. Both must follow intellectual property and copyright regulations. This includes the author's protecting his/her own rights, or a public domain statement, as s/he chooses.

Writers of technical or scientific material may need to write for many non-technical audiences. Some readers have no technical or scientific background; others do, but not in the same field as the authors. Government and corporate policymakers and budget managers need technical information they can understand for decision-making. Citizens affected by technology and/or science are another audience. Non-governmental organizations can encompass many of the preceding groups. Elementary and secondary school programs also need non-technical language for presenting technical subject matter. Reasons that technical authors need to write using non-technical language include: for communicating messages as opposed to denser content; for informing colleagues, both within and without one's field; for obtaining support for a budget or project; and for better informing a wider range of citizens who have the right to know important information without being stymied by the barrier of jargon or unfamiliar terminology and vocabulary.

Copyright © Mometrix Media. You have been licensed one copy of this document for personal use only. Any other reproduction or redistribution is strictly prohibited. All rights reserved.

Authors in technical fields may write using non-technical language to serve the purpose of collecting consumer responses to surveys of public comprehension, perceptions of, and views toward technology and science. They may use non-technical language in popular representations of science, or to present scientific or para-scientific belief systems. They will need to use it to support school instruction in the sciences. They will also need it for writing about the history of science education and the history of popular science. If they write about science and the media, they will need to use non-technical language. Authors with scientific backgrounds who also write science fiction must be equally able to use non-technical language to reach this reading audience. They must use it for scientific lobbying. Reporting studies they may conduct evaluating interactive science centers and science exhibits also requires non-technical language, as do public scientific information services. Popular "anti-science" protests are another purpose. Writing about science and applicable technologies in developing countries also needs non-technical wording.

When authors of technical information must write about their subjects using non-technical language that readers outside their disciplinary fields can comprehend, they should not only use non-technical terms, they should also use normal, everyday language to accommodate non-native-language readers. For example, instead of writing that "eustatic changes" like "thermal expansion" causing "hazardous conditions" in the "littoral zone," an author would do better to write that a "rising sea level" is "threatening the coast." When technical terms cannot be avoided, authors should also define and/or explain them using non-technical language. Although authors must cite references and acknowledge others' work they use, they should avoid the kinds of references or citations that they would use in scientific journals—unless they reinforce author messages. They should not use endnotes, footnotes, or any other complicated referential techniques because non-technical journal publishers usually do not accept them. Including high-resolution illustrations, photos, maps, or satellite images and incorporating multimedia into digital publications will enhance public non-technical writing about technical subjects. Technical authors may publish using non-technical language in e-journals, trade journals, specialty newsletters, and daily newspapers.

Persuasive techniques

To appeal using reason, writers present logical arguments, such as using "If... then... because" statements. To appeal to emotions, authors ask readers how they would feel about something or to put themselves in another's place, present their point as making them feel best, and tell readers how they should feel. To appeal to character, morality, or ethics, authors present their points to readers as the right or most moral choices. Authors cite expert opinions to show readers that someone very knowledgeable about the subject or viewpoint agrees. Testimonials, via anecdotes about and/or quotations from someone who agrees, add support. Bandwagon appeals persuade readers that everybody else agrees with author views. Authors appeal to greed by presenting their choice as cheaper, free, and/or more valuable for less cost. They appeal to laziness by presenting their views as more convenient, easy, or relaxing. Authors also anticipate potential objections and argue against them before audiences think of them, thereby depicting those objections as weak.

Authors can use comparisons like analogies, similes, and metaphors to persuade audiences. For example, a writer might represent excessive expenses as "hemorrhaging" money, which the author's recommended solution will stop. Authors can use negative word connotations to make some choices unappealing to readers, and positive word connotations to make

Copyright © Mometrix Media. You have been licensed one copy of this document for personal use only. Any other reproduction or redistribution is strictly prohibited. All rights reserved.

others more appealing. Using humor can relax readers and garner their agreement. However, writers must take care: ridiculing opponents works with readers who already agree, but otherwise can backfire by angering other readers. Rhetorical questions need no answer, but create effect that can force agreement, such as asking the question, "Wouldn't you rather be paid more than less?" Generalizations persuade readers by being impossible to disagree with; writers can make these appear to support their viewpoints, like saying, "We all want peace, not war" regarding more specific political arguments. Transfer and association persuade by example: if advertisements show attractive actors enjoying their products, audiences imagine they will experience the same. Repetition, which is repeating certain statements frequently, can also sometimes effectively persuade audiences.

Critical evaluation of effectiveness of persuasive methods

First, readers should identify the author's thesis—what s/he argues for or against. They should consider the argument's content and why the author saw a need to present it. Does the author offer solutions to problems raised? If so, are they realistic? Note all central ideas and evidence supporting the author's thesis. Research any unfamiliar subjects or vocabulary. Readers should then outline or summarize the work in their own words. Identify which type(s) of appeal(s) the author uses. Readers should evaluate how well the author communicated meaning from the reader's perspective: Did they respond emotionally to emotional appeals with anger, upset, happiness, etc.? If so, why? Decide if the author's reasoning sufficed for changing the reader's mind. Determine whether the content and presentation were accurate, cohesive, and clear. Readers should also ask themselves whether they found the author believable or not, and why or why not they did.

Classical author appeals

In his *On Rhetoric,* ancient Greek philosopher Aristotle defined three basic types of appeal used in writing. He called these pathos, ethos, and logos in Greek. *Pathos* means suffering or experience and refers to appeals to the emotions (the English word "pathetic" comes from this root). Writing that is meant to entertain audiences, by making them either happy, as with comedy, or sad, as with tragedy, uses pathos. Among criteria for writing tragedy in his *Poetics*, Aristotle included its evoking the emotions of terror and pity. *Ethos* means character and connotes ideology (the English word "ethics" comes from this root). Writing that appeals to credibility, based on academic, professional, or personal merit uses ethos. *Logos* means "I say" and refers to a plea, opinion, expectation, word or speech, account, opinion, or reason. (The English word "logic" comes from this root.) Aristotle used it to mean persuasion that appeals to the audience through reasoning and logic to influence their opinions.

Logical fallacies

Post hoc ergo propter hoc is Latin for "After this, therefore because of this." This equates to reasoning that because X happened before Y, X must have caused Y. But just as correlation does not imply causation, neither does chronological sequence. For example, one cannot assume that because most rapists read pornography as teenagers that pornography causes rape. A red herring is irrelevant information introduced to distract others from the pertinent issue. For example, one author claims that welfare dependence raises crime rates, while another argues plausibly that some increase in crime is justified in addressing poverty. However, if the second author argued instead, "But how can the poor survive

Copyright © Mometrix Media. You have been licensed one copy of this document for personal use only. Any other reproduction or redistribution is strictly prohibited. All rights reserved.

without help?" that would be a red herring. Slippery slopes, when fallacious, are arguments that one thing will cause others without demonstrating any cause-and-effect relationship—hence non-sequiturs. For example, arguing that legalizing one drug will cause all drugs to be legalized is obviously false. Straw man is refuting an exaggeration or caricature of someone's argument, not the real argument.

Rationales for knowing logical fallacies
For writing persuasion and argumentation, logic is necessary, but so are supporting facts, insights, and the plausibility of an argument. Although logic by itself may show that the answer to a question discussed is unknown, the most plausible argument can still convince audiences. One reason for knowing the names of, and processes involved in, logical fallacies is enabling writers to identify flawed reasoning by those presenting opposing viewpoints—and identify them precisely by supplying a Latin name for each. This also indicates an author may better understand the opposite position than its presenter does. Another reason is that by identifying logical fallacies, the author does not simply make an opponent's argument weaker or less convincing, but s/he actually eliminates it from the discussion/debate instead. Rather than counterarguments—allowing opponents' rhetoric proving their arguments' importance—this makes audiences question the validity, even existence, of the opposing argument. If the other author cannot justify it strongly, that argument can be negated, and so the audience does not even consider it.

Steps or strategies to draw attention to logical fallacies in opposing arguments
The writer should first restate the targeted opposing argument. Then s/he points out this argument is a logical fallacy, providing the Latin name for the fallacy identified. The writer then explains the meaning of this logical fallacy, and why it involves erroneous reasoning. Writers must not let their language become pompous or pedantic in tone during this explanation. Instead, they appeal more to audiences by stating the meaning of the fallacy as though their perceptive readers and listeners already know it, and they recognize this audience knowledge. For example, if a writer identifies an opposing writer's use of an appeal to public opinion, s/he defines this by pointing out that majority agreement with a position does not make it right. Writers then give overt examples of a fallacy's incorrectness—such as historical beliefs that the world was flat or that slavery was acceptable did not make such beliefs correct. Lastly, writers state the erroneous argument should be ruled out entirely, leaving opponents only (an) inadequate remaining argument(s) and an untenable position.

Argumentum ad antiquitatem means an argument to tradition or antiquity. We have often read or heard this used when people write or say, "We have always done it this way." An example might be that the governments of all major societies have always supplied state funding for cultural pursuits and the arts. However, it is not logical that the fact of people always having done something intrinsically warrants continuing to do it. An inherent weakness of this argument is that others can refute it easily just by drawing attention to it. Therefore, it should not be a writer's first choice. If one feels the need to use this argument, one way to provide it with more support than simply presenting it by itself is offering a reason for respecting the tradition cited. One might support arguing for a tradition with the evolutionary principle of natural selection—such as saying that the reason all known civilizations practice this tradition is because those that ignored it failed to survive.

Argumentum ad hominem is against the person, not the person's statements/ideas. The arguer attacks a person's motives or character, not what s/he wrote or said. This is less

Copyright © Mometrix Media. You have been licensed one copy of this document for personal use only. Any other reproduction or redistribution is strictly prohibited. All rights reserved.

often by name-calling, such as "He is a communist/fascist/greedy capitalist," but more common by attacking the person as information source. If one cites ending the Vietnam War, signing environmental laws, and opening China as positive accomplishments of Richard Nixon, and quotes him regarding free trade, then the *ad hominem* arguer might cite the Watergate scandal as evidence Nixon was a "crook" and liar, so nobody can believe anything he said. Arguments *ad hominem* also are used against people arguing for anything that would benefit them and against anything that would disadvantage them—like owners of corporate conglomerates arguing against anti-trust laws—shifting focus away from the argument's validity to focus on who makes it. *Ad hominem* is not fallacious against statements by those with vested interests in deception. Many *ad hominem* arguments may be restated about ideas versus people—such as not claiming someone is a fascist, but his/her position is.

Argumentum ad ignorantiam is an argument appealing to ignorance. In other words, the arguer presumes the truth of something based on its not being proven untrue. For example, one would do better by presenting actual data to prove climate change than by arguing it is true because nobody has proven it false. The burden of proof is a key factor for determining whether this argument is fallacious or not. As an analogy, in the United States legal system, a defendant is innocent until proven guilty—rather than guilty until proven innocent as in some other court systems. Thus defense attorneys can argue that their client is not guilty because the prosecution has not proven him/her guilty. However, prosecuting attorneys cannot argue that the defendant must be guilty of committing a crime because s/he has no alibi. Both arguments constitute *ad ignorantiam*, but in the American legal system, the burden of proof is on the prosecution rather than the defense. Similarly, in rhetoric, the proposer typically has the burden of proof.

The logical fallacy *argumentum ad logicam*, or argument/appeal to logic, presumes something is untrue based on somebody's invalid argument or proof. It is fallacious to deem a proposal false just because of unsound reasoning defending it. There could exist other, valid arguments or proofs for the proposal. The *argumentum ad logicam* frequently occurs within the context of the *straw man* fallacy, which argues against a distortion or exaggeration of a position, not the actual position. The *ad logicam* appeal is determined as fallacious or not through the burden of proof: If the proposer of the original position does not prove it, s/he loses the debate even though other arguments not presented could have proven it. Also, if one side disproves another's point as invalid, it will be judged invalid, regardless whether the proposer could have proven it with a better argument because s/he did not do so; the burden of proof is on the proposer. This determination of fallacy or validity via burden of proof is comparable to that used with *argumentum ad ignorantiam*.

Argumentum ad misericordiam means argument/appeal to pity. This is often employed by those pleading to others for donations and other assistance to help starving children, abused animals, and poor people. Of course many pity such victims and want to help, but what makes this appeal illogical is that by itself, it cannot make expenses free, make true something untrue, or render something possible that is impossible. It is valid, however, to emphasize a problem's significance as a way of supporting one's proposing a particular solution to that problem. The proposer of the solution must then be able to address such objections as whether that solution is possible or feasible; what negative impacts it could have on others, even while providing positive impacts on those it would help; and its expenses and how to provide for those. Appealing to pity is acceptable to support

Copyright © Mometrix Media. You have been licensed one copy of this document for personal use only. Any other reproduction or redistribution is strictly prohibited. All rights reserved.

arguments that a proposal's benefits justify its costs, but unacceptable as the sole response to objections without otherwise addressing them.

Argumentum ad nauseam translates literally as argument to the point of nausea. In other words, this tactic involves repeating one's point over and over until listeners are so disgusted at hearing it that they cannot tolerate hearing it any longer. Reiterating a true statement over and over is not fallacious in itself, but expecting such repetition to replace actual logic is. Despite the absence of reasoning, repetition has a powerful effect of making one's listeners remember the statements repeated. This makes *argumentum ad nauseam* very popular. When one side in a spoken or written debate or controversy has used this technique of constant repetition without supplying any evidence to support or document the assertion, this is an opportunity for the other side to point out the use of repetition alone, and moreover, to call attention to the fact that the other has not presented any information to substantiate the repeated statement. Making clear that the other person has repeatedly stated a point without proving it will refute it.

Argumentum ad numerum, translated as argument or appeal to numbers, is a rhetorical device of citing mathematical figures as "proof" that something is true. For example, one might argue, "80 percent of the public supports this legislation." The fallacy here is that the agreement of the majority does not make something true. The 80 percent of the public that supports a law could be wrong in doing so—like in the antebellum Southern United States, where the majority of the public supported slavery. They had considerable incentive to take this position to preserve the entire foundation of their economy and way of life, but they were not morally justified in doing so. *Argumentum ad numerum* resembles *argumentum ad populum*—appeal to popularity or to the people. Their minor difference is that arguing to the people appeals directly to the nearby public, while appealing to numbers attempts to persuade others based on citing how many other people agree. These are similar enough to be often used interchangeably in rhetoric.

The meaning of *argumentum ad verecundiam* is arguing or appealing to authority. This is attempting to prove one's position by citing the opinion of someone who is not an expert in the specific subject at issue. For example, Enrico Fermi and Albert Einstein were both pacifists, and objected strenuously to having their science applied for building bombs. While some agree and some do not, the fact is that Fermi and Einstein were experts in nuclear physics, but not in politics or foreign policy. Citing or quoting authorities in the subject under discussion, though, is not fallacious. It is also acceptable to quote a non-expert who nevertheless made an eloquent statement appropriate to one's argument. Unacceptable uses of the appeal to authority, which opponents are justified in calling out and criticizing, include using unqualified sources to verify facts unaccompanied by any other sources that are qualified, and/or implying that a given position has to be correct just because somebody thought that it was.

Circulus in demonstrando is Latin for a circular argument. This means that by trying to use the assertion or idea they want to prove is itself a part of their proof, people using circular argumentation are actually "talking in circles." As an example, someone argues, "X is illegal. Because it is illegal, one should not do it. Because one shouldn't do it, the government should prevent people from doing it. This is why it is illegal." In this example, the circular nature of the argument is obvious. However, some arguments are circular but less easily recognized. Some politicians and political commentators can be notorious for using circular arguments. To refute the fallacy of *circulus in demonstrando,* one can summarize the

Copyright © Mometrix Media. You have been licensed one copy of this document for personal use only. Any other reproduction or redistribution is strictly prohibited. All rights reserved.

arguer's statement as "You are saying that X is true because X is true," and then additionally point out that the arguer has not provided any information as to why X is true—in other words, they have provided no actual proof.

"Complex question" refers to a rhetorical tactic wherein a speaker or writer forms a question to presume implicitly something not established as true. An obvious example is when reporters or lawyers ask someone, "Have you stopped embezzling?" when there is no proof that the person questioned ever embezzled. This tactic is employed to trick people into admitting things they would not admit in direct questioning. A less obvious example is asking someone, "Since most African-Americans are poor, do you believe the measures proposed would be effective?" The first clause is not true, but the person questioned could be so focused on the second clause and how to answer it as to overlook the falsehood. This is more effective in spoken than written language: in real-time spoken interactions, it can confuse someone; in a written piece, the reader has time to reconsider it and realize it is untrue. A major drawback is that if the person questioned notices the falsehood and confronts the questioner, it makes the questioner appear foolish.

Cum hoc ergo propter hoc means in Latin, "With this, therefore because of this." In other words, because these occur together, one causes the other. A parallel fallacy in scientific research is assuming that correlation indicates causation. Things can occur together out of coincidence: people may attribute economic improvement to a certain president's administration when it may be more due to technological advances. Things can occur together, but one is an effect of prior causes: an improved economy during one president's administration can be the result of an earlier president's actions. Things can occur together and be unrelated to each other, but both related to a common reason: as an economic remedy, one president enacts downsizing measures, which many voters dislike, so they consequently elect a different president, and benefits of the previous president's downsizing appear after the election of the subsequent president. Whereas correlation can never mean causation in scientific research, in rhetoric one may attribute causation to correlation if one can provide sufficiently convincing reasons for it.

The Latin *dicto simpliciter* literally means "spoken simply," a figuratively sweeping generalization. When people make sweeping proclamations they presume are always true, they are stereotyping—which is another term for this. An example is generalizing that as a group, women are not as strong physically as men and assuming that therefore, they cannot serve equally in the military. While the first statement is true in general, it is not always true of specific individuals: some women are far stronger than the average of women as a group. In rhetoric, it is typically sufficient simply to state why a sweeping generalization does not prove someone's point without using the official terminology or pointing out its logical fallacy. Sweeping generalizations are understood by the public without instruction in rhetorical devices. Hence, experts also advise that naming the fallacy in Latin in this case seems condescending. Non-fallacious generalizations are always true individually, such as "Normal human females have two X chromosomes; normal human males have an X and a Y chromosome."

The appeal to nature assumes that anything natural or part of nature is good, and/or that anything not natural is bad. For example, some people may argue that birth control or homosexuality is wrong because these are not natural. In addition to the problem of defining the meaning of "natural," it is also illogical to equate "unnatural" or non-natural with wrong. Human beings use fire, construct and use tools, wear clothing, and farm the

Copyright © Mometrix Media. You have been licensed one copy of this document for personal use only. Any other reproduction or redistribution is strictly prohibited. All rights reserved.

soil; these can be deemed not "natural," yet they are both common and beneficial. Because of these inherent weaknesses, this argument is not effective. For instance, defending environmentalism only on the basis of preserving natural resources or wildernesses does not provide strong enough reasons. However, this important cause can be defended more strongly by appealing to humans on the basis of their own survival by arguing that humans live within a complex ecosystem that is easily damaged by certain human activities which could destroy both the ecosystem and thus humanity as a part of it.

In the naturalistic fallacy, one draws conclusions regarding values—in other words, right and wrong or good and bad—based only on factual statements. This is fallacious because any logical inferences based on facts alone will constitute simply more statements of fact, rather than statements of value. In order to come to conclusions related to values, the axioms, principles, premises, or assumptions that one states must include a statement(s) of value as well. Having given an axiom of value rather than of fact, then one can use it together with facts to make conclusions about values. For instance, the statement, "This medication will keep you from dying" might seem to connect to a conclusion, "You should take this medication." However, the former is a statement of fact, the latter one of value. For the conclusion to be logically valid, an additional premise is needed, "You should do what you need to do to stay alive."

Argumentum ad antiquitatem, or appeal to tradition—that is, something is right because it has always been done, and the appeal to nature—or that something is right because it is natural, are forms of the naturalistic fallacy: they draw conclusions about values using statements of fact without any statement(s) of value to connect logically with conclusions. Facts represent what is; values represent what ought to be. Philosopher David Hume described these fallacies as attempts to bridge the "is-ought gap." Initial axioms of value are not necessarily justifiable via pure logic. However, rhetoric is not limited to pure logic. Three ways to rebut an axiom of value, such as "Anything natural is good," are: (1) Ask if anybody—yourself, the judge of a debate, or even your opponent who stated it—truly believes this; (2) present another value axiom that competes with it, like "Anything that improves people's lives is good," so the judge is forced to choose between the two; and (3) cite logical ramifications of the statement's contradiction of basic morality.

In Latin, *non sequitur* means "It does not follow." If someone says, for instance, "Racism is wrong; thus affirmative action is necessary," this conclusion does not logically follow the initial premise. If one says instead, "Racism is wrong; affirmative action would decrease racism; thus affirmative action is needed," the logical connection is supplied. Some rhetoricians include *non sequiturs* in their opening arguments strategically—to avoid giving away to their opponents a counterargument they anticipate. Except in the cases of significant, obvious counterarguments that should be anticipated and answered early, it is more strategic to wait for an opponent to raise an argument to rebut, rather than waste time and energy answering unstated objections. It is inadvisable to claim *non sequitur* whenever an opponent does not anticipate each of one's counterarguments. The best application for pointing out this fallacy is when an opponent attempts to show a causal chain without proving each link. Identifying each unsubstantiated step ultimately reveals such attempted chains as weak and implausible.

Petitio principii means "begging the question": when attempting to prove something, one assumes the same thing one wants to prove. In terms of logical structure, this is the same as using a circular argument. Although the meaning of "begging the question" is quite specific,

Copyright © Mometrix Media. You have been licensed one copy of this document for personal use only. Any other reproduction or redistribution is strictly prohibited. All rights reserved.

many people misuse this term in rhetorical arguments. A question is begged if it is asked during a conversation but never answered, and meanwhile the parties in the discussion come to a conclusion about a related issue. For example, someone might argue, "Some people campaign for legalizing pornography because it is a medium for freedom of expression. However, this 'begs the question' of what freedom of expression means." This uses the term incorrectly. Some issues and discussions motivate questions rather than begging them. A more correct example of "begging the question" would be if someone argued, "Because we believe that pornography should be legalized, this means it constitutes a valid medium of free expression. Being free expression, it therefore should not be banned."

Translated from Latin, *tu quoque* means "you too." The old saying "Two wrongs don't make a right" addresses this fallacy. In rhetoric, one commits an error in logic—for example, making unproven claims—and defends it by rejoining that the opposition did the same. That both sides made the same error does not excuse either one. Though *tu quoque* is an obvious fallacy, it is often used to significant advantage in rhetoric: Disregarding whether any proposition is true or false, debaters can show which side made the better performance in arguing. For example, if both sides have equally appealed to audience pity (*argumentum ad misericordiam*), or both have used equal *ad hominem* arguments (attacking the person, not what s/he says), then to be fair a judge must penalize both equally, not just one. Additionally, it is not fallacious to show that "non-unique" advantages or disadvantages that apply equally to both sides cannot warrant preferring either position. *Tu quoque* can ensure that judging is only according to differentiating factors between sides.

Author's argument in argumentative writing

When an author writes in argumentative mode, the argument is a belief, position, or opinion that the author wants to convince readers to believe as well. For the first step, readers should identify the issue the author discusses. Some issues are controversial, meaning people disagree about them. For example, gun control, foreign policy, and the death penalty are all controversial issues. Readers should consider whether the author's selected issue is controversial. The next step is to ask oneself what the author's position about the chosen issue is. That position or viewpoint constitutes the author's argument. Readers should then identify the author's assumptions: things s/he accepts, believes, or takes for granted without needing proof. Inaccurate or illogical assumptions produce flawed arguments, causing readers not identifying author assumptions to be misled. Readers should identify what kinds of supporting evidence the author offers—research results, personal observations or experiences, case studies, facts, examples, expert testimony and opinions, and comparisons. Readers should decide how relevant or directly related this support is to the argument.

The first three reader steps to evaluate an author's argument are to identify the assumptions the author makes about the issue discussed in the writing, identify what kinds of evidence the author gives to support the argument, and decide how relevant the supporting evidence is. For example, if an author is not an expert on a particular topic, then that author's personal experience or opinion might not be very relevant. The fourth step in evaluating an author's argument is to assess how objective the author is. For example, consider whether the author introduces clear, understandable supporting evidence and facts to support the argument. The fifth step is evaluating whether the author's argument is complete or not. When authors give sufficient support for their arguments and also

- 53 -

Copyright © Mometrix Media. You have been licensed one copy of this document for personal use only. Any other reproduction or redistribution is strictly prohibited. All rights reserved.

anticipate and respond effectively to opposing arguments or objections to their points, their arguments are complete. However, some authors omit information that could detract from their arguments. If instead they stated this information and refuted it, it would strengthen their arguments.

In order, readers should identify the author's assumptions about the issue s/he writes about, then identify what supporting evidence the author presents, assess the relevance of that evidence, evaluate the author's objectivity, and consider the completeness of the author's argument. Authors may omit detracting information rather than presenting and refuting it. Authors may also not present enough supporting information. The sixth step in evaluating an author's argumentative writing is to assess whether the argument is valid. Providing clear, logical reasoning makes an author's argument valid. Readers should ask themselves whether the author's points follow a sequence that makes sense, and whether each point leads to the next. The seventh step is to determine whether the author's argument is credible, meaning that it is convincing and believable. Arguments that are not valid are not credible, so step seven depends on step six. Readers should not feel overwhelmed at several steps; be mindful of their own biases during evaluation; and not expect authors to prove their arguments conclusively, but rather to reason and support arguments effectively.

Literature, body of literature, research question, problem statement, and review of literature

In research, literature refers to writing on a research topic. The body of literature is all writing and supporting data published on a given topic or research question. A research question or problem is what a researcher wants to find an answer to or resolve. In a research paper, the problem statement clearly identifies the issue, tells why the researcher cares about this issue, defines the scope of the research by focusing on specific variables, and shows why those variables matter. The problem statement follows the title and abstract in the research paper, supplying context for the rest and getting reader attention. Whether professionals or students, when researchers conduct academic research projects, their literature reviews, which thoroughly examine the extant body of literature on their chosen research topic, form a necessary component of the project by showing what work has already been done toward answering the research question that they have chosen to investigate.

Primary and secondary sources

When one conducts research and then writes a research paper reporting the results of that investigation, an essential part of the paper is a literature review. In reviewing the literature, one may examine both primary and secondary sources. Primary sources contain original information, like reports other researchers have made of their findings and other first-hand accounts written by experimenters or witnesses of discoveries or events. They may be found in academic books, journals and other periodicals, and authoritative databases. Secondary sources refer to information originally given by other people or found in other places. They may be cited, quoted, or described in books, magazines, newspapers, films, audio and video materials, databases, and websites. Accounts of research and its results are always informed and directed by reviews of the pertinent literature. These depict the present research as a cumulative process integral to the scientific method.

Copyright © Mometrix Media. You have been licensed one copy of this document for personal use only. Any other reproduction or redistribution is strictly prohibited. All rights reserved.

Literature reviews also test the research question one wants to answer relative to the existing knowledge about the topic.

Addressing research questions

When asking a research question, the researcher may find through making a careful review of the existing literature that the question s/he has chosen has already been answered definitively. In this case, the researcher should modify the question or ask a different one. If their research question has not been answered in the literature, researchers should consider the following: What knowledge exists about the topic, in what chronological sequence the knowledge about this topic has been developed, whether there are any gaps in the knowledge about this topic, what needs and opportunities for additional research other researchers and writers have identified, and how one plans to fill in these gaps. Researchers should also consider whether consensus or controversy exists about pertinent matters and, with the latter, which positions exist. Research trajectories suggested by others' work, and the most productive direction for one's research the literature indicates are also considerations. Researchers should realize there are no absolute answers: they must decide in the context of their work what is important.

Literature review

One main part of a literature review is searching through the existing literature. The other is actually writing the review. Most voluntary researchers enjoy knowledge, so they must take care not to get lost among all the data available without making any progress in their literature review. A remedy is to prepare by writing or printing one's research question and keeping it nearby when searching, and by making a search plan and establishing a time limit in advance. Finding a seemingly endless number of references indicates a need to revisit the research question because it is too broad. Finding too little material means the research question and/or topic is too narrow, in which case one should reconsider the area to investigate. With cutting-edge research, one may find that nobody has ever investigated their question and/or area of interest. This requires systematic searching: with abstracts in periodicals for an overview of available literature; research papers or other specific sources to explore its references; and books and general sources, using their references to find a specific topic.

When searching published literature on a research topic, one must take plenty of thorough notes. We often happen upon references we are not ready for at the time but could use later, without making notes, it becomes frustrating when we want to read the entire reference we saw before but cannot find it again. It is easy to start a word processing document along with the Internet browser to take running notes while searching. Practicing online resource use helps: researchers and students should connect to the Internet regularly, view resources for their research often, learn how to use resources correctly and efficiently, experiment with resources available within the discipline(s), open and examine databases, become familiar with reference desk materials, find publications with abstracts of articles and books on one's topic, use papers' references to locate the most utile journals and important authors, identify keywords for refining and narrowing database searches, and peruse library catalogues online for available sources—all while taking complete notes.

As one searches the literature available about a given subject, one will gradually develop an overview of the body of literature. This signals the time to prepare for writing the literature

- 55 -

Copyright © Mometrix Media. You have been licensed one copy of this document for personal use only. Any other reproduction or redistribution is strictly prohibited. All rights reserved.

review. The researcher should assemble the documents with all the notes s/he has taken while searching, copies of all the journal articles made, and all the books acquired. Then one should again write the research question at the top of a page, and list below it all of the author names and keywords discovered while searching. It is also helpful to observe whether any groups or pairs of these stand out when viewing the list. These activities are parts of structuring one's literature review—the first step for writing a thesis, dissertation, or research paper. Writers should rewrite as necessary rather than expecting to make only one draft. However, they should also not become stuck in rewriting any portion, which impedes momentum; skipping to a less problematic portion and revisiting the earlier part later is better.

Editing and revising

After composing a rough draft of a research paper, the writer should edit and rewrite it. The purpose of the paper is to communicate the answer to one's research question in an efficient and effective manner. The writer should edit the draft to make it as concise and clear as possible. This is often easier to do after writing the first draft than during it, as writers get some distance and objectivity when reviewing their first efforts. If the paper will include an abstract and an introduction, the writer should compose these after writing the rest. Because the point is to communicate ideas and information, writing should have consistency as well as succinctness and clarity. Not all readers understand technical terminology or long words: whenever possible, writers should use these only sparingly, and otherwise replace them with shorter, simpler words that do not change the meaning. Many writing and style guides exist for researchers lacking writing experience and/or confidence to consult.

Writing bodies and conclusions of literature review papers

Writers should first write a rough draft of their literature review paper. Then they should edit it to increase its clarity, eliminate verbiage and make the writing more concise, and change wording and terminology that could confuse some readers to simpler and more understandable language with the same meanings. Writers should always reread what they write. They should also ask others to read it and give them honest feedback. Additionally, the writer should read the paper aloud to hear how it sounds. Then s/he should rewrite and revise the paper based on the information gleaned. Throughout a literature review, the writer should not only summarize and comment on each source reviewed and what s/he has learned from it, s/he should also relate these findings to the original research question. The writer should explicitly state in the conclusion how the research question and pertinent literature interaction is a learning process devloped throughout the body, reflecting on insights gained through the process.

Citing sources

Formal research paper writers must cite all sources used—books, articles, interviews, conversations, and anything else that contributed to the research. One reason is to give others credit for their ideas and words. Otherwise, writers can be accused of stealing others' ideas; using others' words without quoting and citing sources is plagiarism. Another reason is to help readers find more information about the paper subject to read and research further. An additional reason is to make one's paper academically authoritative. To prepare, research writers should keep a running list of sources consulted, in an electronic file or on

Copyright © Mometrix Media. You have been licensed one copy of this document for personal use only. Any other reproduction or redistribution is strictly prohibited. All rights reserved.

file cards. This prevents frantic last-minute searches for missing source information. For every source used, the writer needs the following: Author and/or editor name, title, publication date, city, and publisher name for books; author name, title, journal (or magazine or newspaper) name, volume and issue number, publication date, and page numbers for articles; and in addition to the information for articles, the URL, database name, name of the database's publisher, and the date of access for electronic resources.

Three common reference styles are MLA (Modern Language Association), APA (American Psychological Association), and Turabian (by expert author Kate Turabian). Each style formats citation information differently. Professors and instructors often specify that students use one of these in their syllabus. If not, students can ask them. Sometimes it is obvious: APA style is used in psychology and sociology papers, and MLA style is used in English literature papers and similar scholarly projects. Historically, book titles were underlined to differentiate them from articles and other titles. However, today, underlines frequently signal hyperlinks to Internet documents and pages. To eliminate confusion, book, journal, magazine, newspaper and other titles formerly underlined are now italicized instead. Poem and short story titles are enclosed in quotation marks. Article titles are neither underlined nor italicized in the three major styles, but titles of journals where they appear are italicized. Article titles are enclosed in quotation marks in MLA and Turabian style, but not APA style. Government document titles are italicized in all three, while their sources (like the U.S. Congress and the Senate) are italicized in APA and Turabian, but not MLA.

MLA uses quotation marks around magazine article titles, but APA and Turabian do not. All three italicize magazine names. The manuals differ in ordering issue number, publication year, and page numbers. APA places (year) after article title, then magazine name, month, and page numbers. MLA follows article title with magazine title, then (year), number, month, and page numbers. Turabian puts magazine name after article title, then issue number, month, year, and page numbers. MLA and Turabian use quotation marks around print journal article titles, APA does not. APA puts publication year after author name(s); MLA and Turabian after journal name, issue, and volume numbers, but before page numbers. Turabian and APA put city and publisher after page numbers, MLA before. APA places (year, month, date) of print, microfilm, or microfiche newspaper articles after author name(s); MLA and Turabian place date, month, and year after newspaper name. Journal and newspaper articles from databases are cited similarly to print, microfilm, and microfiche, but with database name, retrieval date, and URL added. Websites need not be in bibliographies, but URLs and access dates should be included in the text.

When citing articles or chapters in books, APA style follows article title with a comma and book title; MLA uses a period, then book title. Turabian uses a period, then "In" followed by book title. When citing books, APA style uses authors' first initials; joins author names with an ampersand (&); follows with publication year in parentheses, period; title, period; city, colon; and publisher name. MLA and Turabian spell out authors' first names, join author names with "and," separate parts with periods like APA, and follow publisher names with publication year. For citing government documents, APA separates with commas, starting with title, government body name, Congress, its number, session number, year, page number. MLA separates with periods; starts with government body/division names; continues with title, Congress and session numbers when applicable; adds resolution number; and finishes with publication city, colon, publisher, comma, year. Turabian is separated by periods and includes government body/division names, title, comma, Congress

Copyright © Mometrix Media. You have been licensed one copy of this document for personal use only. Any other reproduction or redistribution is strictly prohibited. All rights reserved.

number when applying, and date. Sequencing within titles (such as committees/hearings) differ among manuals.

Citations of whole websites need only the URL (web address) in the body of the paper's text and enclosed within parentheses. Websites need not be included in the paper's bibliography, references, or works cited page. APA provides additional information about this at the following web address: http://www.apastyle.org/elecsource.html. For citing single documents found on websites, APA uses this format: Author last name, comma; author first initial, period; (year, month, date); title without quotation marks, period; publication city, colon, publisher/website owner, period; "Retrieved" month, date, year "from the World Wide Web:" URL on a separate line. MLA uses this format: Author last name, comma; author first name, period; title in quotation marks, period; italicized title, period; publisher/website owner, period; and date, month, year, period; URL on a separate line. Turabian uses this format: Author last name, comma; author first name, period; title in quotation marks, period; title, without italics or quotation marks, period; "Available from" and URL in the same line, period; and "Accessed" date, month, year.

To refer to authoritative sources for citing more complicated or specialized resources used in research, such as legislative publications, audiovisual resources, or manuscripts, at http://library.csudh.edu/cyberlib/research.htm is the section on Research and Writing Resources of California State University Dominguez Hills (CSUDH) University Library's website. The APA Manual is available in print: *Publication Manual of the American Psychological Association,* 6th ed., July 2009, and electronically in a Kindle edition. (The sixth is the latest edition as of February 2014.) APA has also adapted from this edition the *APA Style Guide to Electronic References,* and a pocket guide, *Concise Rules of APA Style.* Garner and Smith's *The Complete Guide to Citing Government Information Resources: A Manual for Writers and Librarians,* June 1993 (revised edition) is available in paperback on Amazon.com. *MLA Handbook for Writers of Research Papers* (7th edition, 2009) is available at MLA Bookstore's website. Turabian's *A Manual for Writers of Research Papers, Theses, and Dissertations* (8th edition, revised, 2013) is available from the University of Chicago Press website.

Integrating references and quotations

In research papers, one can make an argument and, without disrupting it, mention studies whose conclusions agree with one's position (Reed 284; Becker and Fagen 93), and those disagreeing (Limbaugh 442, Beck 69) by including parenthetical citations (for example, in this sentence). Quotations should be selective: writers should compose an original sentence and incorporate only a few words from a research source. If students cannot write more, or at least the same number of words as are in the quotation to analyze and concur with or rebut it, they are likely padding their compositions. When quoting sources, students and other writers should work to include quotations and references seamlessly into their sentences, instead of interrupting the flow of their own argument by summarizing the import of a source. Summarizing others' content is often a student ploy to bolster papers' word counts, a technique that is not intellectually original or engaging. Writing that analyzes the content, evaluates it, and synthesizes material from various sources demonstrates critical thinking skills and is thus more valuable.

Copyright © Mometrix Media. You have been licensed one copy of this document for personal use only. Any other reproduction or redistribution is strictly prohibited. All rights reserved.

Incorporating outside sources

Writers do better to include shorter quotations rather than longer ones. For example, six to eight long passages quoted within a 10-page paper are excessive. It is also better to avoid wording like "This quotation shows," "As you can see from this quotation," or "It talks about." These are amateurish, feeble efforts to interact with other authors' ideas. Also, writing about sources and quotations wastes words more effectively used to develop one's own ideas. Quotations should stimulate discussion, not quash it. Ending a paragraph, section, or paper with a quotation is not incorrect per se, but using it to prove a point, without anything more in one's own words regarding the point or subject, is avoiding thinking critically about the topic and considering multiple alternatives. It can also be a tactic to dissuade readers from challenging one's propositions. Writers should include references and quotations that disagree as well as agree with their thesis. Presenting evidence on both sides of an issue makes it easier for reasonably skeptical readers to agree with a writer's viewpoint.

Informative/explanatory vs. argumentative writing

Informative/explanatory writing begins on the basis that something is true or factual, while argumentative writing strives to prove something that may or may not be true or factual. Whereas argument is intended to convince readers that something is true or persuade readers to agree with the author's position, informative/explanatory text is instead intended to provide information and insight to readers. Rather than persuading readers, informative/explanatory writing concentrates on informing readers about why or how something is as it is. This includes offering new information to readers, explaining how a process works to readers, and/or developing a concept for readers. In accomplishing these objectives, the writing may emphasize such naming and differentiating various kinds of things within a category; providing definitions of things; providing details about the parts of something; explaining a particular function or behavior; and giving readers explanations for why a fact, object, event, or process exists or occurs.

Necessary skills for informative/explanatory writing

For students to write in informative/explanatory mode, they must be able to locate and select information pertinent to their topic from primary and secondary sources. They must also combine their own experiences and existing knowledge with this new information they find. They must not only select facts, details, and examples relevant to their topics, but also learn to incorporate this information into their writing. Students need at the same time to develop their skills in using various writing techniques, such as comparing and contrasting, making transitions between topics/points, citing scenarios and anecdotes related to their topics, and other strategies in the craft of writing. In instruction of explanatory/informative writing, teachers must "read like writers" to use mentor texts to consider author craft and technique. They can find mentor texts in blogs, websites, newspapers, novels, plays, picture books, and many more. Teachers should know the grade-level writing standards for informative/explanatory writing to select classroom-specific, appropriate mentor texts.

Narrative writing

Put simply, narrative writing tells a story. The most common examples of literary narratives are fictional novels. Non-fictional biographies, autobiographies, memoirs, and histories also

Copyright © Mometrix Media. You have been licensed one copy of this document for personal use only. Any other reproduction or redistribution is strictly prohibited. All rights reserved.

use narrative. Narratives should tell stories in such a way that the readers learn something, or gain insight or understanding. Students can write more interesting narratives by relating events or experiences that were meaningful to them. Narratives should not begin with long descriptions or introductions, but start with the action(s) or event(s). Students should ensure that there is a point to their story by describing what they learned from the experience they narrate. To write effective description, students should include sensory details. They can access these by reviewing all five senses, asking themselves what they saw, heard, felt/touched, smelled, and tasted during the experiences they describe. In narrative writing, the details supplied should be concrete rather than abstract. Using concrete details enables readers to imagine everything that the writer describes.

Sensory details and concrete vs. abstract descriptions

Students need vivid description to write descriptive essays. When writing narratives, they must also include description—of characters, things, and events. Students should remember to describe not only the visual detail of what someone or something looks like, but details from all senses—how people and things sound, feel, smell, and taste. For example, they can contrast the feelings of a sea breeze versus a mountain breeze, describe how they think something inedible would taste, and sounds they hear in the same location at different times of day and night. Readers have trouble visualizing images or imagining sensory impressions and feelings from abstract descriptions, so concrete descriptions clarify and make these more real to readers. Concrete language provides information that readers can grasp and may empathize with, while abstract language can leave readers feeling disconnected, empty, even confused. "It was a lovely day" is abstract, but "The sun shone brightly, the sky was blue, the air felt warm, and a gentle breeze wafted across my skin" is concrete.

Students should avoid abstract language in description because it will not help readers understand what they want to express. Concrete language conveys to readers impressions, images, and feelings they want to experience. Abstract language is more general, concrete language more specific. For example, "Ms. Couch was a good teacher" uses abstract language. It gives only a general idea of the writer's opinion. But "Ms. Couch could really help us take our ideas and turn them into good essays and stories" uses concrete language, giving more specific examples of what Ms. Couch did that made her a good teacher. "I like writing poems but not essays" gives readers a general idea that the student prefers one genre over another, but not why. But by saying, "I like writing short poems with rhythm and rhyme, but I hate writing five-page essays that go on and on about the same ideas," readers understand that the student prefers the brevity, rhyme, and meter of short poetry over the length and redundancy of longer prose.

Journals

A journal is typically an individual's personal account of events, experiences, feelings, and thoughts in that individual's life. Many people write journals to confide their feelings and thoughts and/or help them process experiences they have had. When people write such journals as private documents not meant for sharing with others, they may not be concerned with grammar, spelling, or other writing mechanics. However, authors may write journals that they expect or hope to publish someday; in this case, they not only express their thoughts and feelings and process their experiences, but they additionally attend to their craft in writing them. Some authors compose journals to document particular time

Copyright © Mometrix Media. You have been licensed one copy of this document for personal use only. Any other reproduction or redistribution is strictly prohibited. All rights reserved.

periods or series of related events, such as cancer diagnosis, treatment, surviving the disease, and how these experiences have changed/affected them; experiences in recovering from addiction; journeys of spiritual exploration and discovery; trips to or time spent in another country; or anything else someone wants to personally document. Journaling can also be therapeutic: some people use them to work through feelings of grief over loss.

Books written in diary form

The Diary of a Young Girl by Dutch Jewish Anne Frank (1947) contains her life-affirming, nonfictional diary entries from 1942-1944 while her family hid in an attic from World War II's genocidal Nazis. *Go Ask Alice* (1971) by Beatrice Sparks is a cautionary, fictional novel in the form of diary entries by an unhappy, rebellious teen who takes LSD, runs away from home and lives with hippies, and eventually returns home. The title quotes lyrics from the Jefferson Airplane song *White Rabbit* (1967), written and sung by Grace Slick, comparing the effects of LSD via extended metaphor to Lewis Carroll's (1865) depiction of *Alice's Adventures in Wonderland*. Frank's writing reveals an intelligent, sensitive, insightful girl, raised by intellectual European parents, who believes in the goodness of human nature despite surrounding atrocities. Character Alice, influenced by early 1970s counterculture, becomes less optimistic. However, adolescent searches for personal identity are evident in both books. Frank died in a Nazi concentration camp; the fictitious Alice died in a drug overdose.

Letters

Letters are typically messages written to communicate with other people. In addition to letters written between individuals, some writers compose letters to the editor of newspapers, magazines, and other publications; some write "Open Letters" to be published and read by the general public. Open letters, while intended for everyone to read, may also identify a group of people or a single person whom the letter directly addresses—or not. In everyday use, the most-used forms are business letters and personal or friendly letters. Both kinds share common elements, like business or personal letterhead stationery; the writer's return address at the top; the addressee's address next; a salutation, such as "Dear [name]" or some similar opening greeting, followed by a colon (:) in business letters or a comma (,) in personal letters; "To Whom it May Concern:" in business letters without specific individual addressees; the body of the letter, with paragraphs as indicated; and a closing, like "Sincerely/Cordially/Best regards/etc." or "Love," in intimate personal letters.

The Greek word for "letter" is *epistolē*, wherefrom English derives the word "epistle." The earliest literary letters were called epistles, including the New Testament's Epistles from the Apostles to the Christians. In ancient Egypt, the writing curriculum in scribal schools included the epistolary genre. Epistolary novels frame a story in the form of letters. For example, 18th-century English novelist Samuel Richardson wrote the popular epistolary novels *Pamela* (1740) and *Clarissa* (1749). Henry Fielding's satire of *Pamela*, entitled *Shamela* (1741) mocked epistolary writing. French author Montesquieu wrote *Lettres persanes* (1721); Jean-Jacques Rousseau wrote *Julie, ou la nouvelle Héloïse* (1761); and Pierre Choderlos de Laclos penned *Les Liaisons dangereuses* (1782), which was adapted into a screenplay for the multiple Oscar-winning 1988 English-language movie *Dangerous Liaisons*. German author Johann Wolfgang von Goethe wrote *The Sorrows of Young Werther* in epistolary form. Frances Brooke also wrote the first North American novel, *The History of Emily Montague* (1769) using epistolary form. In the 19th century, epistolary novels

- 61 -

Copyright © Mometrix Media. You have been licensed one copy of this document for personal use only. Any other reproduction or redistribution is strictly prohibited. All rights reserved.

included Honoré de Balzac's *Letters of Two Brides* (1842) and Mary Shelley's *Frankenstein* (1818).

Essays

The basic format of an essay can be said to have three major parts: the introduction, the body, and the conclusion. Further, the essay's body can be divided into the writer's main points. Short and simple essays may have three main points, while essays covering broader ranges and going into more depth can have almost any number of main points, depending on length. An essay's introduction should answer three questions: (1) What is the subject of the essay? For example, if a student writes an essay about a book, the answer would include the title and author of the book and any additional information needed—such as what the book is about if the title does not indicate this. (2) How does the essay address the subject? To answer this, the writer identifies the essay's organization by briefly summarizing main points and/or evidence supporting them. (3) What will the essay prove? This is the thesis statement, usually the first paragraph's last sentence, clearly stating the writer's message.

An essay consists of an introduction, a body, and a conclusion. The introduction gives the essay's topic, previews its organization by summarizing its main points and supporting evidence, and introduces the thesis statement—the writer's major point. The body elaborates on all the main points related to the thesis and evidence supporting them. The conclusion restates the content of the introduction, and may also summarize the argument or description contained in the body. In the essay's body, the writer should introduce one main point; explain the meaning of this point; make quotations, cite facts, and offer other evidence to support the point; and then explain how this point and the evidence given to support it are related to the thesis. The writer should then repeat this procedure in a new paragraph with each of the additional main points. In addition to relating each point to the thesis, clearly restating the thesis in at least one sentence of each paragraph is also advisable.

An essay's basic parts are its introduction, body, and conclusion. The introduction tells essay's subject, how the essay's structure addresses this subject, and the author's major point or thesis statement. The body is where the writer introduces a series of main points related to the thesis, and provides evidence to support each of these points. The last part, the conclusion, reiterates the content of the introduction, including the thesis, to review them for the reader. The essay writer may also summarize the highlights of the argument or description contained in the body of the essay, following the same sequence originally used in the body. For example, a conclusion might look like Point 1 + Point 2 + Point 3 = Thesis, or Point 1 → Point 2 → Point 3 → Thesis Proof. Good organization makes essays easier for writers to compose, and provides a guide for readers to follow in reading them. Well-organized essays hold reader attention better, and are more likely to get readers to accept their theses as valid.

Speeches

Speeches are compositions written to be delivered or read in spoken language in public, to various groups of people, at formal or informal events. Some generic types include welcome speeches, thank-you speeches, keynote addresses, position papers, commemorative and dedication speeches, and farewell speeches. Speeches are commonly written in present tense. Speeches begin with an introduction, wherein the speaker greets the audience. At

Copyright © Mometrix Media. You have been licensed one copy of this document for personal use only. Any other reproduction or redistribution is strictly prohibited. All rights reserved.

official functions, specific audience members are named ("Chairperson [name]," "Principal [name], teachers, and students") and when audiences include a distinguished guest, s/he is named as well. Then the speaker introduces himself/herself by name, position, and department/organization as applicable. The speaker then introduces the topic. Then s/he states the purpose of the speech. The body of the speech follows, similarly to the body of an essay, stating its main points, their elaboration, and supporting evidence. Finally, in the conclusion, the speaker states his/her hope for accomplishing the speech's purpose and thanks the audience for attending and listening to the speech.

Blogs

The word "blog" derives from "web log" and refers to writing done exclusively on the Internet. Readers of reputable newspapers expect quality content and layouts that enable easy reading. These expectations also apply to blogs. For example, readers can easily move visually from line to line when columns are narrow; overly wide columns cause readers to lose their places. Blogs must also be posted with layouts enabling online readers to follow them easily. However, because the way people read on computer, tablet, and smartphone screens differs from how they read print on paper, formatting and writing blog content is more complex than writing newspaper articles. Two major principles are the bases for blog-writing rules: (1) Whereas readers skim print articles to estimate their length, online they must scroll down to scan; therefore, blog layouts need more subheadings, graphics, and other indications of what information follows. (2) Onscreen reading is harder than reading printed paper; therefore, legibility is crucial in blogs.

Writing forms

When authors write narrative, their purpose is telling a story. Even when they mean to teach lessons or provide insight through relating events and experiences, they still do so by telling stories. Descriptive writing aims to recreate a moment, scene, event, or experience by conveying details vividly to appeal to readers' senses, imaginations, and emotions. Expository writing aims to provide information, explain ideas and processes, and/or give step-by-step directions how to do something. Persuasive/argumentative writing aims to convince readers to agree with the author's viewpoint, opinion, or position, by both providing supporting evidence, and using subjective/expressive language to sway readers' opinions and influence their feelings and beliefs. Speculative writing, rather than informing or explaining as expository/informational writing does, aims to explore ideas and, rather than convincing readers to agree, aims to encourage readers also to consider ideas and various potential thoughts and reactions associated with them. Points are less clear and definitive, and structures looser, in speculative writing than in exposition or argumentation.

Dialect

Dialect is the form of a language spoken by people according to their geographical region, social class, cultural group, or any distinctive group. It includes pronunciation, grammar, and spelling. Literary authors often use dialect when writing dialogue to illustrate the social and geographical backgrounds of specific characters, which supports character development. For example, in *The Adventures of Huckleberry Finn* (1885), Mark Twain's novel is told in the first person by protagonist Huck in the dialect of the young and uneducated white Southern character, opening with this sentence: "You don't know about me without you have read a book by the name of The Adventures of Tom Sawyer, but that

Copyright © Mometrix Media. You have been licensed one copy of this document for personal use only. Any other reproduction or redistribution is strictly prohibited. All rights reserved.

ain't no matter." Twain uses a different and exaggerated dialect to represent the speech of the African-American slave Jim: "We's safe, Huck, we's safe! Jump up and crack yo' heels. Dat's de good ole Cairo at las', I jis knows it."

In *To Kill a Mockingbird,* author Harper Lee used dialect in the characters' dialogue to portray the speech of uneducated Southern American people: "Reckon I have. Almost died the first year I come to school and et them pecans—folks say he pizened 'em." She also uses many Southern regional expressions, such as "right stove up," "What in the sam holy hill...?", "sit a spell," "fess" (meaning "confess"), "jim-dandy," and "hush your fussing." These contribute to Lee's characterization of the people she describes, who live in a small town in Alabama circa the 1930s. In *Wuthering Heights* (1847), Emily Bronte reproduces Britain's 18th-19th-century Yorkshire dialect in the speech of servant Joseph: "Running after t'lads, as usuald!... If I war yah, maister, I'd just slam t'boards i' their faces all on 'em, gentle and simple! Never a day ut yah're off, but yon cat o' Linton comes sneaking hither; and Miss Nelly, shoo's a fine lass!" Emily's sister Charlotte also used this dialect in *Jane Eyre* for a farm woman: "T'pig don't want it."

In addition to using dialects to support character development in novels, plays, poems, and other literary works, authors also manipulate dialects to accomplish various purposes with their intended reading audiences. For example, in an English Language Arts lesson plan for eighth graders (Groome and Gibbs, 2008), teachers point out author Frances O'Roark Dowell from Boone, North Carolina, set her Edgar Allan Poe and William Allen White Award-winning teen novel *Dovey Coe* (2000) in the Western North Carolina mountains of 1928. Dowell writes protagonist Dovey's narration in the regional Appalachian Mountain dialect to remind readers of the significance of the novel's setting. This lesson plan further includes two poems by African-American author Paul Laurence Dunbar: "When Malindy Sings" and "We Wear the Mask." Students are asked why Dunbar wrote the former poem in Southern slave dialect and the latter in Standard English. Exercises include identifying dialect/Standard English features, rewriting dialect in Standard English, identifying audiences, and identifying how author choices of dialects or Standard English affect readers and accomplish author purposes.

Dialect vs. diction
When written as characters' dialogue in literary works, dialect represents the particular pronunciation, grammar, and figurative expressions used by certain groups of people based on their geographic region, social class, and cultural background. For example, when a character says, "There's gold up in them thar hills," the author is using dialect to add to the characterization of that individual. Diction is more related to individual characters than to groups of people. The way in which a specific character speaks, including his or her choice of words, manner of expressing himself or herself, and use of grammar all represent individual types of diction. For example, two characters in the same novel might describe the same action or event using different diction: One says "I'm heading uptown for the evening," and the other says "I'm going out for a night on the town." These convey the same literal meaning, but due to their variations in diction they are expressed in different ways.

Simple survey research into linguistic dialects
To learn about different dialects spoken in different geographic regions, social classes, and cultural groups, students can undertake simple surveys of small groups of informants. Students should first make a list of words they have heard used in certain dialects. Then they can ask their respondents to identify the words in the list whose meanings they know.

- 64 -

Copyright © Mometrix Media. You have been licensed one copy of this document for personal use only. Any other reproduction or redistribution is strictly prohibited. All rights reserved.

Students can also ask respondents which words they have heard of before, but whose meanings are unfamiliar to them. Using their lists of dialect words, students can ask informants to identify which of the words they personally still use in their day-to-day conversations. They might want to ask respondents a combination in the same survey, of both which words they know and which they still use in their speech. For a more multidimensional survey, a student can ask the sampled informants all three—words that they know, those that they have heard of but do not know the meanings, and those that they use in their speech.

Influences on regional dialect

Linguistic researchers have identified regional variations in vocabulary choices, which have evolved because of differences in local climates and how they influence human behaviors. For example, in the Southern United States, the Linguistic Atlas of the Gulf States (LAGS) Project by Dr. Lee Pederson of Emory University discovered and documented that people living in the northern or Upland section of the Piedmont plateau region call the fungal infection commonly known as athlete's foot "toe itch," but people living in the southern or Lowland section call it "ground itch." The explanation for this difference is that in the north, temperatures are cooler and people accordingly wear shoes, so they associate the itching with the feet in their description, but in the south, temperatures are hotter and people traditionally went barefoot, so they associated the itching with the ground wherefrom they presumably contracted the infection. Additional variations identified between northern and southern parts of the Gulf States include "chigger" versus "red bug," "dragonfly" versus "snake doctor," and "wishbone" versus "pullybone."

Considerations to teach students about occasions, purposes, and audiences

Teachers can explain to students that organizing their ideas, providing evidence to support the points they make in their writing, and correcting their grammar and mechanics are not simply for following writing rules or correctness for its own sake, but rather for ensuring that specific reader audiences understand what they intend to communicate. For example, upper-elementary-grade students writing for lower-elementary-grade students should write in printing rather than script, use simpler vocabulary, and avoid writing in long, complex, compound, or complex-compound sentences. The purpose for writing guides word choice, such as encouraging readers to question opposing viewpoints or stimulate empathy and/or sympathy. It also influences narrative, descriptive, expository, or persuasive/argumentative format. For instance, business letters require different form and language than parent thank-you notes. Persuasive techniques, like words that evoke certain reader emotions, description that appeals to reader beliefs, and supporting information can all affect reader opinions.

Questions to ask to determine content and format

When student writers have chosen a viewpoint or idea about which to write, teachers can help them select content to include and the writing format(s) most appropriate to their subject. They should have students ask themselves what their readers need to know to enable them to agree with the viewpoint in the writing, and/or to believe what the writer is saying. Students can imagine another person hearing them say what they will write about, responding, "Oh, yeah? Prove that!" Teachers should have students ask themselves what kinds of evidence they should supply to prove their positions/ideas to skeptical readers. They should have students consider what points they will make in writing with which

- 65 -

Copyright © Mometrix Media. You have been licensed one copy of this document for personal use only. Any other reproduction or redistribution is strictly prohibited. All rights reserved.

readers might disagree. Students should consider what knowledge their reading audience shares in common with them. They should also consider what information they need to share with their readers. Teachers can have students adapt various writing formats, organizing techniques, and writing styles to different purposes and audiences to practice with choosing writing modes and language.

Appropriate kinds of writing for different tasks, purposes, and audiences

Students who are writing to persuade their parents to grant them some additional privilege, such as permission for a more independent activity, should use more sophisticated vocabulary and diction that sounds more mature and serious to appeal to the parental audience. Students who are writing for younger children, however, should use simpler vocabulary and sentence structure, as well as choosing words that are more vivid and entertaining. They should treat their topics more lightly, and include some humor as is appropriate. Students who are writing for their classmates, regardless whether they are writing in expository, argumentative, narrative, or speculative form, might use language that is more informal, as well as age-appropriate. Students wanting to convince others to agree with them should use persuasive/argumentative form. Those wanting to share an experience with readers should use descriptive writing. Those wanting to relate a story and what can be learned from it should write narratives. Students can use speculative writing to invite others to join them in exploring ideas.

Main ideas, supporting details, and outlining a topic

Writers often begin their first paragraph by stating their main idea or point, also known as their topic sentence. In the rest of the paragraph, they supply particular details that develop and support the main point. One way to visualize the relationship between the main point and supporting information is as a table: the tabletop is the main point, and each of the table's legs is a supporting detail or group of details. Both professional authors and writing students can benefit in planning their writing by first making an outline of the topic. Outlines facilitate quick identification of the main point and supporting details without having to wade through the intervening language that will exist in the fully developed essay, article, or paper. Outlining can also help readers to analyze a piece of existing writing for the same reason. The outline first summarizes the main idea in one sentence. Then, below that, it summarizes the supporting details in a numbered list, also of one sentence each.

Words that signal introduction of successive details

When someone writes a paragraph beginning with the topic sentence, the second sentence may begin with a phrase like "First of all," introducing the first supporting detail/example. The writer may introduce the second supporting item with words or phrases like "Also," "In addition," and "Besides," among others. The writer might introduce succeeding pieces of support with wording like, "Another thing," "Moreover" "Furthermore," or "Not only that, but..." The writer may introduce the last piece of support with "Lastly," "Finally," or "Last but not least." Writers get off the point by presenting "off-target" items not supporting the main point. For example, a main point "My dog is not smart" is supported by the statement, "He's six years old and still doesn't answer to his name." But "He cries when I leave for school" is not supportive, as it does not indicate lack of intelligence. Writers stay on the point by presenting only supportive statements that are directly relevant to and illustrative of their main point.

Copyright © Mometrix Media. You have been licensed one copy of this document for personal use only. Any other reproduction or redistribution is strictly prohibited. All rights reserved.

Paragraph

A paragraph is generally a group of sentences that forms a unit separate from (but connected to) other paragraphs. Typically, all of one paragraph's sentences relate to one main idea or point. Two major properties that make paragraphs effective or ineffective are focus and development, or lack thereof. Paragraphs with poor focus impede comprehension because the sentences they contain seem unrelated. When writers attempt to include too many ideas in a paragraph rather than focusing on the most important idea, or fail to supply transitions between ideas, they produce unfocused or at least inadequately-focused paragraphs. Undeveloped or inadequately-developed paragraphs may use good writing, but are still not convincing or effective. When writers misunderstand their reading audience, depend overly upon generalization, and fail to offer specific details, their paragraph development is poor. They may omit key term definitions, supporting evidence, setting description, context for others' ideas, background, and other important details because they assume that readers already know these things and think they would bore readers by repeating them.

The first thing a writer should do to write good paragraphs is to focus upon one main idea as a paragraph's subject or topic. Writers may introduce a paragraph by stating this main idea in a topic sentence. However, the main idea may be so obvious that writers can imply it rather than state it overtly and readers can easily infer it. Another thing writers should do is to use specific details to develop the main idea. Details should capture readers' attention and also explain author ideas. Insufficient detail makes a paragraph too abstract, which readers find boring and even confusing. Excessive detail makes a paragraph unfocused, which readers find overwhelming, and again, even confusing. A third thing writers should do is to develop paragraphs using structural patterns. Paragraphs have a nearly limitless range of structures, but certain patterns appear more often, including narration, description, definition, example and illustration, division and classification, comparison and contrast, analogy, cause and effect, and process.

Narration, description, definition, example and illustration, and division and classification: In narration, a paragraph develops its main idea by using a story or a portion of a story. Writers may use stories as anecdotal evidence to support the main point. In description, the writer helps readers to construct a clear image of a scene or event by including specific, sensory and other details that depict a person, thing, place, and/or time. Description shows readers instead of telling them. In definition, the writer uses a paragraph to provide readers with a detailed definition of a term that is central to the piece of writing. In example and illustration, the writer provides the readers with one or more examples that illustrate the point that the writer wants to make. Paragraphs using division divide one whole thing into its component parts according to some particular principle—for example, body parts or experiment steps. Paragraphs using classification group separate things into categories by their similarities or commonalities, also according to some particular principle—such as mammals and insects, tragedies and comedies, and so on.

Analogy, cause and effect, and process: Paragraphs that compare two or more things make note of their similarities, i.e., all or many of the characteristics that those things share in common. Paragraphs that contrast two or more things make note of how they differ from one another. Another common paragraph technique is both comparing and contrasting two or more items within the same paragraph, showing both similarities and differences.

Copyright © Mometrix Media. You have been licensed one copy of this document for personal use only. Any other reproduction or redistribution is strictly prohibited. All rights reserved.

Analogy compares two things in a way that they are not usually compared, often because they are things belonging to very different categories. This can afford new reader insight. Writers may use analogies to develop their ideas. Writers also develop their ideas in paragraphs through cause and effect, which either explains what caused some event or result, or shows the effects that something produced. Paragraphs may start with cause(s) and proceed to effect(s), or begin with effect(s) and then give cause(s). Process paragraphs describe and/or explain some process. They often sequence the stages, phases, or steps of the process using chronological order.

When a paragraph is coherent, its parts or details fit together such that readers clearly perceive it, and its parts flow well from each to the next. Writers produce more coherent paragraphs when they select structural patterns appropriate to the conceptual content. There are several techniques writers can use to make paragraphs more coherent. Repetition connects sentences by repeating key words, phrases, and/or pronouns referring to these. This not only helps sentences flow together, it also signals to readers the significance of the ideas these words and phrases communicate. Parallelism uses parallel structure, within and also between and among sentences. Humorist Bill Maher once said, "We're feeding animals too sick to stand to people too fat to walk." His parallelism emphasized and connected two issues: using downed cows as food, and the obesity epidemic. Consistency keeps the viewpoint, tone, and linguistic register consistent within the paragraph or piece. Finally, transitions via connective words and phrases aid coherence immensely.

Transitions

Transitions between sentences and paragraphs help guide readers from idea to idea. They also indicate relationships between sentences and paragraphs. Writers should use transitions judiciously: they should not overuse these, and should take care to select the right transition for their purpose. For example, transitional words and phrases indicating time include: thereafter, afterward, immediately, earlier, meanwhile, recently, lately, later (on), now, (ever) since, soon, as soon as, when, then, until, before, in the past, presently, simultaneously, so far, thus far, previously, at that time, and at last. Transitions indicating sequence include: too, first, second, third, further, furthermore, moreover, also, again, and, and then, next, still, too, besides, and finally. Transitions specifying comparison include: similarly, in the same way, likewise, also, again, and once more. Transitions that indicate contrast include: but, even so, even though, although, despite, however, instead, in spite of, nonetheless, nevertheless, on the one hand... on the other hand, regardless, irrespective, though, still, yet, contrastingly, differently, and in contrast.

<u>Transitional words and phrases</u>
Transitions indicating examples include: for example, for instance, the following example, such as, to illustrate, indeed, in fact, of course, namely, specifically, and after all. Transitions indicating cause and effect include: because, consequently, hence, thus, therefore, thereupon, then, to this end, since, so, as a result, if... then, and accordingly. Transitions indicating place include: near, nearby, far, faraway, here, there, to the left, to the right, next to, above, below, adjacent to, beyond, opposite, across from, beside, alongside, at the back, in the front, in front of, behind, to the side, and abreast of. Transitions expressing concession include: granted that, naturally, of course, I admit that, it may seem that, it may appear, and although it is true that. Transitions showing repetition, summary, or conclusion include: as mentioned earlier, as we have seen, as noted, in other words, in any event, in short, on the whole, to summarize, therefore, as a result, to conclude, and in conclusion.

Copyright © Mometrix Media. You have been licensed one copy of this document for personal use only. Any other reproduction or redistribution is strictly prohibited. All rights reserved.

These tell readers how a sentence relates to the previous one(s), and directs their thinking across ideas.

Coherence vs. cohesion

Cohesive writing flows, making readers feel ease in moving from sentence to sentence and that all sentences hold together. Coherent writing contains sentences that are not only clear individually, but also combine into a unified paragraph or passage focusing on a group of ideas that fit together. While we are often warned against using passive voice, sometimes a paragraph or passage is more cohesive using a passive construction when it allows sentences to flow together better. For example, "Scientists are studying black holes. A black hole is made when a dead star collapses..." The passive voice allows repetition of "black hole" from the end of the first sentence to the beginning of the second, connecting this idea. Making one sentence follow from the previous one is the "old-to-new" technique. If the second sentence in active voice read, "When a dead star collapses, it becomes a black hole..." The term "black hole" would be further away from the first sentence and they would not connect or flow as well.

Writers can make text cohesive with the old-to-new principle: starting sentences with information familiar to readers, and ending them with information unexpected to readers. Someone can write a cohesive paragraph because sentences flow together well: each new sentence refers to a word or idea in the previous one. However, a cohesive paragraph may still not be coherent, as when the writer connects words or ideas between sentences, but changes the subject with each new sentence. When writing is coherent, readers can make sense of paragraphs or passages because sentence ideas integrate into a unified whole with interrelated concepts. Coherent writing enables readers to recognize individual sentence topics readily, and realize how they combine into a group of connected ideas. Readers feel more comfortable when sentence topics appear earlier in sentences, and when a sequence of sentences indicates the import of the entire paragraph or passage. Beginning sentences with familiar information in short and simple phrases, keeping topics consistent, and making movement between ideas obvious will help produce cohesive and coherent writing.

Writing style and linguistic form

Linguistic form comes from the phonological, morphological, syntactic, and semantic parts of a language. It encodes the literal meanings of words and sentences. Writing style consists of different ways of encoding that meaning, and indicating figurative and stylistic meanings. The stylistic choices that writers make accomplish three basic effects upon their reading or listening audiences: (1) they communicate meanings beyond linguistically dictated meanings; (2) they communicate the author's attitude, such as persuasive/argumentative effects accomplished through style; and (3) they communicate or express feelings. Within style, component areas include: narrative structure; viewpoint; focus; sound patterns; meter and rhythm; lexical and syntactic repetition and parallelism; writing genre; representational, realistic, and mimetic effects; representation of thought and speech; meta-representation (representing representation); irony; metaphor and other indirect meanings; representation and use of historical and dialectal variations; gender-specific and other group-specific speech styles, both real and fictitious; and analysis of the processes whereby readers infer meanings from writing.

- 69 -

Copyright © Mometrix Media. You have been licensed one copy of this document for personal use only. Any other reproduction or redistribution is strictly prohibited. All rights reserved.

Introduction

Because readers encounter the introduction first, writers should design introductory paragraphs to capture reader interest. Introductions should state the main point, thesis, or topic sentence soon and logically. Writers should use introductions to prepare readers for the content of the body of the essay or piece. To do this, writers should narrow their topics to a main idea. They should determine which main points support the main idea, and then decide in what sequence to order those points. Then they should list all of the details that support each of those main points, and organize these details in sequential order. Some techniques for sequencing include strongest-to-weakest and weakest-to-strongest, logical progression, or sequencing by association. Writers should compose a thesis statement, which may contain their plan for the piece's structure and organization. Then they make a first draft of the body of the document, including transitions between sentences and paragraphs. Finally, they write the introduction, focusing on getting the reader's attention and engaging his/her interest, integrating the thesis into the introduction, and maintaining the document's organization and structure.

Body

In the introduction to an essay, a writer has established the thesis or main idea, and may have indicated how the rest of the piece will be structured. In the body of the piece, the writer elaborates upon, illustrates, and explains the thesis statement. How writers sequence supporting details and their choices of paragraph types are development techniques. Writers may give examples of the concept introduced in the thesis statement. If the subject includes a cause-and-effect relationship, the author may explain its nature and causality. A writer may explain and/or analyze the main idea of the piece. Authors will often present arguments for the veracity or credibility of their thesis statement. If they use ambiguous terms, writers may use development to define or clarify them. Writers may organize paragraphs within the body using natural sequences, like space and/or time. They may employ inductive reasoning, using multiple details to establish a generalization or causal relationship, or deductive reasoning, proving a generalized hypothesis or proposition through a specific example/case.

Conclusion

Two important principles to consider when writing the conclusion of a written piece are strength and closure. When a conclusion is strong, it gives the reader the sense that the main points made by the author were meaningful and important, and that the facts and arguments that the author presented to prove or support those main points were convincing, solid, and well-developed. When a conclusion achieves closure, it gives the reader the sense that the writer has stated what needed stating and the work is complete, rather than that the writer simply stopped writing upon reaching the number of words specified. Some things to avoid when writing concluding paragraphs include: introducing a completely new idea in the conclusion; beginning with "In conclusion" or "To summarize," which is overly obvious and unoriginal; apologizing for one's opinions and/or writing; repeating the thesis word for word, rather than rephrasing it; and believing that the conclusion must always summarize the piece.

Copyright © Mometrix Media. You have been licensed one copy of this document for personal use only. Any other reproduction or redistribution is strictly prohibited. All rights reserved.

Parts of speech

Nouns are words for persons, places, or things. The words *girl, town*, and *house* are all nouns. Nouns are frequently the sentence subjects. Proper nouns are names. Pronouns replace nouns, including personal pronouns specifying person, number, gender, or case. Some common pronouns are *I, you, he, she, it, none,* and *which*. Personal pronouns may be subjective, such as sentence/clause subjects, or objective, like the objects of verbs or prepositions. Verbs are words for actions or states of being. Verbs are often sentence predicates. Adjectives are descriptive words modifying nouns, for example, *big* girl, *red* house, or other adjectives, such as *great* big house. Adverbs are descriptive words modifying verbs, adjectives, or other adverbs (including clauses), often ending in *–ly*. Examples include running *quickly* and *patiently* waiting. Conjunctive adverbs connect two clauses. The words *also, finally, however, furthermore, consequently, instead, meanwhile, next, still, then, therefore, indeed, incidentally,* and *likewise* are all conjunctive adverbs. Prepositions connect nouns/pronouns/phrases to other words in sentences, such as *on, in, behind, under, beside, against, beneath, over,* and *during*. Prepositional phrases include prepositions, their objects, and associated adjectives/adverbs. Conjunctions connect words/phrases/clauses. Common conjunctions include *and, when, but, or/nor, for, so,* and *yet.*

Phrases, clauses, and independent and dependent clauses

A clause has a subject and a predicate and the other elements of a sentence. An independent clause can stand on its own as a sentence. A dependent clause has a subject and a predicate, but it also has a subordinating conjunction, a relative pronoun, or some other connecting word or phrase that makes it unable to stand alone without an accompanying independent clause. For example, "I knew she was not at home" is an independent clause that can be a sentence on its own. But "because I saw her leave" is a dependent clause due to the subordinating conjunction "because," which makes it depend on the independent clause. The two clauses, joined together, form the complex sentence, "I knew she was not at home because I saw her leave." A phrase is neither a complete sentence nor a clause. It lacks a subject, or a predicate, or both. For example, "late at night" is an adverb phrase; "into the house" is a prepositional phrase. Phrases modify other sentence parts.

Simple, compound, and complex sentences

A simple sentence is the same thing as an independent clause. It states a complete thought and includes a subject and predicate/verb. An example is, "Some students cram before tests." "Students" is the subject; "some" is a modifying adjective. "Cram" is the verb; "before tests" is a modifying prepositional phrase. A compound sentence includes two independent clauses connected by a coordinator (*for, and, nor, but, or, yet, so*). For example, "Andrew likes history, but Cynthia prefers math" is a compound sentence. Independent clauses can also be joined by a semicolon instead of a coordinator: "Andrew likes history; Cynthia prefers math." A complex sentence has an independent clause and dependent clause, joined by a subordinator: "While Andrew likes history, Cynthia prefers math." The subordinating conjunction "while" makes the first clause dependent on the second. In the complex sentence, "Students are tired on exam day when they have crammed all night," the second clause, made subordinate by "when," depends on the independent clause that came first.

Copyright © Mometrix Media. You have been licensed one copy of this document for personal use only. Any other reproduction or redistribution is strictly prohibited. All rights reserved.

Compound, complex, and compound-complex sentences

Compound sentences consist of two independent clauses, joined by a coordinating conjunction or punctuation like a semicolon, a colon, or sometimes a comma (for example, "He likes coffee, she likes tea"). Complex sentences consist of an independent clause and a dependent clause, connected by a subordinating word, making one clause subordinate to/dependent on the other. A compound-complex sentence includes two independent clauses, plus one or more dependent clauses. "Susan likes art, and Emily prefers science" is a compound sentence. "Although Susan likes art, Emily prefers science" is a complex sentence. An example of a compound-complex sentence is, "Susan, who draws well, likes art, but Emily, who is very methodical, prefers science." "Susan likes art" is an independent clause. "Who draws well" is a dependent clause with subordinator "who" modifying subject "Susan." "Emily prefers science" is another independent clause. "Who is very methodical" is another dependent clause with subordinator "who" modifying subject "Emily." "But" is the coordinating conjunction joining the two independent clauses.

Fragments and run-on sentences

A sentence fragment is missing some essential component: a subject, predicate, or a dependent clause with no independent clause. An example of the latter is: "Although I knew that." This is incomplete because "although" makes it a dependent clause with no independent clause to complete the thought. By adding an independent clause, the sentence becomes complete: "Although I knew that, I forgot it." The statement "Going to dinner" has a subject (the gerund "going," a verbal functioning as a noun) and a prepositional phrase ("to dinner") but it does not have a proper subject. Again, adding a subject solves the problem: "We are going to dinner." To repair the statement "The friendly woman Mary," simply add a verb: "The friendly woman is Mary." Run-on sentences lack necessary punctuation and/or connecting words: "We went to their party we had a very good time we plan to go again." This can be corrected several ways: "We went to their party. We had a very good time. We plan to go again." Or, less choppily: "We went to their party; we had a very good time, and we plan to go again."

Colons vs. semicolons, its vs. it's, and saw vs. seen

Semicolons separate independent clauses, such as "She likes music; she likes to dance." Colons separate clauses when the second explains or illustrates the first: "She likes music: she likes to dance to it." People often misuse semicolons. For example, business letter salutations should use colons. "Dear Mr. Johnson:" for example. Semicolons are never correct here ("Dear Mr. Johnson;"). Another common error is inserting an apostrophe into "its" to indicate possession. For example, the sentence, "The house is old; *its* paint is peeling" is correct. People often incorrectly spell this possessive personal pronoun as "it's." Their error is because some possessive nouns/pronouns use apostrophes, such as "Barbara's idea" or "the man's hat." But "its," along with "yours," "hers," and "theirs" (without noun objects) do not. The only correct usage of "it's" is as a contraction of "it" and "is," as in "It's raining outside." "Saw" is the past tense of "to see." "Seen" is the perfect tense, used with auxiliary verbs to form present perfect "have seen," or past perfect, "had seen." This is why "I seen you" and "I have saw" are both incorrect.

Copyright © Mometrix Media. You have been licensed one copy of this document for personal use only. Any other reproduction or redistribution is strictly prohibited. All rights reserved.

Lie vs. lay

"To lie" is the infinitive form of the verb, as in "It is restful to lie down on a bed." Many people incorrectly use "lay down" instead. "To lay" is always a transitive verb, which means that it requires an object, and it means to make something lie down or to set something down, as in, "Lay that book on the table." The non-infinitive "lay" is the past tense of "to lie," e.g., "Yesterday I lay down." But the past tense of the transitive verb "to lay" is "laid," as in, "Yesterday I laid the book on the table." The present perfect and past perfect tenses of the intransitive verb "to lie" are both "lain," as in "I have lain here a long time" or "I had lain there all day before they came." However, the present and past perfect tenses of the transitive verb "to lay" are both "laid," as in "I have laid this book down for now" and "I had laid this book down last week."

Compound words

Compound words are words that consist of two single words that are used together to give a more specific meaning so commonly or often that they have been combined to form one word. These may be any part of speech, but are often nouns or adjectives. Some examples of nouns are *footsteps, heartbeat, countertop, gunshot, housewife, household, bookshelf, songbook, storybook, timetable, halfway, aftermath,* and *upkeep.* Some examples among adjectives include *paint-chipped, two-person* or *four-person* (as in *four-person* table or *two-person* serving), *beat-up, pock-marked, war-torn, world-weary,* and *evidence-based.* Compound adjectives may be hyphenated while compound nouns may not, but the reverse can also be true, as it is the compound adjective *bloodstained.* Also, authors may create compound adjectives when writing descriptively, as in *acne-scarred, hail-pitted,* and *flower-adorned,* to name a few. Some inexperienced writers make errors in spelling compound words as two words, such as *up keep, foot steps, after math,* and *half way,* among others.

Dangling participles and squinting modifiers

Dangling participles are common writing errors. They occur when someone writes a participial ("-ing") phrase followed by a clause, but the syntax makes the participle seemingly modify that clause when it really modifies something else that is unstated. Consider the following sentence, "Always getting into trouble, her life changes." The participle "getting" should modify an absent "she," but it incorrectly modifies "her life" instead. Her life is not always getting into trouble, she is. Or another example, "After eating his lunch, we left the restaurant." The dangling participle makes it sound as if we both ate his lunch. If the writer meant to indicate he ate, it should read, "After he ate his lunch, we left the restaurant." "Joanne's mother left when she was young" has a squinting modifier, making unclear who was young when the mother left—Joanne, her mother, or both. Possible corrections include: "Her mother left when Joanne was young," "Joanne's mother left as a young woman," or "Her young mother left when Joanne was a young child."

Misplaced modifiers

Misplaced modifiers are in the wrong part of a sentence, appearing to modify the wrong thing. For example, "This author creates a drama revolving around one character's journey in his new publication." This sounds like the new publication is a part of the character's journey, not the author's creation. Correction involves moving the prepositional phrase: "In his new publication, this author creates a drama revolving around one character's journey."

Copyright © Mometrix Media. You have been licensed one copy of this document for personal use only. Any other reproduction or redistribution is strictly prohibited. All rights reserved.

Some other simple examples of how modifier placement affects meaning include: "She ate only fruit" versus "She only ate fruit." The first sentence means she ate nothing except fruit; the second means she did not plant, pick, wash, or cook fruit, but only ate it. Or, "He failed nearly every class he took" versus "He nearly failed every class he took." The former means he actually failed most of the classes he took, while the latter means he passed every class he took, but just barely. "Covered with flowers, she admired the field" means she was covered with flowers; "She admired the field covered with flowers" is correct.

Inconsistent verb tenses and non-parallel structure

While changing verb tenses in writing can indicate temporal relationships, switching tenses in a sentence if both or all verbs represent the same time frame is incorrect. For example, "The professor explained the theory to students who ask questions" uses inconsistent verb tenses. The verbs should be either "explained" and "asked" or "explains" and "asks." It is also incorrect to maintain the same verb tense when the time frame shifts among actions. The sentence, "Before they even saw the evidence, they decided" should actually read, "Before they even saw the evidence, they *had* decided" because "decided" occurred prior to "saw." "Susie loves the puppy she adopted" is correct: present-tense "loves" is true currently, while past-tense "adopted" is something Susie did previously and is not doing currently. An example of non-parallel structure is: "She enjoys skating, skiing, swimming, and to sail a boat." Because the first three objects are all gerunds ("-ing" participles used as nouns), the fourth should be "sailing" to be consistent, not the inconsistent infinitive "to sail."

Inconsistent verb tense

A narrative includes the following: "Anticipating the explosion, the insurgent watched the Humvees drive out of range. He frowned. Impatiently he jerks at the wire connected to the grenade's pin. But the handle was caught on something and had not detonated the grenade. Staring incredulously at the pin, he reaches over to turn off the radio. But another part of his mind thought it was better that the grenade did not explode. His survival instinct was being triggered. He gets out of the car and shuts the door." This narrative switches tenses. To correct this, the verbs should be consistent in tense. They should then read as one of the following. The verb tenses should be "watched... frowned... jerked... was (caught)... had not detonated... reached... thought... had not exploded... was being triggered... got out... shut." Conversely, they could also be "watches... jerks... is (caught)... has not detonated... reaches... thinks... did not explode... is being triggered... gets out... shuts." When the main narrative is in the past tense, the reference to something occurring earlier should be in the past perfect tense; when narrative is in the present tense, the reference should be in the present perfect tense.

Phrases vs. clauses and transitive vs. intransitive verbs

A clause makes a complete sentence, which can be just a subject and verb. However, the verb must be intransitive—one that does not require an object—for the sentence to be complete. For example, "I am," "I live," and "I love" are all complete sentences, but "I like" (or "I hate") is not because "like" needs an object—I like what? "I like it," "I like this," "I like you," "I like food," "I like to eat," and "I like eating" are all examples of complete sentences and independent clauses. A phrase lacks either a subject or a verb. For example, while "I like to go swimming" is a clause/sentence, "to go swimming" is a phrase: it has a verb but no subject. "You understood" is an example of an acceptable unstated subject. The imperative

Copyright © Mometrix Media. You have been licensed one copy of this document for personal use only. Any other reproduction or redistribution is strictly prohibited. All rights reserved.

"Go now" is a complete sentence wherein the subject "you" is understood; the meaning is "[You] go now."

Punctuation errors in possessive pronouns

Many people make the error of misspelling the possessive pronoun "its" as "it's" when the apostrophe is only ever used in the contraction of "it is," and never in the possessive. Another common error is misspelling other possessive pronouns by using apostrophes, such as "your's" and "her's." These are always incorrect. A possessive pronoun taking a noun as its object, such as "his hat," "your hat," or "her hat" is not complicated by any –s ending. However, when the possessive pronoun does not have any noun object, the –s ending is added: "It is hers," "That hat is yours," or "She is a friend of theirs." Just like other possessive pronouns without –s endings ("That hat is his" or "This is mine"), the possessive pronouns ending with –s never include an apostrophe. With the proliferation of websites with large amounts of text written and typed by people not expert or even basically educated in grammar, errors such as these are more frequently visible than ever.

Drawbacks to wordprocessing spell checkers

Microsoft Word is one of the most popular word processing programs. It has many excellent features facilitating composition. However, students and other writers must realize that its spell checkers, and those of similar programs, are far from perfect. One cannot rely on them without paying attention to what they do. For example, a college student writing a paper on Sophocles' *Oedipus Rex* correctly typed the name of key character Laius, king of Thebes and father of Oedipus, throughout his paper. However, his spell checker, not recognizing the name, "corrected" it to Louis. The student only realized this at the last minute while on his way to class, paper in hand, without a computer or printer nearby, and he had to rewrite every instance of the name by hand. Spell checkers commonly fail to recognize proper names and foreign language words. To eliminate the red zigzag underline that Word uses to indicate a misspelling, simply right-click and select "Add to dictionary" from the drop-down menu. Students and writers must consciously proofread everything they write, rather than assume spell checkers are always correct.

Microsoft Word's grammar check identifies many common errors, but is often incorrect. It does not recognize reflexive verbs, such as "assess themselves" or "do it for themselves," and suggests changing "themselves" to "them." Many writers and students get perplexed when writing a complete sentence to find Word underlining it with a green zigzag, labeling it a "fragment." Sometimes this reflects a true error, like leaving the verb out of a clause. But other times, it makes no sense by current writing standards. Sometimes one simply reverses the order of two clauses and the markup disappears. Microsoft Word's grammar check also inexplicably mistakes things like subject-verb agreement with number. For example, a writer can type, "A given number of posters costs" and grammar check will incorrectly suggest changing "costs" to "cost." The subject is the singular "number," not plural object "posters." Right-clicking, selecting "Grammar" from the drop-down menu, and selecting "Ignore rule" eliminates such wrong "corrections." (Another option is to simply ignore the markups.) If their grammatical knowledge is insufficient, writers and students can consult reputable grammar experts' websites about suspect "corrections."

The grammar checkers in popular word processing software programs like Microsoft Word can catch many inadvertent errors often caused by hurried typing and/or careless writing.

Copyright © Mometrix Media. You have been licensed one copy of this document for personal use only. Any other reproduction or redistribution is strictly prohibited. All rights reserved.

However, these programs are not always correct, and in fact are often incorrect. Not only will Word's grammar checker incorrectly label some constructions incorrect when they are not, but it will also fail to identify other errors. For example, Noam Chomsky's famous sample sentence, "Colorless green ideas sleep furiously" is grammatically, morphologically, and syntactically correct in its construction, but makes no sense semantically—which was Chomsky's point. Grammar checkers are not people who can think, reason, and understand; they are simply programmed to identify certain things categorized as errors. So the grammar checker has no problem with Chomsky's sentence and does not flag anything in it as wrong. This is an example of how grammar checkers not only over-correct by identifying correct usages as incorrect, but also under-correct by not identifying incorrect usages. Writers and students must use their own judgment and knowledge and consult grammatical experts and/or their websites when needed.

Active student listening

Active listening is described as having multiple dimensions. It involves listening processes required of people for their engagement in constructing meaning out of what they hear; being agile, reflective, and creative in considering and manipulating information they receive; and making competent decisions rich in ideas. The natural properties of speech and thought are conducive to active listening: the typical speed of speaking is roughly 125 words a minute, whereas the estimated speed of thinking is roughly 500 words a minute. Therefore, students have around 375 words a minute of spare time to think about the speech they hear. As an educator (Carbone, in TILT Posts 2013-2014) points out, students' minds can wander during this extra time, so teachers can instruct them to use the time instead to summarize lecture information mentally—a form of active listening. Listening and learning share common characteristics of being social and reciprocal. They also both allow and require students to process and consider speech they hear and stimulate their curiosity about subsequent information.

Whole-class learning circles

Forming whole classes into learning circles requires student application of skills for listening to teacher lessons/lectures; synthesizing information they heard, read, reviewed, and studied; and summarizing information received. Teachers can prepare students by articulating central discussion points; identifying next steps in thought, question forming, analysis, and action; guiding student analysis and construction of meaning from what they have read, observed, and experienced; and asking students questions beginning with "What...? So What? and Now What?" Basic ground rules for learning circles include: (1) No student interrupts another. (2) Students may skip a turn until others have taken turns, but no student speaks out of turn. (3) Each student has a certain length of time for speaking. (4) Each student starts by restating what was said previously by another/several other students (e.g., summarizing shared points, differing points, missed points, or points not discussed fully). (5) After every student has had one turn, general discussion is open, possibly guided by teacher-provided questions.

Procedures and ground rules for smaller groups
Teachers can develop student discussion skills integrating listening, reading, and speaking skills by assigning small discussion groups to tackle teacher-supplied problems and topics. Teachers/students may use established groups, new teacher-assigned groups, or student-formed groups. Each group should contain 4-5 students. Teachers read a text passage they

Copyright © Mometrix Media. You have been licensed one copy of this document for personal use only. Any other reproduction or redistribution is strictly prohibited. All rights reserved.

or students choose; describe a scenario; or pose a question to discuss. They give students several minutes to review homework/notes, briefly read new related material, and/or review essay/paper drafts. Teachers then give each student in each group a specified number of uninterrupted minutes to speak in turn. After every group/circle student has taken a turn, the teacher opens general discussion, setting the following ground rules: (1) Students can only speak about others' ideas. However, (2) teachers and classmates can ask students to clarify their ideas, give examples, connect them more closely to what they read, or elaborate. (3) Small groups can summarize overall points they established for other groups, including shared points, differences, and potential topics they missed.

Incorporating active student listening into lessons

Teachers should make clear to students the subject underpinning a day's activities and identify the learning objectives incorporated in those activities to give students a view of the "big picture." They should also give students a single word/phrase to summarize the prior day's subject and a single word/phrase to preview the current day's subject. Teachers should not only establish this recall, retrieval, prediction, and planning process as a daily habit; by doing so, they should also prompt students to develop the same daily habit in their note-taking. Teachers should review main concepts addressed earlier, and/or have students summarize the last lecture's main ideas, to make connections with preceding lessons. In both cueing and queuing student listening, teachers supply spoken presentation/lecture transitions analogously to those in written research papers/articles. By cueing students to write marginal notes/Word comments with questions or summaries at the ends of sections, teachers also help students demonstrate their comprehension.

Teachers can allow students to take photos, videos, and audio recordings of lessons/lectures to review as many times as they need. To encourage students to reword and recall instructional input, teachers can let students download class outlines from GoogleDocs, including hard-to-spell terminology/vocabulary words, jargon of specific disciplines, and links reminding students to follow up by accessing resources and readings to inform notes they take. Teachers should give outlines a two-column format: on the right, a wider column with teacher notes, to which students can add, and on the left, a narrower column for students to place notes and questions about previous lectures and reading. They should advise students to take their own notes in similar formats. Students and teachers alike can learn through speaking, writing, listening, and reading when they contribute narratives to supplement visual graphics they both provide, e.g., photos, concept maps, charts, advance organizers, illustrations, diagrams, etc. to support challenging concepts they analyze and explain.

Educator techniques to improve and augment classroom discussions

Students who feel comfortable with the teacher and the class are more likely to engage openly in discussion. Teachers who learn students' names encourage this. Lively discussions with all students participating are evidence teachers have made students comfortable. Teachers should pose questions rather than make comments: teacher comments discourage student creativity; questions invite various responses. A variety of student answers is evidence the questioning technique works. When student discussions stray off the subject, learning goals the teacher identified will not be met. Teachers redirect discussion by restating topics and questions they previously announced, and introducing new questions related to identified topics. When conversation refocuses on stated topics,

Copyright © Mometrix Media. You have been licensed one copy of this document for personal use only. Any other reproduction or redistribution is strictly prohibited. All rights reserved.

teachers can identify specified learning goals/objectives students are meeting in their discussion on a checklist. In most classes, some students dominate conversations. Teachers can pose less challenging questions, which anyone can answer even without being prepared, to engage more reticent students, and then graduate to higher-level questions. They can evaluate all students' participation using attendance roll-based checklists.

Teaching strategies to encourage discussion

During class discussions, students often contribute erroneous information. Teachers must be tactful in correcting them. If students they correct then withdraw from the conversation or cease further contributions, the teacher has not corrected them appropriately. If corrected students continue to contribute, the teacher has succeeded in providing positive reinforcement rather than punishment with the correction. Some ways to do this include acknowledging how the student came to a conclusion but explaining it does not apply to the current context or explaining how the student's response might be correct in another situation. Teachers can also provide incentives for students to contribute to class discussions. Teachers may incorporate a component of participation in their course syllabi, keep records to tally whenever each student contributes to a discussion, or assign different students to lead class discussions in turn. These are some ways teachers can evaluate individual student participation in classroom discussions, and hence the effectiveness of their teaching strategies to encourage such participation.

Students often feel intimidated if "put on the spot" to answer/discuss questions without warning. Teachers can put them at ease by allowing time to prepare: Announce topics and questions for class discussion. Give students five minutes to jot notes for responses. Give five more minutes for exchanging and reflecting on notes with classmates before beginning whole-class conversation. Teachers may distribute discussion topics/questions at the end of one class for the next day's conversation or post questions/topics online the night before class. One technique for evaluating discussion is asking students early in the term to write papers about the characteristics of good and bad class discussions, and then talk about these. Teachers then compose a list of classroom discussion goals and give all students copies. Another technique is an informal survey: ask students around midterm to evaluate the overall quality of class discussions. Share responses with the class, and inform them of teacher plans incorporating student feedback for enhancing discussions during the rest of the term.

Teachers can encourage in-class discussion by promoting group meetings and discussions outside the classroom. Interacting with students outside class also promotes a sense of community. Teachers demonstrate to students that they care about them as individual persons and about their educational development by asking them about their holiday/summer plans, about how they are feeling during midterm and final exam periods, and about their other classes. Teachers can find online articles related to class material and e-mail or text-message their students links to these for review. They can allow time at the beginnings of classes for announcements. They can also arrange classroom chairs in a semicircle to encourage conversation. These methods are all found effective in promoting a sense of community, which in turn encourages class discussions. To address different student learning styles and abilities, teachers can vary the levels and types of questions they ask them: asking them to give simple information, describe, compare, analyze, justify, compare, generalize, predict, or apply information.

Copyright © Mometrix Media. You have been licensed one copy of this document for personal use only. Any other reproduction or redistribution is strictly prohibited. All rights reserved.

Rubric for assessing student writing

A rubric is basically a checklist to verify what students have learned or accomplished. Teachers can take the lesson objectives they have identified for their lesson to form the basis of a rubric. The teacher should explain the rubric to the students before they begin a writing assignment. During their writing exercise, the students can refer to the rubric to guide what and how they write. After the students have completed their writing assignments, the teacher can then apply the rubric to assess their work as to whether they have met all of the learning objectives they included in the rubric. Students will be less confused and/or frustrated when teachers have given them well-planned, clearly expressed guidelines and instructions for their writing activities. In addition to stating clearly their learning goals, objectives, and expectations of students for each assignment, teachers should model what kinds of performance they expect. Doing these things enables better student performance. Teachers should connect lesson and assignment goals obviously and clearly with student achievement.

Formative and summative assessments

Summative assessments evaluate what a student can demonstrate s/he has learned at the end of a lesson, unit, course, or term. Final examinations are an example. Formative assessments are ongoing evaluations to demonstrate what a student is in the process of learning and has learned thus far. Formative assessments are not just for evaluation: they are also important for teachers to use in their classrooms as teaching tools. As teachers conduct ongoing evaluations via formative assessments, they can and should use both formal and informal assessment instruments. Teachers should never use only one formal or informal assessment of a class as a reason to group students on a permanent basis. They should only place students into groups after administering, scoring, and interpreting a number of different assessments. Teachers should also create student groups that take into account individual differences among the students in every group, and they should accordingly make these groupings sufficiently flexible to accommodate these individual student differences.

Observation

Observational assessment is very appropriate for evaluating student skills acquisition and status, and for evaluating effectiveness of instruction and learning. A teacher can create a checklist of skills, requirements, or competencies that students should attain. The teacher can then observe individual students or student groups and check off each of the skills or competencies they have seen the student or group demonstrate. For example, if a teacher has been instructing a class in how to listen carefully, s/he can compose a checklist with items such as paying attention, refraining from interrupting others, summarizing what ideas the other students have expressed, and asking other students questions. The teacher can then initiate a student discussion and observe the students' behaviors during it. The teacher can check off the checklist items s/he observes the students performing. Or, when teaching interview skills, a teacher can make a checklist including confidence, personal appearance, mannerisms, and directly answering interviewer questions; observe students participating in mock or real interviews; and identify which items the students satisfy.

By observing their students as they work on assignments and learning or practice exercises, teachers can obtain a lot of valuable information. With kindergarten and first-grade classes,

- 79 -

Copyright © Mometrix Media. You have been licensed one copy of this document for personal use only. Any other reproduction or redistribution is strictly prohibited. All rights reserved.

many school districts inform parents of children's progress by filling out "report cards" or inventories. Through experience, long-term teachers typically develop their own methods of making ongoing skills assessments of their students. Books about reading instruction typically include informal reading assessments. Experts recommend that teachers assess student progress in naturalistic ways on a continual basis. They find that teachers and parents continually observing students regarding their status and progress in the physical, cognitive, emotional, and social domains yields the most relevant assessment—particularly with young children. Experts also approve of portfolio assessments and performance assessments for more complete pictures of overall progress than standardized test scores. They also find that writing narrative reports about young children depicts the whole child better than giving them number and/or letter grades.

Observational checklists
When observing student behaviors as an informal assessment measure, using observational checklists to identify skills attained has an advantage over formal written tests because informal, naturalistic observation enables teachers to record behaviors that traditional written tests cannot include. For example, if teachers want to know whether students can follow all steps of a science experiment in the correct sequence, how many baskets they can make in free throws on the basketball court, or whether they can remember all of the significant parts to include in a speech they write and deliver to the class, they can record these by observing and marking such items on a checklist they have designed in advance—but they could not record any such behaviors through standard "pencil-and-paper" tests. The structure of checklists has the advantage of being consistent, but also the disadvantage of being inflexible. Teachers can remedy the latter by including a place at the end of the checklist to write open-ended comments on their observations of student performance.

Running record

To identify what students are able and unable to do, one informal assessment measure teachers can use is a running record. For example, the teacher can listen to a student reading aloud from text such as an essay, a speech, a novel, or a class subject textbook. While listening, the teacher marks a copy of the text to show words the student pronounces incorrectly. The teacher draws a line through each word the student skips, draws an arrow under words the student repeats, and writes the student's incorrect pronunciation of words above the printed words in the text copy. Teachers may also mark student hesitations at certain words. If the teacher then calculates that the student correctly read 95 percent of the words, the student reads this text at the Independent level. If the student correctly reads 90-94 percent of the words, s/he reads this text at the Instructional level, indicating satisfactory performance with teacher assistance. Reading 89 percent or fewer words correctly indicates the Frustration level, where comprehension may be inadequate.

Anecdotal records

Anecdotal records can provide good information to teachers for making formative assessments. For example, when students conduct science experiments or complete class projects, their teachers can use anecdotal records to help instruct them in how to write reports that explain the procedures they followed. When students in group learning activities solve a problem(s) together, teachers can use anecdotal records to document the process the students used for problem-solving. Such anecdotal documents not only provide the teacher with formative assessment information, but teachers can also use them to give

Copyright © Mometrix Media. You have been licensed one copy of this document for personal use only. Any other reproduction or redistribution is strictly prohibited. All rights reserved.

feedback to the group of students. Two disadvantages of using anecdotal records is that they can take more time for teachers to complete than other informal assessments, and that it can be hard to use them for assigning grades. Two advantages are that anecdotal records can encompass all pertinent information, whereas other assessments may not, and that teachers may use them only for giving students feedback, which eliminates the need to base grades on them.

Portfolio assessment

In portfolio assessment, teachers and/or students create a folder, accordion file, or box and deposit a student's best work products, accumulated over time. In language arts, teachers often collect student writing samples in portfolios for a whole year. Some language arts teachers additionally transmit year-long portfolios to the following year's teacher to aid them in student assessment. Teachers can use portfolio assessments in any subject to enable students to assume greater responsibility for planning, organizing, and implementing what they learn. The combined products in the portfolio afford concise depictions of what students have achieved during specific time periods. Portfolios can include handwritten and/or printed essays, stories, and articles; videos; computer files of multimedia presentations; or any combination thereof. Teachers should help students develop guidelines about which materials to place in portfolios, and how to self-assess their own work. Portfolios' advantages over tests include not being damaged by one bad test score, helping students develop self-assessment skills, and giving clearer pictures of student progress.

Research-based assessment techniques

To assess student attitudes, educators can give them various situations and observe and document their responses, and require students to make choices among behaviors to demonstrate. To assess cognitive strategies, teachers can give students learning tasks, require them to select useful strategies for learning new information independently, and expect them to explain and discuss what methods they use for different learning tasks. To assess student comprehension, teachers give them topics and assign them to restate and summarize information, have students apply information in teacher-supplied new contexts, give students statements with words differing from the original lesson, and have them identify the right meanings. To assess student concept understanding, teachers give students new examples and "non-examples," having students classify these into the right categories. To assess student creativity, teachers can give students new problems— including products, presentations, or performances—to study, resolve, or "turn upside down"; have students fit solutions and products into specified resources and functions; and give them situations needing novel responses or approaches.

To assess student critical thinking, teachers can ask students to evaluate outcomes or information, and have them perform research and analysis. To assess student insight, teachers should give them opportunities to engage in inquiry and discovery activities, and offer students situations they can or must manipulate. To assess student metacognition, teachers should give students a variety of problems or situations to address, and assign students to identify different kinds of thinking strategies they can use for analysis and evaluation of their own thought processes. To assess multiple intelligences (cf. Gardner), teachers should give students learning experiences in each of the modalities they target, like verbal, musical, and physical. They should offer students choices of several different

Copyright © Mometrix Media. You have been licensed one copy of this document for personal use only. Any other reproduction or redistribution is strictly prohibited. All rights reserved.

modalities. They should also require students to perform in the modalities selected. To assess motor skills, teachers must supply resources and situations wherein students can perform the skills, and the teachers can evaluate using checklists. To assess problem-solving, teachers have students choose appropriate strategies to solve different provided problem situations, including simple, complex, structured, and unstructured.

To assess student knowledge of principles, rules, and procedures, teachers supply situations requiring students to identify using these correctly with everyday problems. They have students state principles, rules, and procedures, and choose which apply to various scenarios. To assess student scientific inquiry skills, teachers give students problems or situations that necessitate their speculating about them, inquiring into them, and formulating hypotheses about them. Teachers should also give students hands-on activities wherein they must conduct research and draw conclusions about the results they find. To assess student thinking skills, teachers can have students give summaries of different kinds of thinking strategies. They provide situations wherein students must select the best thinking strategies to apply. Teachers assign students to observe examples of open-mindedness versus closed-mindedness, and examples of accurate versus inaccurate, and responsible versus irresponsible applications of thinking methods. They design scenarios requiring student persistence for analyzing and discovering answers to particular questions, and have them apply certain thinking strategies in real-life circumstances. To assess verbal knowledge, teachers require information recall, restatement, and comprehension.

Research-based strategies to teach effective writing

Experts have reviewed multiple, controlled, valid and reliable studies of writing instruction strategies that met research quality standards. These studies identify teaching strategies that improve overall writing performance. Some of these include: Explicitly teaching students techniques to plan, revise, and edit their writing, and including such things as brainstorming for planning and steps to follow for writing argumentation essays. Teacher modeling and independent student practice of strategies are recommended. Summarizing text they read is an effective strategy for helping students practice writing clearly, concisely, and accurately about main text ideas. Teachers can teach this explicitly, and/or model with gradual fading. Collaborative writing helps students plan, write, edit, and revise writing cooperatively. Teachers should supply structure and individual performance expectations within groups. Classmates can take turns reviewing each other's writing, giving both positive feedback for reinforcement and constructive feedback for improvement. Setting specific goals for writing assignments promotes motivation and accomplishment. Teachers and/or students can develop goals, such as incorporating certain genre elements or including more ideas in a paper.

The word processing functions of computers constitute a valuable student strategy for planning, writing, and editing compositions. Another strategy is explicitly instructing students to produce more sophisticated and complex sentences via sentence combining. Teachers model for students how to combine two or more related sentences, and encourage them to apply these skills when writing compositions. The process writing approach is a strategy whereby teachers give students opportunities for extended practice with planning, writing, and review; student peer interactions throughout the process of writing; taking personal responsibility for their writing; writing for authentic reader or listener audiences; and self-evaluation of their writing. Inquiry strategies include setting clear goals for writing;

Copyright © Mometrix Media. You have been licensed one copy of this document for personal use only. Any other reproduction or redistribution is strictly prohibited. All rights reserved.

examining concrete data, like through observation of others and documenting their own responses; and application of learning to compositions. Prewriting strategies help students generate and organize ideas, access background knowledge, research topics, and/or visualize their ideas graphically. Another strategy is giving students good models of expected writing types, analyzing models with students, and inviting students to emulate effective and critical model elements in their own writing.

Some researchers have found that students with writing challenges achieve strongly positive results when teachers explicitly model composition strategies and the writing process for them. When students collaborate with classmates and participate in conferences with teachers that inform them with useful feedback, students also improve in writing. Using mnemonic devices, checklists, graphic organizers, outlining, and other procedural strategies are found to help students plan and revise their writing. Students who have difficulties with transcribing text benefit from dictation and other ways of limiting those obstacles. Teaching students to ask themselves questions and make self-statements enhances their self-regulation abilities, which also promotes writing improvement. Studies find cognitive strategies aid students of all ability levels and ages. Teaching self-regulation increases maintenance and generalization of writing strategies by improving self-reflection and self-awareness of writing strengths and weaknesses, promoting more strategic writing efforts, better self-management of inhibiting emotions and behaviors, and empowerment to adapt strategies as needed. Explicit instruction, modeling, think-aloud sessions, and scaffolding are effective; exposure to writing processes alone is not enough.

Teaching strategies to address student and family diversity

Teachers must recognize that each student is unique. When a teacher respects individual student differences, s/he communicates this attitude to students. Research finds that cultural differences influence human behavior, and hence play a part in classrooms. Teacher acknowledgement of students' cultural differences prevents student isolation. To educate students from diverse backgrounds effectively, teachers need understanding of a student's culture and his or her individual characteristics—as well as disabilities when these exist. Teacher and school involvement with students' families promote student success during and after school. This requires educators to avoid ethnocentric approaches. Diverse families may need instruction in the school culture of collaboration and communication. Schools also must initially meet family needs physically, socially, and economically to enable involvement, requiring school knowledge of supportive community programs. Communications must be translated for families speaking different languages. Educators need willingness to interact outside of school hours and grounds. They can also recruit parent liaisons with similar cultural backgrounds. Teachers should open parent communications with positive feedback about children.

Inclusive educational programs require meaningful, effective collaboration of educators, students, and families. Teachers must not only meet student and family needs, they must also communicate their own needs effectively, and be willing to find solutions to their unfulfilled needs through team-based approaches to problem-solving. Collaboration allows outcomes that individuals cannot achieve alone. Researchers have discovered that despite the challenges of cooperation among all school staff members, the more teachers interact with each other, the greater educational change is achieved successfully. Understanding of cultural communication differences, respectful disagreement, respect for confidentiality, willingness to compromise, responsible communication of opinions and emotions (such as

Copyright © Mometrix Media. You have been licensed one copy of this document for personal use only. Any other reproduction or redistribution is strictly prohibited. All rights reserved.

using "I" statements), tolerance for others' various perspectives, and careful listening to others are communication skills needed for effective communication to enable collaboration. Some educators advocate multicultural awareness days involving all school personnel, families, and community members when each school year starts. Culturally responsive standards-based instruction (CRSBI) incorporates caring, communication, curriculum, and standards-based instruction. Educators must also foster positive student-teacher relationships, and assure positive role models for every student.

Creating safe educational environments

Teachers need to establish and sustain classroom environments for students wherein they feel nurtured, and feel that the teacher is open to receiving their communications of feelings, thoughts, and ideas. Teachers are responsible for developing respect for individual differences and openness to discussions in their classrooms. They may need to explain to students the difference between fairness and equality. For example, students who need eyeglasses cannot be deprived of them, but neither should all students be made to wear them. Teachers can use such examples to illustrate to students that fairness does not mean everybody gets the same thing: while every student deserves whatever help s/he needs, that help will differ for different students. Teachers must create student-teacher relationships of mutual trust, and assure all students know teachers care about them, both academically and personally. Teacher beliefs, attitudes, and performance expectations and how teachers communicate these establish this knowledge. Teachers must know student and family languages, communication styles, and home literacy practices, and build on these in their classrooms.

Copyright © Mometrix Media. You have been licensed one copy of this document for personal use only. Any other reproduction or redistribution is strictly prohibited. All rights reserved.

Reading Theory, Research, and Instruction

Connections and distictions among elements in text

One of the Common Core State Standards in English Language Arts for reading informational texts is for students to be able to analyze how an informational text makes connections and distinctions among ideas, events, or individuals, such as by comparing them or contrasting them, making analogies between them, or dividing them into categories to show similarities and differences. For example, teachers can help eighth-graders analyze how a biology text author divides animals into categories of carnivores, which eat only meat; herbivores, which eat only plants; and omnivores, which eat both meat and plants. Teachers and students can identify the author's comparisons and contrasts of groups. Teachers can help students analyze these processes by supplying sentence frames. For example, "A _____ is a _____, so" and "A _____ is a _____ which means." The students fill these empty spaces in, such as, "A frog is a carnivore, so it eats only meat," and "A rabbit is an herbivore, which means it eats only plants."

Structures or organizational patterns in informational texts

Some informational text is descriptive: It uses sensory imagery that helps readers to see, hear, feel, taste, and smell its information and/or it informs readers about what, who, when, where, and why related to the text's subject or topic. Another structure or pattern of informational text is sequence and order: Chronological texts relate events in the sequence that they occurred, from start to finish, while how-to texts organize information into a series of instructions in the sequence in which the steps should be followed. Comparison-contrast structures of informational text describe various ideas to their readers by pointing out how things or ideas are similar and how they are different. Cause and effect structures of informational text describe events that occurred, and identify the causes or reasons that those events occurred. Problem and solution structures of informational text introduce and describe problems, and then offer one or more solutions for each problem described.

Text features in informational texts

The title of a text gives readers some idea of its content. An appendix, at the back of the book or document, adds important information not in the main text. Captions, below or beside illustrations or photos, explain what those images show or contain. Charts and tables are visual forms of information that making something easier and faster to understand. Diagrams are drawings that show relationships between things or explain how they work. Glossaries, usually found at the backs of books, list technical terms alphabetically with their definitions to aid vocabulary learning and comprehension. Graphs visually show relationships of multiple sets of information plotted along vertical and horizontal axes. Headings separate sections of text and show the topic of each. An index, at the back of a book, lists the book's important topics alphabetically with their page numbers to help students find them easily. Maps show geographical information visually to help students understand the relative locations of places covered in the text.

Copyright © Mometrix Media. You have been licensed one copy of this document for personal use only. Any other reproduction or redistribution is strictly prohibited. All rights reserved.

Illustrations and photographs are pictures visually emphasizing important points in text, helping to make it more interesting. Boldface print is used to emphasize certain words, often identifying words included in the text's glossary where readers can look up their definitions. The table of contents is a list near the beginning of a text, showing the book's sections and chapters and their coinciding page numbers. This gives readers an overview of the whole text, and helps them find specific chapters easily. A timeline is a visual graphic showing historical events in chronological order to help readers see their sequence. A subheading divides subject headings into smaller, more specific categories to help readers organize information. Footnotes, at page bottoms, give readers more information, such as citations, links, or further details and discussions of statements or references in main text. Bullet points list items separately, making facts and ideas easier to see and understand. A sidebar is a box of information to one side of the main text giving additional information, often on a more focused or in-depth example of a topic.

Standards for citing textual evidence for grade levels 6-12

Reading standards for informational texts expect sixth-graders to cite textual evidence to support their inferences and analyses. Seventh-graders are expected additionally to identify several specific pieces of textual evidence to defend each of their conclusions. Eighth-graders are expected to differentiate strong from weak textual evidence. Ninth- and 10th-graders are expected to be able to cite thorough evidence as well as strong evidence from text. Eleventh- and 12th-graders are expected, in combination with the previous grade-level standards, to determine which things are left unclear in a text. Students must be able to connect text to their background knowledge and make inferences to understand text, judge it critically, draw conclusions about it, and make their own interpretations of it. Therefore, they must be able to organize and differentiate between main ideas and details in a text to make inferences about them. They must also be able to locate evidence in the text.

Making inferences about informational text

With informational text, reader comprehension depends not only on recalling important statements and details, but also on reader inferences based on examples and details. Readers add the information they have read in the text to what they already know to draw inferences about the text. These inferences help the reader to fill in the information that the text does not explicitly state, enabling them to understand the text better and answer more questions about it. When reading a nonfictional autobiography or biography, for example, the most appropriate inferences for the reader to make might concern the events in the book, the actions of the subject of the autobiography or biography, and the message the author means to convey. When reading a nonfictional expository (informational) text, the reader would best draw inferences about problems and their solutions, and causes and their effects. When reading a nonfictional persuasive text, the reader will want to infer ideas supporting the author's message and what the author is trying to convince the intended audience.

Technical language

Technical language, like what is found in scientific texts, is more impersonal than literary and vernacular language. Passive voice tone makes tone impersonal. For example, instead of writing, "We found this a central component of protein metabolism," scientists write, "This was found a central component of protein metabolism." While science professors

Copyright © Mometrix Media. You have been licensed one copy of this document for personal use only. Any other reproduction or redistribution is strictly prohibited. All rights reserved.

traditionally instructed students to avoid active voice because it leads to first-person ("I" and "we") usage, science editors today find passive voice dull and weak. Many journal articles combine both. Tone in technical science writing should be detached, concise, and professional. While one writes in the vernacular, "This chemical has to be available for proteins to be digested," professionals write technically, "The presence of this chemical is required for the enzyme to break the covalent bonds of proteins." Science writers also must achieve balance in mood between self-deprecating and grandiose. For instance, self-deprecating: "With fewer than ten reproducible assays, our findings are insignificant." Grandiose: "From our findings, we conclude everybody needs these supplements." And balanced: "We conclude more research is needed to isolate the mechanism this chemical initiates."

Explicit and implicit information

When informational text states something explicitly, the reader is told by the author exactly what is meant, which can include the author's interpretation or perspective of events. For example, a professor writes, "I have seen students go into an absolute panic just because they weren't able to finish administering the Peabody [Picture Vocabulary Test] in the time they were allotted." This explicitly tells the reader that the students were afraid, and by using the words "just because," the writer indicates their fear was exaggerated out of proportion relative to what happened. However, another professor writes, "I have had students come to me, their faces drained of all color, saying 'We weren't able to finish the Peabody.'" This is an example of implicit meaning: the second writer did not state explicitly that the students were panicked. Instead, he wrote a description of their faces being "drained of all color." From this description, the reader can infer the students were so frightened that their faces paled.

Identifying author's point of view or purpose

In some informational texts, readers find it easy to identify the author's point of view and/or purpose, as when the author explicitly states his or her position and/or reason for writing. But in other texts which are difficult, and/or whose authors give neutral or balanced viewpoints, it is harder. This is particularly true in scientific texts, wherein authors may state the purpose of their research in the report, but never state their point of view except by interpreting evidence or data. To analyze text and identify point of view or purpose, readers should ask themselves the following four questions: (1) With what main point or idea does this author want to persuade readers to agree? (2) How do this author's choices of words affect the way that readers consider this subject? (3) How do this author's choices of examples and/or facts affect the way that readers consider this subject? And (4) What is it that this author wants to accomplish by writing this text?

Use of rhetoric

There are many ways authors can support their claims, arguments, beliefs, ideas, and reasons for writing informational texts. For example, authors can appeal to readers' sense of logic by communicating their reasoning through carefully sequenced series of logical steps to help "prove" the points made. Authors can appeal to readers' emotions by using descriptions and words that evoke feelings of sympathy, sadness, anger, righteous indignation, hope, happiness, or any other emotion to reinforce what they express and share with their audience. Authors may appeal to the moral or ethical values of readers by

Copyright © Mometrix Media. You have been licensed one copy of this document for personal use only. Any other reproduction or redistribution is strictly prohibited. All rights reserved.

using words and descriptions that can convince readers of the idea that something is right or wrong. By relating personal anecdotes, authors can supply readers with more accessible, realistic examples of points they make, as well as appealing to their emotions. They can provide supporting evidence by reporting case studies. They can also illustrate and illuminate their points by making analogies to which readers can better relate.

<u>Rhetorical devices</u>

An anecdote is a brief story authors may relate, which can illustrate their point(s) in a more real and relatable way. Aphorisms concisely state common beliefs and may rhyme. For example, Benjamin Franklin's "Early to bed and early to rise / Make a man healthy, wealthy, and wise" is one. Allusions refer to literary or historical figures to impart symbolism to a thing or person, and/or create reader resonance. A literary example is that in John Steinbeck's *Of Mice and Men,* protagonist George's last name is Milton, alluding to John Milton who wrote *Paradise Lost*, to symbolize George's eventual loss of his dream. Satire is a writing style that ridicules or pokes fun at human foibles or ideas. Jonathan Swift and Mark Twain are two examples of authors who wrote satirically. A parody is a form of satire that imitates another work to ridicule its topic and/or style. Paradox is a statement that is true despite appearing contradictory. Hyperbole is overstatement using exaggerated language. Oxymoron combines seeming contradictions, such as "deafening silence" or "jumbo shrimp."

Analogies compare two things sharing some common elements. Similes (stated comparisons using the words "like" or "as") and metaphors (implied comparisons) are considered forms of analogy. When using logic to reason with audiences, syllogism refers either to deductive reasoning or a deceptive, very sophisticated, or subtle argument. Deductive reasoning moves from general to specific, inductive reasoning from specific to general. Diction is author word choice establishing tone and effects. Understatement achieves effects like contrast or irony by downplaying or describing something more subtly than warranted. Chiasmus uses parallel clauses, the second reversing the order of the first. Examples include T. S. Eliot's "Has the Church failed mankind, or has mankind failed the Church?" and John F. Kennedy's "Ask not what your country can do for you; ask what you can do for your country." Anaphora regularly repeats a word or phrase at the beginnings of consecutive clauses or phrases to add emphasis to an idea. A classic example of anaphora was Winston Churchill's emphasis of determination: "We shall fight in the trenches. We shall fight on the oceans. We shall fight in the sky."

Figurative vs. literal language, denotation vs. connotation, and technical language

As in fictional literature, informational text also uses both literal language, which means just what it says, and figurative language, which imparts more than literal meaning. For example, an informational text author might use a simile or direct comparison, such as writing that a racehorse "ran like the wind." Informational text authors also use metaphors or implied comparisons, like describing "the cloud of the Great Depression." Similar to literal and figurative, denotation is the literal meaning or dictionary definition of a word whereas connotation is feelings or thoughts associated with a word not included in its literal definition. For example, "politician" and "statesman" have the same denotation, but in context, "politician" may have a negative connotation while "statesman" may have a positive connotation. "Inexpensive" and "cheap" both denote "not costly," but the former has a neutral connotation while the latter can have a negative one. Technical language is vocabulary related to a specific discipline, activity, or process. For example, in closet-

Copyright © Mometrix Media. You have been licensed one copy of this document for personal use only. Any other reproduction or redistribution is strictly prohibited. All rights reserved.

organizing instructions, "itemize" is technical language; in fire-building instructions, "kindling" is technical language.

Connotation and denotation

While denotation is a word's definition/literal meaning, its connotation is an implied meaning that readers infer. Teachers can help students understand positive or negative connotations of words depending on their sentence contexts. For example, the word "challenge" has a positive connotation in this sentence: "Although I finished last, I still accomplished the challenge of running the race." Teachers can give students a multiple-choice game wherein they choose whether "challenge" here means (A) easy, (B) hard, (C) fun, or (D) taking work to overcome. The word "difficult" has a negative connotation in this sentence: "I finished last in the race because it was difficult." Students choose whether "difficult" here means (A) easy, (B) hard, (C) fun, or (D) lengthy. Positive and negative connotations for the same word can also be taught. Consider the following sentence: "When the teacher asked Johnny why he was in the restroom so long, he gave a *smart* answer." In this context, "smart" means disrespectful and carries a negative connotation. But in the sentence, "Johnny was *smart* to return to class from the restroom right away," the same word means wise and carries a positive connotation.

Affixes

Affixes in the English language are morphemes that are added to words to create related but different words. Derivational affixes form new words based on and related to the original words. For example, the affix *–ness* added to the end of the adjective *happy* forms the noun *happiness.* Inflectional affixes form different grammatical versions of words. For example, the plural affix *–s* changes the singular noun *book* to the plural noun *books*, and the past tense affix *–ed* changes the infinitive or present tense verb *look* to the past tense *looked.* Prefixes are affixes placed in front of words. For example, *heat* means to make hot; *preheat*, using the prefix *pre-*, means to heat in advance. Suffixes are affixes placed at the ends of words. The *happiness* example above contains the suffix *–ness.* Circumfixes add parts both before and after words, such as how *light* becomes *enlighten* with the prefix *en-* and the suffix *–en.* Interfixes compound words via central affixes: *speed* and *meter* become *speedometer* via the interfix *–o–.*

Word roots, prefixes, and suffixes to determine meanings of words

Many English words were formed from combining multiple sources. For example, the Latin *habēre* means "to have," and the prefixes *in-* and *im-* mean a lack or prevention of something, as in *insufficient, inordinate, intemperate,* and *imperfect.* Latin combined *in-* with *habēre* to form *inhibēre,* whose past participle was *inhibitus.* This is the origin of the English word *inhibit,* meaning to prevent from having. Hence by knowing the meanings of both the prefix and the root, one can decipher the word meaning. In Greek, the root *enkephalo-* refers to the brain. This informs the meanings of many medical terms used in English: *encephalitis, hydrocephalus, electroencephalogram, anencephaly,* and so on. And knowing prefix and suffix meanings, like *–itis* meaning inflammation, *hydro-* meaning water, *electro-* meaning electrical, *–gram* meaning writing/drawing/record, and *an-*meaning not/without, informs the rest of the words' meanings: brain inflammation, water/fluid on the brain, an electrical brain record, and the condition of not having a brain.

Copyright © Mometrix Media. You have been licensed one copy of this document for personal use only. Any other reproduction or redistribution is strictly prohibited. All rights reserved.

Prefixes

While knowing prefix meanings helps ESL and beginning readers learn new words, other readers take for granted the meanings of known words. However, prefix knowledge will also benefit them for determining meanings or definitions of unfamiliar words. For example, native English speakers and readers familiar with recipes know what *preheat* means. Knowing that *pre-* means in advance can also inform them that *presume* means to assume in advance, that *prejudice* means advance judgment, and that this understanding can be applied to many other words beginning with *pre-*. Knowing that the prefix *dis-* indicates opposition informs the meanings of words like *disbar, disagree, disestablish,* and many more. Knowing *dys-* means bad, impaired, abnormal, or difficult informs *dyslogistic, dysfunctional, dysphagia,* and *dysplasia.* With technical terminology, as in medicine, specific prefixes can indicate organs and systems: knowing *hepat(o)-* refers to the liver and *splen(o)* to the spleen informs *hepatitis* and *hepatosplenic.* Knowing *macro-* means large and *micro-* means small informs terms like *macroglossia, microglossia, macrocephaly,* and *microcephaly.* Knowing *hydro-* refers to water informs *hydrocephalus, hydration,* and *anhydrous.*

Suffixes

In English, certain suffixes generally indicate both that a word is a noun, and that the noun represents a state of being or quality. For example, *-ness* is commonly used to change an adjective into its noun form, as with *happy* and *happiness, nice* and *niceness, sturdy* and *sturdiness, quick* and *quickness,* and so on. The suffix *–tion* is commonly used to transform a verb into its noun form, as with *converse* and *conversation, convene* and *convention, move* and *motion,* and *locomote* and *locomotion.* Thus, if readers are unfamiliar with the second form of a word, knowing the meaning of the transforming suffix can help them determine meaning, especially if they know the meaning of the first form (which knowledge of word roots will help). With medical terminology, knowing that the suffix *–osis* can mean a diseased/abnormal condition can help them define many words, such as *sclerosis, leukosis, cirrhosis,* and *arthrosis,* to name a few. And knowing that *–itis* means inflammation informs many word meanings like *appendicitis, bronchitis, laryngitis, arthritis, pneumonitis,* and many more.

Context clues to determine meanings of words

If readers simply bypass unknown words in reading, they can reach unclear conclusions about what they read. However, if they look for the definition of every unfamiliar word in the dictionary, it can slow down their reading progress. Moreover, the dictionary may list multiple definitions for one word; then readers must still examine surrounding context to determine which definition is the one that applies. Hence context is important to new vocabulary regardless of reader methods. Four types of context clues are examples, definitions, descriptive words, and opposites. Authors may use a certain word, and then follow it with several different examples of what it describes. Sometimes authors actually supply a definition of a word they use, which is especially true in informational and technical texts. Authors may use descriptive words that elaborate upon a vocabulary word they just used. While this may be done to make their prose colorful or memorable, it nonetheless affords context clues for readers. Authors may also use opposites with negation that help define meaning.

Examples and appositives

An author may use a word and then give examples that illustrate its meaning. Consider this text: "For students who are deaf or hard of hearing, teachers who do not know how to use

Copyright © Mometrix Media. You have been licensed one copy of this document for personal use only. Any other reproduction or redistribution is strictly prohibited. All rights reserved.

sign language can help them understand certain instructions by using gestures instead, like pointing their fingers to indicate which direction to look or go; holding up a hand, palm outward, to indicate stopping; holding the hand(s) flat, palm(s) up, curling a finger toward oneself in a beckoning motion to indicate 'come here'; or curling all fingers toward oneself repeatedly to indicate 'come on', 'more', or 'continue.'" The author of this text has used the word "gestures" and then followed it with examples of gestures. A reader unfamiliar with the word "gestures" can deduce from the examples given that this word means hand motions in this context. Readers can find examples by looking for signal words "for example," "for instance," "like" (as in the text presented above), "such as," and "e.g."

While readers sometimes have to look for definitions of unfamiliar words in a dictionary and/or do some work to determine a word's meaning from its surrounding context, at other times an author may make it easier for readers by defining certain words they use. For example, an author may write, "The company did not have sufficient capital, that is, available money, to continue operations." The author defined "capital" as "available money," and heralded the definition with the phrase "that is." Another way that authors supply word definitions is with appositives. Rather than being introduced by a signal phrase like "that is," "namely," or "meaning," an appositive comes after the vocabulary word it defines and is enclosed within two commas. For example, an author may write, "The Indians introduced the Pilgrims to pemmican, cakes they made of lean meat dried and mixed with fat, which proved greatly beneficial to keep settlers from starving while trapping." In this example, the appositive phrase following "pemmican" and preceding "which" defines the word "pemmican."

Descriptions

When readers encounter a word they do not recognize in a text, the author may expand on that word to illustrate it better. While the author may do this to make the prose more picturesque and vivid, the reader can also take advantage of this description to provide context clues to the meaning of the unfamiliar word. For example, an author may write, "The man sitting next to me on the airplane was obese. His shirt stretched across his vast expanse of flesh, strained almost to bursting." The descriptive second sentence elaborates on and helps to define the previous sentence's word "obese" to mean extremely fat. One author described someone who was obese simply, yet very descriptively, as "an epic in bloat." A reader unfamiliar with the word "repugnant" can decipher its meaning through an author's accompanying description: "The way the child grimaced and shuddered as he swallowed the medicine showed that its taste was particularly repugnant."

Opposites with negation to determine meanings of words

Text authors sometimes introduce a contrasting or opposing idea before or after a concept they present. They may do this to emphasize or heighten the idea they present by contrasting it with something that is the reverse. However, readers can also use this author's technique to help themselves with comprehension of new vocabulary words. For example, an author may write, "Our conversation was not cheery. We sat and talked very solemnly about his experience, and a number of similar events." The reader who is not familiar with the word "solemnly" can deduce by the author's preceding use of "not cheery" that "solemn" means the opposite of cheery or happy, so it must mean serious or sad. Or if someone writes, "Don't condemn his entire project because you couldn't find anything good to say about it," readers unfamiliar with "condemn" can understand from the sentence structure that it means the opposite of saying anything good, so it must mean reject,

Copyright © Mometrix Media. You have been licensed one copy of this document for personal use only. Any other reproduction or redistribution is strictly prohibited. All rights reserved.

dismiss, or disapprove. "Entire" adds another context clue, meaning total or complete rejection.

Syntax to determine part of speech and meanings of words

Syntax is sentence structure and word order. Suppose that a reader encounters an unfamiliar word when reading a text. To illustrate, consider an invented word like "splunch." If this word is used in a sentence like "Please splunch that ball to me," the reader can assume from syntactic context that "splunch" is a verb. We would not use a noun, adjective, adverb, or preposition with the object "that ball," and the prepositional phrase "to me" further indicates "splunch" represents an action. However, in the sentence, "Please hand that splunch to me," the reader can assume that "splunch" is a noun. Demonstrative adjectives like "that" modify nouns. Also, we hand someone some*thing*—a thing being a noun; we do not hand someone a verb, adjective, or adverb. Some sentences contain further clues. For example, from the sentence, "The princess wore the glittering splunch on her head," the reader can deduce that it is a crown, tiara, or something similar from the syntactic context, without knowing the word.

Syntax to indicate different meanings of similar sentences

The syntax, or structure, of a sentence affords grammatical cues that aid readers in comprehending the meanings of words, phrases, and sentences in the texts that they read. Seemingly minor differences in how the words or phrases in a sentence are ordered can make major differences in what that sentence means. For example, here are two sentences that use exactly the same words, with the only difference being their order; one phrase is located in a different place in each sentence, with the result being that they have different meanings: (1) "The man with a broken arm sat in a chair." (2) "The man sat in a chair with a broken arm." The first sentence means the man had a broken arm and sat in a chair. The second sentence means the man sat in a chair that had a broken arm. While both indicate a man sat in a chair, differing syntax indicates whether the man's or chair's arm was broken.

Nuances of word meaning relative to connotation, denotation, diction, and usage

A word's denotation is simply its objective dictionary definition. However, its connotation(s) refer(s) to the subjective associations, often emotional, that specific words evoke in listeners and readers hearing and seeing them. Two or more words can have the same dictionary meaning, but very different connotations. Writers use diction (a style element) to convey various nuances of thought and emotion by selecting synonyms for other words that best communicate the associations they want to trigger for readers. For example, a car engine is naturally greasy; in this sense, "greasy" is a neutral term. But when a person's smile, appearance, or clothing is described as "greasy," it has a pejorative connotation. Because of usages that have occurred in recent times, many words have gained additional and/or different meanings. The word "gay" used to have only the meaning of happy, or festive as in the Christmas carol "Deck the Halls" lyrics "Don we now our gay apparel," but by the 20th century, it had also come to indicate a sexual preference.

Figures of speech

A figure of speech is a verbal expression, used not only in speech but also in writing, whose meaning is figurative rather than matching the literal meanings of the words in it. For

Copyright © Mometrix Media. You have been licensed one copy of this document for personal use only. Any other reproduction or redistribution is strictly prohibited. All rights reserved.

example, the figure of speech "butterflies in the stomach" does not literally mean someone has actual butterflies in his or her stomach; it is a metaphor representing the fluttery feelings some people get in their stomachs when they are nervous or excited—or when they "fall in love"—another figure of speech so common we take it for granted, but which does not mean physically falling. "Hitting a sales target" does not mean physically hitting a target with arrows as in archery; it is a metaphor for meeting a sales quota. "Climbing the ladder of success" does not involve physically climbing an actual ladder; it metaphorically likens advancing in one's career to ascending ladder rungs. Similes, such as "light as a feather" (meaning very light, not a feather's actual weight), and hyperbole, like "I'm starving/freezing/roasting," are also figures of speech.

In English, a very common idiomatic expression meaning it is raining very hard is "raining cats and dogs." Foreigners have difficulty translating or understanding such non-literal expressions. The origin of this figure of speech is in Teutonic mythology. Circa 100 B.C., some Celtic or Germanic people living in Jutland believed in the Old Norse religion wherein Odin was the god of war, wisdom, and the main god in charge of the world. The Teutonic belief then was that Odin's dog took the form of the wind, and a cat assumed the form of the rain. During rainstorms, they believed Odin's dog—the wind—was chasing a cat—the rain. When rain poured down, they attributed it to Odin dropping cats and dogs from the sky. Over 2,000 years later, although modern peoples do not believe Odin is responsible or that wind and rain are in dog and cat form, they have still preserved this ancient expression calling a heavy downpour "raining cats and dogs."

The figure of speech "in hot water" is familiar to most native English-language speakers. In the Middle Ages, many countries were governed via feudal systems wherein lords owned land and serfs worked that land. In those days, legal court systems and jury trials had not yet been developed. To determine someone's guilt or innocence, officials often used "trials by ordeal." A crime deemed worthy of the death penalty was tried by an ordeal of fire or hot water. With a hot water trial, the suspect was placed into a large pot of boiling water. If the suspect survived, s/he was judged innocent. If the accused person died from being in the boiling water, s/he was found guilty. Such trials were used to try many crimes, including witchcraft. The original term "in hot water" dates back to when someone accused of a capital crime was literally placed in hot water. Although this practice has long since become obsolete, the expression "in hot water" persists to describe discomfort, difficulty, or danger.

While the meaning of the saying, "Leave no stone unturned" is obvious—to look everywhere when searching for something, and/or to spare no effort in doing work thoroughly—we tend to take this common expression for granted and may not know its original source. The saying actually dates back to ancient Greek mythology. Many ancient Greek myths, plays, poems, popular stories, and other literature include references to consulting the Oracle at Delphi, who they believed could communicate with the gods and thus predict the future and answer all questions. For example, the Oracle at Delphi predicted the eventual fate of Oedipus in Sophocles' tragedy *Oedipus Rex.* Socrates, Homer, and others referred to this Oracle. Tragedian Euripides once related a story that a general, defeated in battle, buried his treasure before fleeing the area. Someone asked the Oracle at Delphi where this treasure was. The reply was that to find the treasure, one should "leave no stone unturned"—in other words, to look everywhere possible.

While "tying the knot" is figurative today, it was done literally in many ancient traditions. For example, in early Hindu tradition, at the end of the wedding ceremony the groom placed

Copyright © Mometrix Media. You have been licensed one copy of this document for personal use only. Any other reproduction or redistribution is strictly prohibited. All rights reserved.

a colored ribbon around the neck of the bride. The father of the bride could demand a higher price of the groom for his daughter before this ribbon was tied, but once it was knotted, he could not, and the marriage was permanent (early Hinduism prohibited separations or divorces). Early Parsees, Indian Zoroastrians descended from Persians, bound grooms at wedding ceremonies with seven-stranded cords. This was both to assure tight bonds, and to show the Parsee belief in seven as a lucky and sacred number. In the ancient Phoenician city-state of Carthage, at weddings the bride and groom were tied together with leather laces around their thumbs. And in Roman weddings, the bride's girdle was tied with a knot so tight it was called a Herculean knot, which the groom had to loosen or untie.

In the 18th and 19th centuries, well-dressed ladies wore corsets, dresses, and shoes, all of which had to be pulled together to fasten them. Corsets, which were early girdles, were very tight: their laces had to be pulled strenuously together. Dresses featured many hooks and eyes to be fastened, which also required pulling the two sides together. Even shoes and boots had leather thongs that had to be pulled together before buckling the outer buckles. Rich women had female assistants to help with this, but other women relied on their husbands for assistance. The phrase "making ends meet" originally referred to the physical efforts required for ladies to dress properly. But over time, innovations in apparel manufacturing made clothes easier to put on and fasten, while fashionable clothing still became more expensive. Accordingly, the meaning of the expression evolved to signify not physical struggles, but the economic struggle of financing a lady's fashionable wardrobe. Eventually this generalized to mean any financial struggle.

Before industrial developments enabled maritime and aerial warfare, wars were fought only on land. Troops were accompanied by musicians—fifes and drums at the least, and often entire bands. In preparation for battle, as soldiers were forming lines, the bands headed up the lines, playing martial music to alert, support, and inspire the troops, who had to "face the music." Before giving the "forward march" command, the first command was "face the music." Another military practice to which this phrase is attributed is the history of the dishonorable discharge, wherein a soldier was literally drummed out of service: the company stood at attention, and the drum and fife bands accompanying the troops played a tune called "Rogue's March," popular with the American army during the Revolutionary War, including drum rolls to "drum out" the disgraced one who had to "face the music." A theatrical application of this figure of speech is the test of an actor's courage when in the spotlight onstage, facing musicians in the orchestra pit.

Influence of existing schemata on reading comprehension

Experts have stated that less-successful readers start reading without thinking, whereas successful readers activate and build upon their existing knowledge before they read—as well as before they write, listen, or speak. Connecting reading to what we already know enables learning new information and constructing meaning. Readers' existing schemata reflect their attitudes, values, experiences, conceptual comprehension, and skills they bring to new texts. For example, before third-graders read a book about Johnny Appleseed, their teachers have them start a KWL chart—a list of what they *Know*, what they *Want* to know or learn, and what they have *Learned* after reading. Before sixth-graders read a letter written by a Japanese national relocated during World War II, teachers ask them to describe their opinions and reactions regarding internment camps. Or before sixth-graders read a piece about a tsunami in Hawaii, their teacher asks them what they know about tsunamis.

Copyright © Mometrix Media. You have been licensed one copy of this document for personal use only. Any other reproduction or redistribution is strictly prohibited. All rights reserved.

Activating existing background knowledge and having students think about texts before reading improves comprehension.

SSBI classroom teaching approach

Language teaching and learning have evolved, from a traditional focus on teaching and teachers to a more current focus on learning and learners. Educators have come to realize that regardless how well teachers perform, if students are not learning and/or not motivated, more emphasis on learners is needed. More learner-centered instruction is necessarily more interactive, self-directed, and independent. However, many students lack awareness of learning strategies. Language acquisition requires not only memory formation and retention, but also relevant and continuing practice. Classroom teachers can train students in purposeful, systematic learning methods to support and facilitate these components. Styles- and Strategies-based Instruction (SSBI) (cf. Oxford, 200a; Cohen and Dörnyei, 2002) combines training activities in learning strategies and styles with day-to-day language instruction. Its basis is a combination of classroom language learning opportunities with more efficient, effective use of language learned. Explicit and implicit instruction in language learning and strategy use are integrated in classrooms to promote strategy awareness, organization, systematic and effective application, and transfers to new learning and contexts of use.

<u>Components</u>
The first component of the SSBI approach is Strategy Preparation. This involves teachers' discovering which learning strategies students already know, and how they are able to apply them. Most students have evolved some strategies, but they often do not apply them systematically or effectively. The second component of SSBI is Strategy Awareness-Raising. Its aim is for teachers to make students aware of learning strategies they may never have considered, or had thought about but have never actually utilized. Five SSBI tasks of awareness raising are: (1) What comprises the learning process; (2) students' individual approaches to learning generally and/or preferences in learning styles; (3) which types of strategies they already use, plus strategies the teachers and classmates suggest; (4) how much responsibility individual students assume for their own learning; and (5) methods to use for assessing students' use of learning strategies. These activities are necessarily explicit in their nature of addressing language-learning strategies.

Following the first two phases of SSBI—Strategy Preparation and Strategy Awareness-Raising—the third component is the Strategy Training phase. This involves explicit instruction by classroom teachers to teach students why, when, and how specific learning strategies are used to support activities for learning and using language. Strategies may be used singly, in clusters, or in sequences. In a typical scenario of classroom training in learning strategies, a teacher would describe strategies that could prove useful to students, model the application of these strategies, and give the students several examples of each strategy to illustrate them. The teacher would also have students contribute more examples from their own personal learning experiences. The teacher leads whole-class and/or small-group discussions about three things: rationales for using various strategies, planning their approaches to specified activities, and assessing the efficacy of the strategies that they select. The teacher can also invite students to experiment with applying a wide array of strategies.

Copyright © Mometrix Media. You have been licensed one copy of this document for personal use only. Any other reproduction or redistribution is strictly prohibited. All rights reserved.

The first three phases of SSBI are Strategy Preparation, Strategy Awareness-Raising, and Strategy Training. The fourth phase is Strategy Practice. Teachers get students to experiment with different learning strategies across a wide range. Awareness of and training in a strategy are insufficient: students must additionally have plenty of opportunities to practice applying them to many different tasks in language learning and use. This phase incorporates activities that are "strategy-friendly," meaning they reinforce strategies that students have previously learned, and they afford ample time for students to combine their learning of subject course content with practice in using the various strategies. SSBI activities are prescribed to refer explicitly to strategies employed for task completion. Hence, either students plan which strategies to use for a certain activity, or teachers call their attention to which strategies they are using at the time. Teachers may also "debrief" students in their strategy applications and their comparative efficacy following an activity.

SSBI includes Strategy Preparation; Strategy Awareness-Raising; Strategy Training; Strategy Practice; and finally, Personalization of Strategies. During this final component, students make personal what they have learned about various systematic strategies for language learning. They self-assess their application of the strategies they have learned, and they examine how they can transfer these strategies to different contexts. Those who plan, write, and implement curriculum within the SSBI approach have the responsibility of ensuring that day-to-day classroom materials and activities have the systematic learning strategies integrated into them, and that the linguistic tasks they assign to students embed these strategies, both implicitly and explicitly, to give students practice using strategies in different contexts. Teachers can begin with existing course matter and then decide which strategies to incorporate, begin with a set of selected strategies and then build activities around these, or they can spontaneously include indicated or suitable strategies during lessons. SSBI activities aim to give students strategy awareness; training; practice; personalization; and spontaneous, independent, and unprompted selection of strategies they prefer.

Research-based instruction for vocabulary development

The National Reading Technical Assistance Center (NRTAC, 2010) has reviewed current research on vocabulary instruction and synthesized salient findings. According to the National Reading Panel (NRP), children often must learn the meanings of specific words to understand specific subject matter and/or lessons. Therefore, teachers must give them direct instruction in the vocabulary words used by specific texts. Researchers also find it important for students to be exposed to vocabulary words multiple times, and they additionally warn that word repetition not be simply drilling, but rather repeated encounters with the same words in varied contexts. Studies demonstrate that students should learn high-frequency vocabulary words that they will be able to apply in multiple and varied contexts, which increases their productive language skills. Vocabulary learning is found to take a developmental course. Researchers also find that teachers should restructure vocabulary exercises as needed because once students understand what a task expects from them, they frequently learn faster.

Research findings about vocabulary instruction

Among a number of conclusions that reviewers of the research literature on vocabulary instruction have made, they find that learners achieve more effective vocabulary acquisition

Copyright © Mometrix Media. You have been licensed one copy of this document for personal use only. Any other reproduction or redistribution is strictly prohibited. All rights reserved.

when vocabulary learning is not limited to knowing word definitions but also involves active student engagement. Some researchers define a child's "knowing" a word as not simply knowing the dictionary definition of a word and how it is related logically to other words, but moreover by the way that the word works in various contexts. Also, research in 2000 by the National Institute of Child Health and Human Development (NICHD) found computer technology very useful in vocabulary instruction, but not many teaching applications revealed in literature. As reviewers were still citing these conclusions in 2010, it is inferred that progress has occurred but still been inadequate, indicating need for further study. Additional research finds that students' long-term vocabulary development is significantly influenced by their reading volume, which promotes incidental learning of vocabulary. Researchers recommend independent reading at home and school, plus structured read-aloud sessions and discussions.

Areas needing further study
According to the National Institute of Child Health and Human Development (NICHD), optimum vocabulary learning by students will not proceed from relying on only one instructional method. Multiple researchers and educators find students must learn not just word definitions, but moreover how words fit into the world's context. Crucial aspects of vocabulary learning include receptive vocabulary understanding versus productive vocabulary expression, printed or written vocabulary versus spoken vocabulary, and vocabulary depth versus vocabulary breadth. These are all topics wherein extant research indicates the need for additional study. Moreover, other researchers have found the means of measuring vocabulary knowledge, in which words teachers are instructing students, student levels of vocabulary knowledge, and variability among students in the sizes of their vocabularies all need to be taken into account to understand vocabulary learning. The National Reading Panel (NRP) reported (NICHD, 2000) that while vocabulary instruction increases comprehension, teaching methods must fit reader ability and age, and that research has not yet definitively identified the best instructional methods for vocabulary.

Consensus conclusions regarding what is most effective
Researchers find that when young children are repeatedly exposed to targeted vocabulary words, as in repeated readings of the same storybooks, they are more likely to understand the words' meanings, remember them, and use them more often than children who hear a story only once. Rereading is also found effective for children at risk for reading problems. Researchers note that children gain semantic and lexical knowledge gradually through frequent exposure to targeted words. Other findings suggest that children with comprehension deficits in lexical learning may experience these due to variations in semantic learning instead of in phonological learning. Studies have shown that explicit instruction of word meanings during read-aloud sessions in addition to rereading increases children's vocabulary comprehension more than rereading alone. Also, students are found to progress even more from explaining their own definitions of target words than from being told explanations for unknown words. Researchers find contextual instructional approaches increase vocabulary more than lessons teaching word definitions.

Multimedia and questions and comments
Studies find that children learn definitions of new words more easily than they can recall their pronunciations, which is harder. Some researchers examined multimedia applications for enhancing read-aloud sessions and vocabulary instruction with preschoolers through second-graders, including both native English speakers and English language learners (ELLs). While findings for adding multimedia with native English-speaking students were

Copyright © Mometrix Media. You have been licensed one copy of this document for personal use only. Any other reproduction or redistribution is strictly prohibited. All rights reserved.

not statistically significant, they were significant for ELL students. Gaps between ELLs and native English speakers were reduced, not just for vocabulary words targeted, but also for more generalized knowledge of English vocabulary. Researchers have also found that when teachers use questions and comments to call attention to target vocabulary words, children are more likely to learn the meanings of those new words. Investigators have ruled out previous knowledge by using storybooks they created themselves that included nonsense words; children still comprehended and remembered meanings assigned to the nonsense words better when teachers asked them questions and gave them comments about the word meanings.

Scaffolding, question demand, and student engagement
Some investigators have evaluated how using low-demand and high-demand questions and scaffolding influence young children's vocabulary learning during storybook read-alouds. The experimenters found when teachers used scaffolding (graduated support) by asking children low-demand questions and gradually adding more complexity until their questions eventually reached high-demand status, preschool children showed more progress in learning new words than they did without such scaffolding. Others have examined engagement in linguistic student-teacher interactions and its effects on vocabulary acquisition. Some have found that amounts of time spent in early literacy activities vary widely among preschool classes; that learning environments cover a range, from language-centered to mainly non-literacy-based learning activities; and furthermore, that even children in the same classrooms have strikingly varied learning opportunities and experiences—indicating a significant relationship of children's experience and background knowledge to their learning results. Other studies show that preschoolers and kindergarteners learn and remember vocabulary better through interactive approaches than through embedded or incidental vocabulary exposure during read-aloud sessions.

Research-based teaching strategies for using metacognitive processes

Competent, active readers evaluate the text and their understanding of it before, during, and after their reading. They consider intuitively whether a work's title is interesting to them; whether in their perception the author depicts reality accurately, or distorts or exaggerates it; and whether the text is something they would recommend to other readers and, if so, to whom. These practices enable them to make connections with text and monitor their own comprehension. For example, before reading an advertisement, sixth-graders think about media techniques attracting them to products. During reading, they identify particular audience persuasion techniques. After reading, they analyze the influences of things like vocabulary choices and concept repetition with the aid of visual graphic organizers. Then they evaluate the advertisement's effectiveness on its audience. For students to succeed in all academic subjects, they must read actively and strategically. Experts find that literacy motivation and learning between ages 10 and 18 are crucial to prepare students for both school and life.

Evidence-based teaching approaches

Evidence-based teaching approaches mean that curriculum and instruction methods have been proven effective by multiple studies, applying rigorous research standards, and obtaining similar results. Their use is justified by their valid and reliable evidence, which educators can trust to be effective: when they correctly apply an evidence-based program of curriculum and instruction, they can expect students to demonstrate academic

Copyright © Mometrix Media. You have been licensed one copy of this document for personal use only. Any other reproduction or redistribution is strictly prohibited. All rights reserved.

improvement. Evidence-based curriculum is founded on existing research, is evaluated locally on an ongoing basis, and is aligned with state educational standards. In evaluating effective instruction, the teaching practices to use should be clearly defined. A monitoring process should be established to make sure teachers adhere to those defined practices. The results of the instruction for students should be evaluated using appropriate and established measures. And a suitable way of comparing students' progress should also be established.

Paired reading strategy to identify main ideas and details

Students can support one another's comprehension of informational text by working in pairs. Each of the two students silently reads a portion of text. One student summarizes the text's main point, and then the other must agree or disagree and explain why. The pair will then develop an agreement as to what the text's main idea is. Then each of the students in the pair takes a turn at identifying details in the text portion that support the main idea that they have identified. After this, the pair of students silently reads the next portion of the text. Then they go through the same steps as before, but with their roles reversed this time. Each pair of students can keep track of the central ideas and supporting details by taking notes in two columns: one for main ideas and the other for the details that support those main ideas.

Text coding

Some experts (cf. Harvey and Daniels, 2009) recommend text coding or text monitoring as an active reading strategy to support student comprehension of informational texts. As they read short independent reading selections that their teachers assign them according to their reading levels, students make text code notations on Post-it Notes or in the margins of the text. Teachers should model text coding for students one or two codes at a time until they have demonstrated all eight codes: A check mark means "I know this." An X means "This is not what I expected." An asterisk (*) means "This is important." A question mark means "I have a question about this." Two question marks mean "I am really confused about this." An exclamation point means "I am surprised at this." An L means "I have learned something new from this." And an RR means "I need to reread this part."

Two-column notes

When students read or listen to an informational text, it can help them find and note its main ideas and supporting details by using the "two-column notes" strategy. Teachers should first introduce this strategy to students, model it, and have them practice using it. As students use two-column notes, they can better organize textual information, find data in text supporting conclusions, and evaluate whether textual evidence supports author claims. For example, in analyzing Abraham Lincoln's Gettysburg Address, students put in the Main Ideas column, "Our founding fathers created the U.S." Next to it in the Details column, they place "Conceived in liberty" and "Dedicated to all men being created equal." Under Main Ideas: "Now the U.S. is in a Civil War." Under Details: "Testing whether our nation as conceived can survive." Main Ideas: "We are here to dedicate the Gettysburg battlefield." Details: "The dedication is to those who died in the war," "This is their final resting place," and "This is a fitting and proper thing to do."

Copyright © Mometrix Media. You have been licensed one copy of this document for personal use only. Any other reproduction or redistribution is strictly prohibited. All rights reserved.

Teacher interpretation of research

Some researchers find most teachers do well at data location in complex graphs and tables. But to manipulate data using calculations comparing scores among student groups, some either overlook necessary data points or become overwhelmed by the cognitive load. More teachers have difficulty with data comprehension, such as manipulating data by calculating proportions of proficiency levels among student groups. For example, significant numbers of teachers reading data results confuse percentages of proficient students with cutoff criteria for proficiency. Another teacher confusion area is absolute values versus proportions. Teachers have more trouble distinguishing histograms from bar graphs, and interpreting histograms: many fail to notice when histogram percentages add up to over 100 percent. Teachers easily locate relevant figures in contingency tables, but often cannot interpret relationships between variables. Many fail to distinguish cross-sectional from longitudinal data. Most teachers can plan data-based differentiated instruction better with individual, real student scores than hypothetical students' inconsistent test results. Data interpretation and question-posing seem most problematic. Teachers make data-informed instructional decisions better in small groups than individually.

Copyright © Mometrix Media. You have been licensed one copy of this document for personal use only. Any other reproduction or redistribution is strictly prohibited. All rights reserved.

Practice Test

Practice Questions

Questions 1-4 are based on the following excerpt:

>   riverrun, past Eve and Adam's, from swerve of shore to bend of bay, brings
>   us by a commodious vicus of recirculation back to Howth Castle and
>   Environs.

1. This is the opening sentence of...
    a. *Ulysses.*
    b. *Finnegans Wake.*
    c. *Adventures in the Skin Trade.*
    d. *A Portrait of the Artist as a Young Man.*

2. In the excerpted sentence, the word "vicus" represents which of the following?
    a. Vicinity
    b. Vico Way
    c. Giambattista Vico
    d. All of the above

3. Why does this opening sentence begin with an uncapitalized word?
    a. This was to make it stand out to the reader as different.
    b. It is really the continuation of the author's previous novel.
    c. It forms the completion of the novel's unfinished last sentence.
    d. A typesetting error in the original edition was preserved in perpetuity.

4. The author of the excerpted work is famous for using a literary technique known as...
    a. Stream-of-consciousness.
    b. The unreliable narrator.
    c. First-person narration.
    d. The author surrogate.

Questions 5-7 refer to the following excerpts:

>   Had we but world enough, and time,
>   This coyness, lady, were no crime.
>   We would sit down, and think which way
>   To walk, and pass our long love's day.
>
>   But at my back I always hear
>   Time's winged chariot hurrying near;
>   And yonder all before us lie
>   Deserts of vast eternity.

Copyright © Mometrix Media. You have been licensed one copy of this document for personal use only. Any other reproduction or redistribution is strictly prohibited. All rights reserved.

5. Who is the author of this poem?
    a. John Donne
    b. Andrew Marvell
    c. George Herbert
    d. Henry Vaughan

6. This poem reflects a thematic tradition known as...
    a. Carpe diem.
    b. Classicism.
    c. Cinquain.
    d. Conceit.

7. What is the meter of the couplets in this poem?
    a. Pentameter
    b. Heptameter
    c. Hexameter
    d. Tetrameter

Questions 8-10 refer to the following excerpt:

> Call the roller of big cigars,
> The muscular one, and bid him whip
> In kitchen cups concupiscent curds.
> Let the wenches dawdle in such dress
> As they are used to wear, and let the boys
> Bring flowers in last month's newspapers.
> Let be be finale of seem.
> The only emperor is the emperor of ice-cream.

8. The excerpted poem was written in...
    a. The 17th century.
    b. The 19th century.
    c. The 20th century.
    d. The 18th century.

9. Which literary device is shown in the third line of the excerpted stanza?
    a. Alliteration
    b. Hyperbole
    c. Onomatopoeia
    d. Metonymy

10. The line "Let be be finale of seem" can be interpreted as reflecting a concept from which of the following?
    a. Ovid's *Metamorphoses*
    b. Dante's *Divine Comedy*
    c. Plato's *Dialogues*
    d. Homer's *Iliad*

Copyright © Mometrix Media. You have been licensed one copy of this document for personal use only. Any other reproduction or redistribution is strictly prohibited. All rights reserved.

I AM assured by our Merchants, that a Boy or a Girl before twelve Years old, is no saleable Commodity; and even when they come to this Age, they will not yield above [an amount of money] at most, on the Exchange; which cannot turn to Account...to the Parents...; the Charge of Nutriment and Rags, having been at least four Times that Value.

I SHALL now therefore humbly propose my own Thoughts; which I hope will not be liable to the least Objection.

I HAVE been assured by a very knowing *American* of my Acquaintance in *London;* that a young healthy Child, well nursed, is, at a Year old, a most delicious, nourishing, and wholesome Food; whether *Stewed, Roasted, Baked,* or *Boiled;* and, I make no doubt, that it will equally serve in a *Fricasie,* or *Ragoust.*

11. The literary form used in the excerpted piece is...
    a. Persuasion.
    b. Satire.
    c. Exposition.
    d. Bathos.

12. The excerpted work was published in which century?
    a. 20th
    b. 19th
    c. 18th
    d. 17th

13. The author of the excerpted piece also wrote which of the following?
    a. *The Canterbury Tales*
    b. *The Faerie Queene*
    c. *Paradise Lost*
    d. *Gulliver's Travels*

Questions 14-17 refer to the following poem:
                    The Thought-Fox

    I imagine this midnight moment's forest:
    Something else is alive
    Beside the clock's loneliness
    And this blank page where my fingers move.

    Through the window I see no star:
    Something more near
    Though deeper within darkness
    Is entering the loneliness:

    Cold, delicately as the dark snow
    A fox's nose touches twig, leaf;
    Two eyes serve a movement, that now
    And again now, and now, and now

Copyright © Mometrix Media. You have been licensed one copy of this document for personal use only. Any other reproduction or redistribution is strictly prohibited. All rights reserved.

Sets neat prints into the snow
Between trees, and warily a lame
Shadow lags by stump and in hollow
Of a body that is bold to come

Across clearings, an eye,
A widening deepening greenness,
Brilliantly, concentratedly,
Coming about its own business

Till, with a sudden sharp hot stink of fox,
It enters the dark hole of the head.
The window is starless still; the clock ticks,
The page is printed.

From *Ted Hughes: Selected Poems 1957-1967.* Copyright © 1972 by Ted Hughes, Harper & Row Publishers, Inc.

14. The primary literary device used by the poet here is...
    a. Foreshadowing.
    b. Irony.
    c. Clichés.
    d. Metaphor.

15. Which of these does this poem really describe?
    a. The process of a fox's natural actions
    b. The process of being inspired by nature
    c. The process of being inspired to write
    d. The process of being attacked by a fox

16. Which of the following best characterizes how this poem portrays the creative process?
    a. The poet exercises tight control of a thought.
    b. The poet is a passive recipient of the thought.
    c. The poet carefully guides the thought to him.
    d. The poet imagines a fox to help him to write.

17. In which of the following forms is this poem written?
    a. In the free verse form
    b. Rhymed and metered
    c. Unrhymed and metered
    d. Rhymed and unmetered

Questions 18-20 refer to the following excerpts:
    I knew I should be grateful to Mrs. Guinea, only I couldn't feel a thing. If Mrs.
    Guinea had given me a ticket to Europe, or a round-the-world cruise, it
    wouldn't have made one scrap of difference to me, because wherever I sat—
    on the deck of a ship or at a street café in Paris or Bangkok—I would be
    sitting under the same glass bell jar, stewing in my own sour air.

Copyright © Mometrix Media. You have been licensed one copy of this document for personal use only. Any other reproduction or redistribution is strictly prohibited. All rights reserved.

I sank back in the gray, plush seat and closed my eyes. The air of the bell jar wadded round me and I couldn't stir.

[Following a successful shock treatment:]
All the heat and fear had purged itself. I felt surprisingly at peace. The bell jar hung, suspended, a few feet above my head. I was open to the circulating air.

"We'll take up where we left off, Esther," she [her mother] had said, with her sweet, martyr's smile. "We'll act as if all this were a bad dream."
A bad dream.
To the person in the bell jar, blank and stopped as a dead baby, the world itself is the bad dream.

Valerie's last, cheerful cry had been "So long! Be seeing you."
"Not if I know it," I thought.
But I wasn't sure. I wasn't sure at all. How did I know that someday—at college, in Europe, somewhere, anywhere—the bell jar, with its stifling distortions, wouldn't descend again?

From *The Bell Jar* by Sylvia Plath, copyright © 1971 by Harper & Row, Publishers, Inc.

18. The bell jar the author refers to is an example of which literary device?
    a. A simile
    b. An allusion
    c. A metaphor
    d. Personification

19. In this book, Plath uses a bell jar to symbolize…
    a. The strictures of reality.
    b. Her own mental illness.
    c. A case of writer's block.
    d. A disorder of breathing.

20. Which of the following statements is accurate about Sylvia Plath?
    a. *The Bell Jar* was her last in a long series of novels, all of them successful.
    b. She ultimately recovered, lived a long life, and wrote many more novels.
    c. Plath wrote only a few poems, but *The Bell Jar* was the first of her books.
    d. She wrote *The Bell Jar* about her initial breakdown almost a decade later.

21. William Shakespeare wrote during which historical and literary period?
    a. Medieval
    b. Renaissance
    c. Restoration
    d. Enlightenment

Copyright © Mometrix Media. You have been licensed one copy of this document for personal use only. Any other reproduction or redistribution is strictly prohibited. All rights reserved.

22. Which of the following was the author of *The Pilgrim's Progress?*
    a. John Bunyan
    b. William Congreve
    c. Daniel Defoe
    d. Samuel Butler

Questions 23-24 are based on the following excerpt:
     Come live with me and be my love,
     And we will all the pleasures prove
     That valleys, groves, hills, and fields,
     Woods, or steepy mountain yields.

23. This is the first stanza of a poem written by…
    a. Andrew Marvell.
    b. Christopher Marlowe.
    c. Sir Walter Raleigh.
    d. William Shakespeare.

24. The rhyme scheme of this stanza is…
    a. ABAB.
    b. ABBA.
    c. AABB.
    d. ABCD.

25. The legend of Faust has been treated in literature by which of the following?
    a. Christopher Marlowe
    b. Johann Wolfgang von Goethe
    c. Thomas Mann
    d. All of the above

26. Of the following works by Alexander Pope, which was written in prose?
    a. *An Essay on Criticism*
    b. *The Rape of the Lock*
    c. *The Universal Prayer*
    d. None of the above

Questions 27-29 refer to the following excerpts:
     [First stanza:] I wake to sleep, and take my waking slow.
     I feel my fate in what I cannot fear.
     I learn by going where I have to go.

     [Last stanza:] This shaking keeps me steady. I should know.
     What falls away is always. And is near.
     I wake to sleep, and take my waking slow.
     I learn by going where I have to go.

From *The Waking* by Theodore Roethke, in *Roethke: Collected Poems,* Doubleday & Company, Inc.
copyright © 1937-1966 by Beatrice Roethke as Administratrix of the Estate of Theodore Roethke;
copyright © 1932-1961 by Theodore Roethke.

Copyright © Mometrix Media. You have been licensed one copy of this document for personal use only. Any other reproduction or redistribution is strictly prohibited. All rights reserved.

[First stanza:] I shut my eyes and all the world drops dead;
I lift my lids and all is born again.
(I think I made you up inside my head.)

[Last stanza:] I should have loved a thunderbird instead;
At least when spring comes they roar back again.
I shut my eyes and all the world drops dead.
(I think I made you up inside my head.)

From *Mad Girl's Love Song* by Sylvia Plath, copyright © 1954 by Sylvia Plath, in A Biographical Note, in *The Bell Jar,* Copyright © 1971 by Harper & Row, Publishers. *Mad Girl's Love Song* first appeared in *Mademoiselle,* August 1953 issue.

[First stanza:] Do not go gentle into that good night,
Old age should burn and rave at close of day;
Rage, rage against the dying of the light.

[Last stanza:] And you, my father, there on the sad height,
Curse, bless, me now with your fierce tears, I pray.
Do not go gentle into that good night.
Rage, rage against the dying of the light.

From *Do not go gentle into that good night* by Dylan Thomas, copyright © 1951, From *The Poems of Dylan Thomas,* Copyright © 1937-1967 the Trustees for the Copyrights of Dylan Thomas. Copyright © 1938-1971 New Directions Publishing Corp.

27. Which is true of all three excerpted poems?
    a. They are all ballads.
    b. They are all sonnets.
    c. They are all villanelles.
    d. They are all different forms.

28. Which of the excerpted poems focus on the nature of reality vs. the imagination?
    a. The second and third
    b. The first and second
    c. The first and third
    d. All three

29. Which of the excerpted poems deal(s) directly with the subject of death?
    a. The third
    b. The second and third
    c. The first and third
    d. All three

Copyright © Mometrix Media. You have been licensed one copy of this document for personal use only. Any other reproduction or redistribution is strictly prohibited. All rights reserved.

Questions 30-35 refer to the following poem:

> I like to see it lap the Miles —
> And lick the Valleys up —
> And stop to feed itself at Tanks —
> And then — prodigious step
>
> Around a pile of Mountains —
> And supercilious peer
> In Shanties — by the sides of Roads –
> And then a Quarry pare
>
> To fit its Ribs
> And crawl between
> Complaining all the while
> In horrid — hooting stanza —
> Then chase itself down Hill —
>
> And neigh like Boanerges —
> Then — punctual as a Star
> Stop — docile and omnipotent
> At its own stable door —

30. This poem describes which of the following?
    a. An aristocratic thoroughbred horse
    b. The recently invented railroad train
    c. An incredible mythological monster
    d. The subject cannot be determined

31. This poem was written around the time of...
    a. The American Revolution.
    b. The French Revolution.
    c. The War of 1812.
    d. The Civil War.

32. An amazing feat in this poem is that the structure of the subject described is mirrored in the poem's...
    a. Vocabulary.
    b. Rhythms.
    c. Syntax.
    d. Tone.

33. The adjectives "docile and omnipotent" in the penultimate line were chosen because they are...
    a. Synonymous.
    b. Nonsensical.
    c. Mechanical.
    d. Contrasting.

Copyright © Mometrix Media. You have been licensed one copy of this document for personal use only. Any other reproduction or redistribution is strictly prohibited. All rights reserved.

34. What is the source of the phrase "And neigh like Boanerges" in the last stanza?
    a. A Greek myth about a creature that inhabits Hades (the underworld)
    b. A New Testament reference to a fiery, strong-voiced preacher/orator
    c. An Old Testament reference to a wrathful prophet seeking vengeance
    d. A Roman name for a mythological animal that lived within a labyrinth

35. This poet famously used dashes for _____ and capitals for _____.
    a. Punctuation; honor
    b. Separation; names
    c. Prosody; emphasis
    d. Continuity; names

Questions 36-38 refer to the following poem:
            Because I could not stop for Death —
            He kindly stopped for me —
            The Carriage held but just Ourselves —
            And Immortality.

            We slowly drove — He knew no haste
            And I had put away
            My labor and my leisure too,
            For His Civility —
            We passed the School, where Children strove
            At Recess — in the Ring —
            We passed the Fields of Gazing Grain —
            We passed the Setting Sun —

            Or rather — He passed Us —
            The Dews drew quivering and chill —
            For only Gossamer, my Gown —
            My Tippet — only Tulle —

            We paused before a House that seemed
            A Swelling of the Ground —
            The Roof was scarcely visible —
            The Cornice — in the Ground —

            Since then — 'tis Centuries — and yet
            Feels shorter than the Day
            I first surmised the Horses' Heads
            Were toward Eternity —

36. The descriptions of Death, of the "Fields of Gazing Grain," and of the setting sun all employ which literary device?
    a. Analogy
    b. Hyperbole
    c. Alliteration
    d. Personification

Copyright © Mometrix Media. You have been licensed one copy of this document for personal use only. Any other reproduction or redistribution is strictly prohibited. All rights reserved.

37. Irrespective of its topic, the tone of this poem would best be described as...
    a. Serious, grave, and portentously dark
    b. Detached, alienated, and numb of feeling
    c. Lighthearted, humorous, and gently ironic
    d. Frantic, agitated, and with a frenzy of fear

38. What is described in the fifth stanza?
    a. A home
    b. A grave
    c. A church
    d. A school

39. A distinguishing feature of the form known as haiku is...
    a. 5/7/5 syllables per line
    b. An ABA rhyme scheme
    c. Perfectly regular meter
    d. Lengthy epic narratives

40. Which of the following accurately identifies *The Diary of a Young Girl* by Anne Frank?
    a. A fictional novel of a 1920s American debutante's diary
    b. A non-fictional Dutch journal influenced by World War II
    c. A long, episodic poem depicting childhood schizophrenia
    d. A British record documenting a sociological diary project

Question 41 refers to the following excerpt:
> When I got to camp I warn't feeling very brash, there warn't much sand in my craw; but I says, this ain't no time to be fooling around. So I got all my traps into my canoe again so as to have them out of sight, and I put out the fire and scattered the ashes around to look like an old last-year's camp, and then clumb a tree.

41. This passage is taken from which of the following?
    a. *The Mysterious Stranger*
    b. *The Adventures of Tom Sawyer*
    c. *The Adventures of Huckleberry Finn*
    d. *The Prince and the Pauper*

42. Which of the following statements is most accurate regarding the characters of Drouet and Hurstwood in Theodore Dreiser's novel *Sister Carrie*?
    a. Drouet has the awareness to be decent, but he lacks the morality.
    b. Hurstwood has the morality, but not the awareness, for decency.
    c. Only one of these characters is representative of the middle class.
    d. Drouet is morally decent but unaware; Hurstwood is the opposite.

Questions 43- 45 refer to the following excerpt:
> I bequeath myself to the dirt to grow from the grass I love,
> If you want me again look for me under your boot-soles.

Copyright © Mometrix Media. You have been licensed one copy of this document for personal use only. Any other reproduction or redistribution is strictly prohibited. All rights reserved.

43. What is the title of the poem from which this is taken?
   a. *To You*
   b. *Thou Reader*
   c. *Song of Myself*
   d. *One's-Self I Sing*

44. Which of the following is the best interpretation of the excerpted lines?
   a. The poet means that he will be dead and buried in the future.
   b. The poet means he is one with and an integral part of nature.
   c. The poet means the person addressed is above him in station.
   d. The poet means the recipient stepped on/walked all over him.

45. The excerpted work was published in which century?
   a. 19th
   b. 20th
   c. 18th
   d. 21st

Questions 46-50 refer to the following excerpts:
   I should have been a pair of ragged claws
   Scuttling across the floors of silent seas.

   Shall I part my hair behind? Do I dare to eat a peach?
   I shall wear white flannel trousers, and walk upon the beach.
   I have heard the mermaids singing, each to each.

   I do not think that they will sing to me.

   We have lingered in the chambers of the sea
   By sea-girls wreathed with seaweed red and brown
   Till human voices wake us, and we drown.

46. What is the title of the work from which these excerpts are taken?
   a. *The Waste Land*
   b. *The Love Song of J. Alfred Prufrock*
   c. *Notes Toward the Definition of Culture*
   d. *The Hollow Men*

47. The second excerpt is speaking about…
   a. Indecision.
   b. A vacation.
   c. Mortality.
   d. Drowning.

48. Which of the following is/are the best interpretation(s) of the meaning in the first excerpt?
   a. The speaker's existence is as significant as the life of a crab.
   b. The speaker loves the sea and wishes he could live under it.
   c. The scavenger can create beauty by reconstructing garbage.
   d. The answers choices in (A) and (C) are valid interpretations.

- 111 -

Copyright © Mometrix Media. You have been licensed one copy of this document for personal use only. Any other reproduction or redistribution is strictly prohibited. All rights reserved.

49. Why does the speaker say, "I do not think that they will sing to me"?
    a. Because he feels the despair of existence.
    b. Because he is becoming deaf with old age.
    c. Because he knows mermaids are not real.
    d. Because he is on the beach, not in the sea.

50. Which of the following is the best interpretation of the final line?
    a. Mermaids protect us from drowning; humans ruin it.
    b. The dream of art is ruined by the intrusion of reality.
    c. Dreaming of mermaids is part of death by drowning.
    d. Mermaids bewitch us from knowing that we drown.

51. Which of Chaucer's *Canterbury Tales* is an example of the literary form known as the fabliau?
    a. *The Physician's Tale*
    b. *The Wife of Bath's Tale*
    c. *The Miller's Tale*
    d. *The Pardoner's Tale*

52. Which of the following pairs are NOT both written in the form of frame tales?
    a. *The Canterbury Tales* by Geoffrey Chaucer and *The Decameron* by Giovanni Bocaccio
    b. The *Mahabharata* by Veda Vyasa and *The Parlement of Foules* by Geoffrey Chaucer
    c. *Frankenstein* by Mary W. Shelley and *Wuthering Heights* by Emily Brontë
    d. *The Great Gatsby* by F. Scott Fitzgerald and *To the Lighthouse* by Virginia Woolf

53. Which of the following works was the first ever published in vernacular Italian?
    a. *De re publica (On the Republic)* by Marcus Tullius Cicero
    b. *Il Decameron (The Decameron)* by Giovanni Bocaccio
    c. *La Divina Commedia (The Divine Comedy)* by Dante Alighieri
    d. *Il Nome della Rosa (The Name of the Rose)* by Umberto Eco

Questions 54-56 are based on the following poem:
Leda and the Swan

A sudden blow: the great wings beating still
Above the staggering girl, her thighs caressed
By the dark webs, her nape caught in his bill,
He holds her helpless breast upon his breast.

How can those terrified vague fingers push
The feathered glory from her loosening thighs?
And how can body, laid in that white rush,
But feel the strange heart beating where it lies?

A shudder in the loins engenders there
The broken wall, the burning roof and tower
And Agamemnon dead.

Being so caught up,

- 112 -

Copyright © Mometrix Media. You have been licensed one copy of this document for personal use only. Any other reproduction or redistribution is strictly prohibited. All rights reserved.

So mastered by the brute blood of the air,
Did she put on his knowledge with his power
Before the indifferent beak could let her drop?

William Butler Yeats, 1923

54. "The broken wall, the burning roof and tower/And Agamemnon dead" refer to…
    a. The Punic Wars.
    b. The Trojan War.
    c. The Peloponnesian War.
    d. A murder but no war.

55. In what form is this poem?
    a. A sonnet
    b. Villanelle
    c. Free verse
    d. A sestina

56. The poet's final question best suggests which of the following ideas?
    a. Humans get godlike knowledge and power from the gods.
    b. Human knowledge and power are necessarily incomplete.
    c. Humans in ancient Greece interacted differently with gods.
    d. Humans conceiving from gods got power, not knowledge.

57. In the Three Cueing Systems model of word recognition in reading instruction, which system most relates to how words are assembled into meaningful language?
    a. Phonological
    b. Semantic
    c. Syntactic
    d. Pragmatic

58. In the word-recognition model of the Three Cueing Systems used in teaching reading, which of the following is most associated with the meanings of words?
    a. Using pragmatic cues
    b. Phonological system
    c. The syntactic system
    d. The semantic system

59. In the model known in reading instruction as the Three Cueing Systems, which of these relate most to how sounds are used to communicate meaning?
    a. Syntactic cues
    b. Semantic cues
    c. Phonological cues
    d. Pragmatic cues

- 113 -

Copyright © Mometrix Media. You have been licensed one copy of this document for personal use only. Any other reproduction or redistribution is strictly prohibited. All rights reserved.

60. In reading instruction, the Three Cueing Systems is one model used. Which of the following represent a valid reading strategy that is NOT a system in the Three Cueing Systems model?
    a. Syntactic cues
    b. Pragmatic cues
    c. Semantic cues
    d. Phonological cues

61. Relative to reading, we should teach students to activate their prior knowledge at which time(s)?
    a. Before reading
    b. During reading
    c. After reading
    d. All of the above

62. Which choice most appropriately fills the blanks in this statement? "Teaching children which thinking strategies are used by _____ and helping them use those strategies _____ creates the core of teaching reading." (*Mosaic of Thought*, Keene and Zimmerman, 1997)
    a. Reading teachers; in different ways
    b. Beginning students; with assistance
    c. Proficient readers; independently
    d. Published writers; more creatively

63. Scholars have identified three kinds of major connections that students make when reading: connecting text to self, text to the world, and text to text. Which of the following student statements best reflect(s) the connection of text to the world?
    a. "These mythic gods have more power, but feel and act like humans."
    b. "This novel is set during a period I learned about in my history class."
    c. "I can relate to how the main character felt about being controlled."
    d. All three statements equally reflect connection of text to the world.

64. When students are taught to use effective reading comprehension strategies, they not only achieve deeper understanding, they also learn to think about how they think when reading. This is known as...
    a. Schemata.
    b. Scaffolding.
    c. Metacognition.
    d. Metamorphosis.

65. Activity settings (Tharp and Gallimore, 1988) are aspects of the sociocultural context that affect how students learn and read. Of five activity settings, one is participant identity, or who the students are. Of the other four, which is most related to motivation?
    a. When the activity is done
    b. Why the activity is done
    c. Where the activity is done
    d. How the activity is done

Copyright © Mometrix Media. You have been licensed one copy of this document for personal use only. Any other reproduction or redistribution is strictly prohibited. All rights reserved.

66. Some experts maintain that teaching reading comprehension entails not just the application of skills, but the process of actively constructing meaning. This process they describe as *interactive, strategic,* and *adaptable.* Which of the following best defines the *interactive* aspect of this process?
    a. The process involves the text, the reader, and the context in which reading occurs.
    b. The process involves readers' using a variety of strategies in constructing meaning.
    c. The process involves readers' changing their strategies to read different text types.
    d. The process involves changing strategies according to different reasons for reading.

67. In first-language (L1) and second-language (L2) acquisition, which of the following is true about developmental stages?
    a. L2 learners do not undergo the first stage called the Silent Period as L1 learners do.
    b. L2 learners undergo all stages, but are urged to skip the first stage more than in L1s.
    c. L2 learners do not undergo the second stage of Formulaic Speech as L1 learners do.
    d. L2 learners undergo the third stage of Structural and Semantic Simplifications later.

68. Which statement is most accurate about social contexts of L1 and L2 acquisition?
    a. Both L1 and L2 learning can occur in equally varied natural and educational contexts.
    b. L1s are only learned in natural contexts, while L2s are learned in educational contexts.
    c. Variations in L2 proficiency can result from the different contexts of learning the L2s.
    d. L2s are not a speaker's natural language and so are never learned in natural contexts.

69. Which of the following is found to be unique to second-language learning?
    a. Zone of proximal development
    b. The critical period hypothesis
    c. Marked/unmarked features
    d. The process of fossilization

70. An ESL student whose L1 is Chinese tends to omit plural endings and articles before nouns. Of the following, which is the best explanation for these errors?
    a. The student has not yet learned these English grammatical forms.
    b. Omission avoids having to choose among irregular English forms.
    c. Incompatible nature and rules of the L1 are transferring to the L2.
    d. The student does not understand how the L1 and L2 forms relate.

71. Which of the following is the most accurate characterization of dialects?
    a. They are non-standard versions of any language.
    b. They are often seen as less socially acceptable.
    c. They include linguistic features that are incorrect.
    d. They indicate poor/incomplete language learning.

72. Of the following, which statement is correct regarding Standard English?
    a. The formal Standard English applies to written language.
    b. Standard English is universal in English-speaking nations.
    c. Speech communities use the Standard English of writing.
    d. The Standard English construct does not include dialects.

Copyright © Mometrix Media. You have been licensed one copy of this document for personal use only. Any other reproduction or redistribution is strictly prohibited. All rights reserved.

73. The Great Vowel Shift occurred during which time span?
    a. 10th to 13th centuries
    b. 12th to 15th centuries
    c. 15th to 18th centuries
    d. 16th to 19th centuries

74. The Great Vowel Shift caused the pronunciation of long vowels in English to shift:
    a. Farther back.
    b. Higher up.
    c. Lower down.
    d. Farther front.

75. Of the following authors, whose English existed *during* the Great Vowel Shift?
    a. William Shakespeare
    b. Geoffrey Chaucer
    c. Emily Dickinson
    d. The Pearl Poet

76. Linguists generally analyze the Great Vowel Shift as having transpired in _____ steps.
    a. Ten
    b. Eight
    c. Six
    d. Four

77. Which of the following areas has been affected in the long term by the Great Vowel Shift?
    a. Written spelling
    b. Teaching reading
    c. Text comprehension
    d. All the above

78. The source of the silent *b* in the English word *debt* was originally...
    a. A Middle English word.
    b. A voiced Old English *b*.
    c. From Latin etymology.
    d. The Greek etymology.

79. We are familiar with the modern English meanings of the word "disaster." But in the 16th century, this word meant...
    a. Catastrophe.
    b. Star-crossed.
    c. A misfortune.
    d. Unflowerlike.

80. The English word "salary" has a 2,000-year-old etymology to a word meaning...
    a. Salt.
    b. Celery.
    c. Money.
    d. Earnings.

Copyright © Mometrix Media. You have been licensed one copy of this document for personal use only. Any other reproduction or redistribution is strictly prohibited. All rights reserved.

81. Which of the following is an example of a portmanteau?
    a. Fax
    b. Brunch
    c. Babysitter
    d. Saxophone

82. The English language word "quark" is an example of the result of which linguistic process?
    a. Blending
    b. Conversion
    c. Neologisms
    d. Onomatopoeia

83. The questions in this test can give you an idea of what kinds of questions you might find on the actual test; however, they are not duplicates of the actual test questions, which cover the same knowledge but may differ somewhat in form and content.
The preceding sentence is which of the following sentence types?
    a. Simple
    b. Complex
    c. Compound
    d. Compound-complex

84. Doctors perform surgery and the patient dies. A doctor reporting this says the surgery had a "negative patient outcome." This is *best* identified as an example of...
    a. Jargon.
    b. Ambiguity.
    c. Euphemism.
    d. Connotation.

85. Which of the following is NOT typically categorized as a prewriting process?
    a. Planning
    b. Reflection
    c. Visualization
    d. Brainstorming

86. Which of the following correctly represents the sequence of stages or steps in the writing process?
    a. Prewriting, drafting, revising, editing, publishing
    b. Prewriting, drafting, editing, publishing, revising
    c. Prewriting, editing, drafting, revising, publishing
    d. Prewriting, drafting, editing, revising, publishing

87. Research has found which of the following outcomes occur for students via revision and rewriting?
    a. Students only correct their mechanical errors in revisions.
    b. Students often incorporate new ideas when they rewrite.
    c. Students retain their original writing goals during revision.
    d. Students' planning in prewriting is unaffected in rewriting.

Copyright © Mometrix Media. You have been licensed one copy of this document for personal use only. Any other reproduction or redistribution is strictly prohibited. All rights reserved.

88. Which of the following have researchers learned about children's writing?
   a. Children's writing reflects as much knowledge as they have on any given topic.
   b. Children stop writing when they have run out of things they want to articulate.
   c. Children stop writing when they cannot adequately articulate their knowledge.
   d. Children's writing commonly covers more than they actually know about a topic.

89. Arthur writes a paper. One classmate identifies ideas and words that resonated with her when she read it. Another describes how reading the paper changed his thinking. A third asks Arthur some questions about what he meant by certain statements in the paper. A fourth suggests a portion of the paper that needs more supporting information. This description is most typical of...
   a. A portfolio assessment.
   b. A holistic scoring.
   c. A scoring rubric.
   d. A peer review.

90. Which of the following is the best definition of Information Literacy?
   a. It is the set of skills required for reading and comprehending different information.
   b. It is the cognitive skill set necessary to amass a comprehensive base of knowledge.
   c. It is the skill set required for the finding, retrieval, analysis, and use of information.
   d. It is the set of skills necessary for effectively communicating information to others.

91. What is the primary reason the early 21st century has been referred to as the Information Age?
   a. Because educational and governmental agencies require greater information
   b. Because there are more sources and outputs of information than ever before
   c. Because students can now learn all they need to know in four years of college
   d. Because college students today are much more interested in new information

92. Of the following statements, which adheres to Information Literacy standards?
   a. Students accessing information must critically evaluate it and its sources before using it.
   b. Students accessing information can ascertain how much of it they need after they find it.
   c. Students accessing information efficiently sacrifice broader scope and incidental learning.
   d. Students accessing information ethically must eschew using it to attain specific purposes.

93. According to the MLA system for documenting sources in literature, which of the following typically combines signal phrases and parenthetical references?
   a. An MLA list of the works cited
   b. MLA in-text citations in a paper
   c. Adding MLA information notes
   d. All of the above

Copyright © Mometrix Media. You have been licensed one copy of this document for personal use only. Any other reproduction or redistribution is strictly prohibited. All rights reserved.

94. According to MLA guidelines for writing research papers, which of the following is correct regarding citations of Web sources if you cannot immediately see the name of a source's author?

a. Assume the author is not named, as this is a common occurrence on the Web.
b. Do not name an agency or corporation as author if it is the sponsor of the source.
c. Author names are often on websites, but need additional looking to discover.
d. It is not permissible to cite the book or article title in lieu of an author's name.

95. When making in-text citations in a research paper, which of the following reflects MLA guidelines for citing Web sources with regard to page numbers?

a. If a Web source does not include pagination, you are advised to avoid citing that source.
b. If page numbers appear on a printout from a website, include these numbers in citations.
c. In-text citations of online sources in research papers should never include page numbers.
d. If the Web source is a PDF file, it is recommended to cite page numbers in your citations.

96. The MLA guidelines for citing multiple authors of the same source in the in-text citations of a research paper are to use the first author's name and "et al" for the other(s) in the case of...

a. More than one author.
b. Two or three authors.
c. Three or more authors.
d. Four or more authors.

97. A movie review is one example of what type and purpose of writing?

a. Narration
b. Description
c. Persuasion
d. Exposition

98. Of the following writing types and purposes, which one can often be the hardest to write?

a. Expository
b. Persuasive
c. Descriptive
d. Narrative

99. Which of the following do *The Adventures of Huckleberry Finn* by Mark Twain, *The Diary of a Young Girl* by Anne Frank, and *The Fall of the House of Usher* by Edgar Allan Poe have in common?

a. They are all examples of the narrative type and purpose of writing.
b. They are all examples of a purely descriptive writing type/purpose.
c. They are all examples of works of primarily expository writing type.
d. They are all examples of writing of the persuasive type and purpose.

Copyright © Mometrix Media. You have been licensed one copy of this document for personal use only. Any other reproduction or redistribution is strictly prohibited. All rights reserved.

100. When you have a writing assignment, which of the following is true about your reader audience?
    a. You need not identify the audience because it is the assigning teacher.
    b. You should consider how your readers are likely to use what you write.
    c. You should know your writing purpose more than a reader's purposes.
    d. You are overthinking to wonder about readers' likely attitude/reaction.

101. Which statement is correct regarding the relationship of your audience profile to the decisions you make in completing a writing assignment?
    a. How much time you spend on research is unrelated to your audience.
    b. Your audience does not influence how much information you include.
    c. The writing style, tone and wording you use depend on your audience.
    d. How you organize information depends on structure, not on audience.

102. Which of the following statements is most accurate about writing the introduction to an essay or paper?
    a. The introduction should use the technique of starting essays with dictionary definitions.
    b. The introduction should leave the most attention-getting material for later in the work.
    c. The introduction should move from the focused and specific to the broad and general.
    d. The introduction should move from the broad and general to the focused and specific.

103. When writing a paper or essay, which of these parts of the introduction should come first?
    a. Your thesis statement for the paper or essay
    b Background on the essay or paper's purpose
    c. Something original to engage reader attention
    d. A "road map" of how you will present the thesis

104. Which of the following is true about effective ways to open the introduction of an essay or paper?
    a. You should summarize your position in your own words, not by quoting another.
    b. Citing a statistic related to the topic that is surprising can grab readers' attention.
    c. Opening with a story or anecdote is counter to the purposes of an essay or paper.
    d. Asking rhetorical questions to open an essay or paper will only frustrate readers.

105. Which of the following is the *worst* way to view the conclusion of an essay or paper you write?
    a. As a means of including all material that would not fit elsewhere
    b. As a means of reiterating the thesis you stated in the introduction
    c. As a means of synthesizing and/or summarizing your main points
    d. As a means of clarifying the context of your discussion/argument

106. In writing, _____ is the overall written expression of the writer's attitude, and _____ is the individual way in which the writer expresses the former.
    a. Voice; tone
    b. Tone; voice
    c. Style; tone
    d. Voice; style

Copyright © Mometrix Media. You have been licensed one copy of this document for personal use only. Any other reproduction or redistribution is strictly prohibited. All rights reserved.

107. _____ is the overall choice of language you make for your writing; _____ are the specific words from a given discipline that you use when writing within or about that discipline.
    a. Vocabulary; diction
    b. Vocabulary; jargon
    c. Diction; vocabulary
    d. Style; vocabulary

108. Which of the following is most accurate regarding writing style?
    a. The kind of diction you use does not affect style.
    b. You add style later to give your writing personality.
    c. Style is unrelated to your control of your content.
    d. Your purpose for writing guides your writing style.

109. When considering strategies for writing assignments, it helps to know the cognitive (or learning) objective(s) your teacher is aiming to meet with an assignment. If the assignment asks you to "describe," "explain," "summarize," "restate," "classify," or "review" some material you read, what is the cognitive objective?
    a. Knowledge recall
    b. Application
    c. Comprehension
    d. Evaluation

110. Your writing assignment asks you to do things like "organize," "plan," "formulate," "assemble," "compose," "construct," and/or "arrange" some material you have read and/or learned. Which of the following cognitive (learning) objectives is the teacher aiming to meet with this assignment?
    a. Analysis
    b. Synthesis
    c. Evaluation
    d. Application

111. Which of the following processes used in writing is the most complex?
    a. Evaluation
    b. Application
    c. Comprehension
    d. Knowledge recall

112. Of the following learning and writing processes, which strategy/strategies is (or are) the most commonly used forms of analysis in college-level writing?
    a. Comparing and contrasting
    b. Explaining cause and effect
    c. Giving support to an opinion
    d. Options A and B

Copyright © Mometrix Media. You have been licensed one copy of this document for personal use only. Any other reproduction or redistribution is strictly prohibited. All rights reserved.

113. Which of the following writing strategies is (or are) among the most commonly used forms of synthesis in college-level writing?
    a. Explaining cause and effect
    b. Comparing and contrasting
    c. Proposing a solution
    d. Using persuasion

114. Among writing projects that can develop from research, which of the following discourse aims is represented by a white paper, an opinion survey, an annotated bibliography, and a problem solution?
    a. Expressive
    b. Exploratory
    c. Informative
    d. Persuasive

115. This treatise developed from an initial idea about the way a plant develops from a seed. The preceding sentence is an example of which literary device and argument method?
    a. Analogy
    b. Allegory
    c. Allusion
    d. Antithesis

116. In the famous balcony scene of William Shakespeare's *Romeo and Juliet,* Romeo says:

> But soft! What light through yonder window breaks?
> It is the east, and Juliet is the sun.
> Arise, fair sun, and kill the envious moon,
> Who is already sick and pale with grief,
> That thou her maid art far more fair than she:
> Be not her maid, since she is envious;
> Her vestal livery is but sick and green
> And none but fools do wear it; cast it off.

The literary device Shakespeare used here is also used in all *but* which of the following?
    a. T. S. Eliot's description of the fog in *The Love Song of J. Alfred Prufrock* (1915)
    b. Robert Frost's entire poem *The Road Not Taken* (1916)
    c. Carl Sandburg's whole short poem *Fog* (1916)
    d. All of these use the same device as Shakespeare

117. Of the following sentences, which one appeals to emotion?
    a. It is dangerous to use a cell phone while driving because you steer one-handed.
    b. Statistics of greater accident risk show cell-phone use while driving is dangerous.
    c. It is really stupid to use a cell phone when you drive because it is so dangerous.
    d. Many state laws ban cell-phone use when driving due to data on more accidents.

118. Which of the following gives an example of a fallacy of inconsistency?
    a. "There are exceptions to all general statements."
    b. "Please pass me; my parents will be upset if I fail."
    c. "He is guilty: there is no evidence he is innocent."
    d. "Have you stopped cheating on your assignments?"

Copyright © Mometrix Media. You have been licensed one copy of this document for personal use only. Any other reproduction or redistribution is strictly prohibited. All rights reserved.

119. In the 1984 comedy movie *All of Me,* a character from another country, who has no experience with either telephones or flush toilets, flushes a toilet and then a phone rings. He flushes again and the phone rings again. After this occurs several times, the character concludes that pulling the toilet's flush handle causes the ringing. This is an example of which type of cognitive bias?
    a. An above-average effect
    b. A clustering illusion
    c. A confirmation bias
    d. A framing bias

120. Archie says, "Asian people are all terrible drivers." The *most precise* definition of this statement is…
    a. A stereotype.
    b. An inference.
    c. An assumption.
    d. A generalization.

Copyright © Mometrix Media. You have been licensed one copy of this document for personal use only. Any other reproduction or redistribution is strictly prohibited. All rights reserved.

Answers and Explanations

1. B: This is the opening sentence of James Joyce's last novel, *Finnegans Wake* (Copyright © 1939 by James Joyce, renewed George Joyce and Lucia Joyce, 1967; Great Britain: Faber and Faber Ltd., 1939; USA: Viking Penguin, Inc., 1939; Viking Compass Edition 1959; Reprinted 1961-1975; Published in Penguin Books 1976). He published *Ulysses* (A) previously, in 1922; and *A Portrait of the Artist as a Young Man* (D) even earlier, in 1916. *Adventures in the Skin Trade* (C) was not written by Joyce but by Dylan Thomas (1938).

2. D: Joyce used the word "vicus" because it means "vicinity" (A) or "lane" in Latin; to refer to Vico Way (B), the name of the shore road running alongside of Dublin Bay; and to allude to Giambattista Vico (C), an Italian philosopher living from 1688-1744 who espoused the cyclic theory of history, a theme in Joyce's novel.

3. C: The lower-case initial letter of the first word was not an error (D). It did not continue Joyce's previous novel (B). And he did not use it to make the opening stand out as different to the reader (A). Rather, it is uncapitalized to show that it completes the book's last sentence fragment, "A way a lone a last a loved a long the—". By having the end of the book be completed and continued only by the beginning, Joyce embodied the cyclical nature of history and of the novel within its sentence structure.

4. A: Joyce is famous for using stream of consciousness in his novels, as he did in *Ulysses* and *Finnegans Wake*. The unreliable narrator (B) is a technique used often in murder mysteries, as by Edgar Allan Poe in *The Tell-Tale Heart, The Cask of the Amontillado* and many other stories and by Agatha Christie in *The Murder of Roger Ackroyd*. Joyce is not famous for using it. He used third-person narration and often included soliloquies, but is not famous for using first-person narration (C. An example of the author surrogate (D) is Socrates in Plato's works; Joyce is not known for using this technique.

5. B: The author of the excerpted poem, *To His Coy Mistress,* is Andrew Marvell. Marvell, Donne (A), Herbert (C), and Vaughan (D) were all members of a group of mainly 17th-century poets known as the Metaphysical Poets for their common time period, themes, content, and style.

6. A: Carpe diem is Latin for "seize the day." This tradition reflects the theme that time flies and that life is fleeting, and thus we should take advantage of the present moment. The tradition of classicism (B) reflects ancient Greek and Roman ideals of beauty and principles of form and discipline (as opposed to Romanticism's principles of emotional impact), as reflected in the works of Alexander Pope and John Dryden. The cinquain (C) is a five-line type of poem in which line 1 is a one-word title, line 2 contains two words describing the title, line 3 has three words telling the action, line 4 contains four words expressing the feeling, and line 5 reverts back to one word that recalls the title. The conceit (D) type of poetry uses a metaphor, simile, or image comparing two very dissimilar things, such as Shakespeare's Sonnet # 18, also known as *Shall I compare thee to a summer's day?*

7. D: Tetrameter means four beats per line, which is the meter of the rhymed couplets in this poem. Pentameter (A) means five beats per line. Heptameter (B) means seven beats per line. Hexameter (C) means six beats per line. Also, beats are only the stressed syllables, not total syllables.

Copyright © Mometrix Media. You have been licensed one copy of this document for personal use only. Any other reproduction or redistribution is strictly prohibited. All rights reserved.

8. C: *The Emperor of Ice-Cream* was written by Wallace Stevens in 1922. The style of the excerpted stanza is typical of modern poetry and does not reflect the conventions of 17th-century (A), 18th-century (D), or 19th-century (B) poems.

9. A: "In kitchen cups concupiscent curds" makes use of alliteration, the repetition of the same initial sound and/or letter in adjoining or nearby words—in this case, the sound /k/ and letter "c." Hyperbole (B) is the device of exaggeration. Onomatopoeia (C) is the device of words sounding like what they mean (for example, "the clang of the bell" or "the gun went bang"). Metonymy (D) is the device of referring to a noun by an associated thing (using "the White House" to mean the U.S. government, or "Hollywood" to mean the American film and television industry).

10. C: Plato's *Dialogues* expound the philosophy of Socrates, including the concept that the mortal life of humanity and the world of the human senses and perception are really the illusion, while the eternal life of the divine and the world of the ideal are really the reality, rather than vice versa. Stevens refers to this concept with "Let be be finale of seem"—meaning that "seem" is what we perceive, and is followed by "be," which is the reality found after life—as the first stanza's boys bringing flowers is continued in the second (final) stanza with references to shrouding a dead woman's body. A main theme in option A is the creation of the world; an allegorical journey through Hell, Purgatory, and Heaven in choice B; and, in option D, a journey home from war, which is also an allegory for every man's life journey.

11. B: The author, Jonathan Swift, wrote the excerpted piece, *A Modest Proposal,* as a satire. He was not literally suggesting that children be cooked and eaten, but lampooning the way the British looked down on the Irish with his "proposal" as an ironic example of a "solution" to the poverty and overpopulation in Ireland. Persuasion (A) is a form of argument to sway the reader rather than make fun of something. Exposition (C) is also a straightforward method of giving information. Bathos (D) is a literary mood of overstated emotion that moves suddenly from the sublime to the ridiculous or pedestrian to create an anticlimactic effect.

12. C: *A Modest Proposal* was published in 1729, i.e., the 18th century. It does not have the modern style of the 20th (A) century. The bulk of Swift's work was published in the 1700s, with several pieces published in the late 1690s (D)—but not this one. Swift died in 1745 and even *A Journal to Stella,* published posthumously, was published in 1766, so the 19th (B) century is incorrect.

13. D: Jonathan Swift, author of the excerpted satirical essay *A Modest Proposal,* also wrote *Gulliver's Travels* (1726, 1735), a novel satirizing human behavior and parodying the travel genre. *The Canterbury Tales* (A) were written by Geoffrey Chaucer in the 14th century. *The Faerie Queene* (B) was written by Edmund Spenser in the 16th century. *Paradise Lost* (C) was written by John Milton in the 17th century.

14. D: Hughes uses (extended) metaphor by describing the concrete presence of an animal, a fox, to represent the abstract entity of an inspiration for the writer to produce poetry. From beyond the blank window, starless sky, and dark forest, the fox, as a totem for the writer's imagination, approaches from without to inspire, its pawprints in the snow symbolizing print appearing on the blank page. Foreshadowing (A) is the literary device of hinting earlier in a work at something that will become more apparent later. Irony (B) is the

Copyright © Mometrix Media. You have been licensed one copy of this document for personal use only. Any other reproduction or redistribution is strictly prohibited. All rights reserved.

device of creating a discrepancy between what is expected and what really occurs (verbal, dramatic, or situational irony). Hughes's work is notable for NOT including any overused expressions known as clichés (C).

15. C: The poem describes how the poet is inspired to write, using the fox to embody the thought that enters the poet's mind (hence the title The Thought-Fox). The fox's natural actions (A) are thus symbolic
rather than literal. The poet is not inspired by nature (B); in this poem, he uses an element of nature (the fox) to represent the thought that he receives and writes. The fox's entering "the head" is not a literal attack (D) but a symbolic representation of having or getting that thought.

16. B: The poet's passivity and lack of control over the thought, or content, of his writing can be interpreted from Hughes's separation of the thought, which does not arise from within his head, but approaches symbolically in the form of a fox from outside of his head, his body, and even his house. This separation is emphasized by the description of the Thought-Fox as "Coming about its own business." The poet as passive recipient is further shown in the last stanza, where the fox "...enters the dark hole of the head." This passivity of the artist is further reflected in the last line, "The page is printed," wherein Hughes uses the passive voice to represent the thought/writing process, rather than saying that he himself prints the page.

17. A: This poem is written in free verse, meaning it has no regular rhyme scheme (options B and D) or metrical pattern (choices B and C). There is some partial rhyming, as in the sight rhyme of "snow" and "now" in stanza 3; the near rhymes of "star" with "near" in stanza 2 and "lame" with "come" in stanza 3; the rhymes of "darkness" and "loneliness" in stanza 2, "snow" and "hollow" in stanza 4, and "greenness" with "business" in stanza 5; and the off rhyme of "fox" with "ticks" in the last stanza. However, these are not regular, like the repeated rhymes of an established rhyme scheme. There is also no regular meter or number of beats per line. Hence the overall form of this poem is free verse.

18. C: The bell jar is a metaphor, an implied comparison between two things. A simile (A) is an overtly stated comparison; it would be a simile if she had written "It was *like* a bell jar." An allusion (B) is an implied, indirect, or incidental reference, usually to a real or fictional person, place, or event. Personification (D) or anthropomorphism is attributing human characteristics to non-human animals or things.

19. B: The bell jar is Plath's metaphor for her mental illness. She describes feeling confined, not by reality (A), but by her own depression and its attendant alienated feelings and distorted perceptions. Writer's block (C) was not the bell jar but a symptom of it (her illness), as when she wrote about fearing she would never be able to write again. (Moreover, though Plath did experience inability to write at times and her fear was genuine, she also produced many great poems as well as this novel during and in spite of her illness.) Her references to "stewing in my own sour air," being unable to stir with the "air of the bell jar wadded round me," closed off from the "circulating air," being "blank and stopped as a dead baby," and "the bell jar, with its stifling distortions," do not signify any literal breathing disorder (D), but rather a metaphorical lack of the fresh air of reality and sanity.

20. D: Sylvia Plath underwent a serious breakdown and hospitalization in 1953; she wrote about this experience in *The Bell Jar* around 1961 (published in England in 1963 and

Copyright © Mometrix Media. You have been licensed one copy of this document for personal use only. Any other reproduction or redistribution is strictly prohibited. All rights reserved.

America in 1971.) *The Bell Jar* was Plath's only novel (A). Plath wrote many poems, not a few (C). She did not recover to live a long life or write more novels (B); she committed suicide in 1963, a month after *The Bell Jar*'s London publication. (There is some evidence she intended to have the suicide attempt discovered and be rescued from it. She recounts a number of suicide attempts in *The Bell Jar,* which were either discovered in time or she found she could not complete.) While she wrote other prose pieces early in her career, *The Bell Jar* was, she wrote, "my world… as seen through the distorting lens of a bell jar." Before her death at age 30, she had intended to write a second novel about "…that same world as seen through the eyes of health."

21. B: Shakespeare (1564-1616) wrote during the Renaissance. The Medieval (A) era (also known as the Middle Ages) was earlier, ending before the 16th century (circa 1485), and included authors like Geoffrey Chaucer, Dante Alighieri, the Pearl Poet and author of *Sir Gawain and the Green Knight,* and Sir Thomas Malory. The Restoration (C) period followed the Renaissance, circa 1660-1700, and included authors like John Dryden, who wrote poetry, satire, and criticism. The Enlightenment (D) occurred from 1700-1785, and included the authors Jonathan Swift, Alexander Pope, Dr. Samuel Johnson and James Boswell.

22. A: John Bunyan (1628-1688) was the author of *The Pilgrim's Progress*, a religious allegory, among many other works. William Congreve (B) (1670-1729) wrote *The Way of the World,* originally a play not successful on the theatre stage, but subsequently highly regarded as a literary exemplar of the comedy of manners. Daniel Defoe (C) (circa 1660-1731) is known for *Robinson Crusoe* and other adventure novels, and *The Apparition of Mrs. Veal,* a ghost story later found to be factually based. Samuel Butler (D) (1612-1680), one of the Augustan poets, wrote the burlesque poem *Hudibras.*

23. B: This is the first stanza of *The Passionate Shepherd to His Love* by Christopher Marlowe (1564-1593). Andrew Marvell (A) also included poems on pastoral themes in his oeuvre, including *The Garden*; however, he lived later (1621-1678) than Marlowe and was one of the Metaphysical Poets. Sir Walter Raleigh (C) was more contemporary (1552-1618) with Marlowe and wrote *The Nymph's Reply to the Shepherd,* among others. William Shakespeare (D) was a contemporary (1564-1616) of Raleigh and Marlowe and also included pastoral themes in his songs and sonnets, including *Shall I compare thee to a summer's day?*

24. C: The rhyme scheme of this stanza, and the rest of the poem, is AABB: The second line rhymes with the first, and the fourth line rhymes with the third. This use of rhyming couplets was popular in the poetry of the time.

25. D: All of the above. The legend of Faust, who sold his soul to the devil in exchange for knowledge (echoing Adam and Eve's fall from grace in Eden caused by their desire for knowledge), has been popular throughout the various literary eras. Marlowe (A) wrote *Dr. Faustus* near the end of the 1500s. Goethe (B) wrote his German dramatic masterpiece *Faust* in the 19th century. Thomas Mann (C), also German, wrote the novel *Doktor Faustus* in the 20th century. In addition to literary works, the contemporary musician Randy Newman composed the musical *Randy Newman's Faust* in 1993.

26. D: None of the above. These are all titles of poems written by Pope. *An Essay on Criticism* (A) is a didactic poem discussing literary theory, modeled after the style, language, and tone of the ancient Roman poet Horace. *The Rape of the Lock* (B) is a satirical poem, like *The Dunciad* and many others; Pope became famous for his satires. *The Universal Prayer* (C) is

Copyright © Mometrix Media. You have been licensed one copy of this document for personal use only. Any other reproduction or redistribution is strictly prohibited. All rights reserved.

also a poem from Pope's *Moral Essays,* stating his beliefs. Pope wrote in a variety of styles on diverse subjects, including romantic, philosophical, political, pastoral, and others as well as satires. He achieved great rhythmic and linguistic diversity among these, but they were all poems; Pope's fame is as a poet.

27. C: The poems excerpted are all villanelles, not different forms (D). The villanelle has nineteen lines with five tercets (three-line stanzas) and an ending quatrain (four-line stanza); alternating repetition of the first stanza's first and third lines in each subsequent stanza's last line; and then the repetition of both those lines, comprising the refrain, at the end of the last stanza. These excerpts are not in ballad (A) form, which often uses quatrains, and rhymes either all alternating lines or second and fourth lines. (A famous example is *The Rime of the Ancient Mariner* by Samuel Taylor Coleridge.) Sonnet (B) form also differs from villanelle form. The Petrarchan sonnet has 14 lines, with a major shift in thinking or *volta* between the octave and sestet. The Shakespearean sonnet's 14 lines are three quatrains with ABAB/CDCD/EFEF rhymes and ending with a pivotal GG couplet. Villanelles typically have ABA rhyme schemes. Sonnets also lack the repetition characteristic of villanelles.

28. B: The first poem excerpted, *The Waking* by Theodore Roethke, is a meditation on the nature of waking reality vs. dreaming imagination and which is which; life vs. death, mortality vs. immortality, process/journey vs. product/destination, world vs. self; the constancy of change; and the inability to control or even understand the mysteries of life, nature, and eternity. The second poem excerpted, *Mad Girl's Love Song* by Sylvia Plath, also contemplates the nature of reality vs. imagination via the existentialist argument that we construct and destroy our own realities, and nothing objective exists beyond these. The third excerpted poem, *Do not go gentle into that good night* by Dylan Thomas (options A and C), focuses instead on how the dying should approach death.

29. A: Dylan Thomas' *Do not go gentle into that good night,* addressed to his dying father, expresses the idea that death should be approached with spirited resistance rather than serene acceptance. The second poem, Sylvia Plath's *Mad Girl's Love Song,* despite its use of the words "drops dead" and "born again," is not dealing with death but rather with the existentialist idea that reality is only what we perceive, imagine, or create and does not exist objectively outside of our own constructs. The first poem, Theodore Roethke's *The Waking,* explores the nature of both reality vs. dreaming and life vs. death, but does not deal directly with the subject of death as Thomas's poem does.

30. B: This poem was written around 1862, during the Industrial Revolution when the railroad had recently been invented. (The poet's father was one of the owners of a local railroad.) The poet describes this "iron horse" by appropriately using the extended metaphor of a horse, but is not describing an actual horse (A) or a mythic monster (C). Thus it is not true that the subject of the poem cannot be determined (D).

31. D: This poem was written circa 1862. The American Revolution (A) was 1775-1783, the French Revolution (B) was 1789-1799, and the War of 1812 (C) was 1812-1815. The Civil War (D) was 1861-1865. Therefore, this poem was written during the Civil War period.

32. C: The poet performs an amazing structural feat in reflecting the composition of a railroad train in the composition of the poem's single, 17-line sentence. The first two words "I like" are the only subject and predicate; everything after the object "it" is a series of verbs complementing that object: "lap," "lick," "stop," "step," "peer," "pare," "crawl," "chase,"

Copyright © Mometrix Media. You have been licensed one copy of this document for personal use only. Any other reproduction or redistribution is strictly prohibited. All rights reserved.

"neigh," and "stop." This syntax mirrors the engine (subject and predicate) pulling the train behind it. The train's structure is not as specifically mirrored in vocabulary (A). The poem's rhythms (B) are typical of this poet, who very often wrote in iambic lines of alternating tetrameter and trimeter. The tone (D), a childlike kind of enthusiasm, is deliberately used to suggest its role as a powerful toy, satirizing the "progress" of the modern invention.

33. D: The poet, Emily Dickinson, chose these words because they both contrast with one another and typify characteristics of domesticated horses, thus carrying out her horse metaphor for the "iron horse" of the railroad train. In this sense, they are not contradictory: horses have great physical power, are larger than humans and could easily kill a human, but domesticated horses, when treated well, are also typically obedient and gentle with humans. Thus these words are contrasting rather than synonyms (A). They are not nonsense words (B). While they describe a mechanical object, they are not mechanical (C) words.

34. B: Dickinson compares the train's whistle, first metaphorically to a horse's neigh, and then in the simile "like Boanerges," the last name/nickname given by Jesus to disciples James and John, sons of Zebedee, in Mark 3:17. This name has since come to mean a fiery and/or vociferous preacher or orator, especially one with a powerful voice. One creature inhabiting Hades in Greek myth (A) was Cerberus, the three-headed guardian dog. A mythological animal in a labyrinth (D) was the Minotaur, slain by Theseus. This was a Greek myth, not a Roman one. (Like most Greek culture, it was later appropriated by the Romans: the Minotaur is described as "part man and part bull" by the Roman poet, Ovid. However, the names and story of the Minotaur, labyrinth, and Theseus are Greek.) One Old Testament prophet who was angry at opponents and prayed for vengeance (C) was Jeremiah.

35. C: Dickinson habitually used dashes as a kind of musical mechanism to establish the prosody of her poems and habitually capitalized the initials of certain words to lend them additional emphasis. The dashes were not simply punctuation (A); she used other punctuation marks conventionally in places, and the dashes were more a rhythmic device. She did not capitalize to honor (A) the capitalized words. The dashes were not to separate (B) words and the capitals were not used only with names (B). The dashes added control to her prosody rather than providing continuity (D).

36. D: The author of this poem, Emily Dickinson, uses personification in describing how Death "kindly stopped for me" and "He knew no haste", describing the grain as "gazing", and describing the setting sun with the saying "He passed Us." Personification is attributing human qualities to non-human entities, a practice also known as anthropomorphism. Dickinson describes death, fields of grain, and the sun as if they were people, using pronouns ("He") and human actions ("stopped," "drove," "knew," "gazing," "passed," "paused"). Analogy (A) is a comparison of different things, like saying that the human heart is like a pump. Hyperbole (B) is exaggeration. Alliteration (C) is repetition of sounds in adjacent or close words. Although "gazing grain" and "setting sun" both use brief alliteration in the poem, the descriptions of Death do not.

37. C: While the topic of this poem is death, it is treated with a lighthearted tone, finding humor in death with a gentle kind of irony. The diction, word choice, rhythms, and conclusion do not convey gravity, portent or darkness (A). The descriptive details of the journey to Eternity, slow yet seemingly over within a day in retrospect, do not convey detachment, alienation, or numbness (B). The deliberate, placid narrative has no frantic,

Copyright © Mometrix Media. You have been licensed one copy of this document for personal use only. Any other reproduction or redistribution is strictly prohibited. All rights reserved.

agitated, frenzied, or fearful (D) qualities. Rather, the poet seems to welcome "Immortality" even as she quietly observes Death's "kindly" character and "Civility"—examples of the aforementioned gentle irony regarding death's inevitability, in that even if we cannot "stop for Death," death will still stop for us regardless.

38. B: The fifth stanza about "a House that seemed/A Swelling of the Ground" is an oblique description of a grave. Its cornice is "in the Ground" and the roof is "scarcely visible," indicating that this "House" was underground. This is not a literal description of a home (A) or a church (C). A school (D) with children at recess is literally described as one of the aspects of life they pass in their journey, in the third stanza. The fifth stanza's description of a grave is in keeping with the whole poem's light, gentle, indirect, yet spiritually accepting treatment of death.

39. A: The haiku, originating in Japanese poetry and since adopted in English-language poetry, is a short poem of only three lines, often with 17 syllables, with the first and third lines having five syllables and the second line having seven syllables. (In Japanese there are many other rules, which become very complicated.) Haiku are typically unrhymed, so they do not have a rhyme scheme (B). Similarly, they do not employ any regular meter (C). Because haiku are typically 17 syllables or fewer, they do not involve long narratives (D).

40. B: This book was the actual diary kept by Anne Frank, a Dutch Jewish teenager whose family and others spent two years hiding in another family's attic before being sent to concentration camps by Nazis during World War II. Frank, 14-15 years old at the time, was intelligent and wrote articulately, depicting both the everyday details and the unusual difficulties of life in hiding and constant fear. The book is invaluable today, not only for its personal perspective on history and details of first-hand experiences with war and Nazism, but also as a testament to a young girl's unshakeable faith in human nature, even in the face of horrible inhumanity: she wrote near the end of her entries (July 15, 1944, only weeks before being arrested by Nazis) in one of the book's most often-quoted passages, "….I still believe, in spite of everything, that people are truly good at heart."

41. C: All answer choices are novels by Mark Twain. However, while *The Mysterious Stranger* (A) is also a first-person narrative written in the literate language of its narrator, while *The Adventures of Huckleberry Finn* is written in its narrator's uneducated and Southern regional dialect. *The Adventures of Huckleberry Finn* followed and referred to *The Adventures of Tom Sawyer* (B), which is a third-person narrative rather than in first person. *The Prince and the Pauper* (D) is also a third-person narrative. The use of a first-person narrative in dialect differentiates the correct choice from the others. (*Tom Sawyer* contains similar dialects as *Huckleberry Finn,* but only in dialogue spoken by characters, not in the actual narration, which is third-person and not narrated by a character.) Also, the subject matter of the excerpt does not fit choices A or D.

42. D: In *Sister Carrie* (1900), the character of Drouet is basically a decent person, but is deficient in the intelligence or awareness for always behaving morally. Therefore, choice A is incorrect. Hurstwood, by contrast, has the intelligence to understand moral behavior, and his awareness allows him to reject his family's superficial values. However, the moral deficiencies of his own character allow him to behave immorally. Therefore, option B is incorrect. In their attitudes toward women, both characters represent the middle class of the time; therefore, choice C is incorrect.

Copyright © Mometrix Media. You have been licensed one copy of this document for personal use only. Any other reproduction or redistribution is strictly prohibited. All rights reserved.

43. C: All choices are titles of poems by the same author, Walt Whitman, and all are published in the volume *Leaves of Grass*. This particular excerpt is taken from *Song of Myself*, Whitman's longest and perhaps most famous poem.

44. B: Whitman's masterpiece is his celebration ("singing") of a mystical experience revealing, among other themes, his unity with the universe and nature. This is reflected in the title, *Leaves of Grass*, that he gave his collection of poems including *Song of Myself*. The meaning of the excerpt is not simply literal (A). It is also not a metaphor for social classes or roles (C), and it does not refer to mistreatment in a personal relationship (D). The overall content of the poem clearly eliminates these choices.

45. A: *Leaves of Grass*, the book of poems containing *Song of Myself*, was first published in 1855, and Whitman continued to make revisions over 36 years, releasing subsequent editions through 1891. Hence all editions were published in the 19th century.

46. B: These excerpts are from *The* Love *Song of J. Alfred Prufrock* by T. S. Eliot. The other choices are also by Eliot. *Prufrock* was one of his earliest poems (published in *Poetry* magazine in 1915 and in a collection, *Prufrock and Other Observations*, in 1917). *The Waste Land* (A), often considered his masterwork, was published in 1922. While these two share several similar themes, *The Waste Land* is far longer, is not written as a dramatic monologue as *Prufrock* is, and does not contain any of the excerpted verses. Option C is by Eliot, but it is an essay, not a poem. He published his poem *The Hollow Men* (D) in 1925.

47. C: The persona in the poem is speaking about his mortality. His rhetorical questions about parting his hair and eating a peach do not indicate indecision (A) but rather allude to conditions of old age (balding and diarrhea), as the imagery of his dress and the beach allude to retirement—not a vacation (B). This excerpt does not mention drowning (D). (The third excerpt does, but there it is not literal.)

48. D: Options A and C both express meanings that can be interpreted from this verse. The speaker compares his existence to that of a crab to show his own sense of unimportance, which is consistent with other parts of the poem expressing his sense of low status (e.g., "No! I am not Prince Hamlet, nor was meant to be... Almost, at times, the Fool"). Moreover, the poet has chosen the image of a crab not only to fit with the poem's other sea imagery, but also because it is a scavenger. Eliot's essay *Tradition and the Individual Talent* and other material wherein he discusses his poetic technique suggest that art can rescue the bleakness of modern life by creating beauty from its refuse. The imagery ("ragged," "scuttling," "silent") reinforces this bleak view rather than expressing a simple, literal wish (B).

49. A: This line is an expression of the despair felt by the speaker, characterizing the poet's view of modern life as broken, fragmented, and both alienating and isolating to the individual. While the speaker often mourns his aging throughout the poem ("I grow old... I grow old..."), the statement about the mermaids is not literal as in options B and D. The mermaids represent the beautiful dream of the world of art; the speaker feels he cannot be included in or belong to it, even though he can perceive it. He is not saying the mermaids are not real (C) as in the previous line, he has said "I have heard the mermaids singing." But they only sing to one another ("each to each"), not to him.

Copyright © Mometrix Media. You have been licensed one copy of this document for personal use only. Any other reproduction or redistribution is strictly prohibited. All rights reserved.

50. B: Hearing the mermaids singing to each other is part of Eliot's imagery symbolizing the beauty found in art, and in the beautiful dreams that both inspire it and are created by it. Prufrock's hearing them singing can also symbolize his glimpses of eternity, immortality, the ideal, and/or Paradise—things that art can portray or even achieve, but which he despairs of experiencing. His hearing them singing to each other but thinking they will not sing to him emphasizes his feelings of isolation and futility, which reflect Eliot's desolate view of the modern condition. The meaning is not primarily literal as in options A, C and D.

51. C: The fabliau is a humorous story including an incident that is nearly always indecent. In *The Miller's Tale,* the cuckolded husband hangs his rear end out of the window and flatulates into the face of his wife's lover. *The Reeve's Tale, The Shipman's Tale, The Summoner's Tale,* and others are additional instances of fabliau in *The Canterbury Tales. The Physician's Tale* (A) is an example of the literary form of the classical legend. *The Wife of Bath's Tale* (B), an Arthurian story, is an example of one version of the literary form of the romance. *The Pardoner's Tale* (D) is an example of the literary form of the *exemplum*, a type of instructional anecdote or story often used by preachers in sermons to illustrate moral points or principles.

52. D: *The Great Gatsby* by F. Scott Fitzgerald (1925) and *To the Lighthouse* by Virginia Woolf (1927) are both novels, the former American and the latter English. Neither novel is a frame tale (a story or stories set within a story). Chaucer's *Canterbury Tales* is a 14th-century work that is rather famous for, among other things, being a frame tale containing multiple stories. Bocaccio's *Decameron* is likewise a 14th-century frame tale containing 100 tales. (A) each story-within-a-story is told by a different character in both. Vyasa's Sanskrit epic the *Mahabharata* (circa 4th century) and Chaucer's 14th-century *The Parlement of Foules (Parliament of Fowls)* also use the frame tale structure—the former for historical, geographical, religious, moral, and other instruction and the latter framed in the form of a dream. The Gothic-Romantic novel *Frankenstein* (1818) by Mary W. Shelley and the Victorian novel *Wuthering Heights* by Emily Brontë (1847) also use the narrative structure of the frame story (C).

53. C: Dante wrote his *Divine Comedy* between 1308 and 1321, consisting of three *canticas* (songs or chants): *Inferno* (Hell), *Purgatorio* (Purgatory) and *Paradiso* (Heaven). It was the first work ever published in vernacular Italian, the everyday language actually spoken by the people. Previously, all publications in Italy were issued in Latin, the language of the Roman Catholic Church. This was also true in other countries dominated by the Roman Empire; throughout the Middle Ages, as vernacular languages developed, books began being published in the languages of their countries. Cicero wrote *De re publica* (*On the Republic*) (A) between 54 and 51 BCE, an ancient Roman work published in Latin. Bocaccio finished writing *Il Decameron* (*The Decameron*) (B) around 1351-1353, after Dante's *Divine Comedy* and hence not the first published in Italian. Umberto Eco's *Il nome della rosa* (*The Name of the Rose*) (D) is a novel published in modern Italian in 1980 (English translation published in 1983).

54. B: In this line, Yeats refers to the Trojan War, which has been indirectly attributed to the rape of Leda by the god Zeus in the form of a swan. This non-consensual union produced the war-gods Castor and Polydeuces and also Helen of Troy and Clytemnestra. Helen's elopement with Paris triggered the Trojan War, a conflict powered by the war-gods. In the war, Agamemnon killed Clytemnestra's first husband and infant and took Clytemnestra as his wife. After his 10-year absence in the war, Clytemnestra killed Agamemnon. As such, this

- 132 -

Copyright © Mometrix Media. You have been licensed one copy of this document for personal use only. Any other reproduction or redistribution is strictly prohibited. All rights reserved.

part of Yeats's poem refers to both a murder *and* a war (D). The Trojan War occurred roughly around the 11th-12th century BCE. The Peloponnesian War (C) between Athens and Sparta occurred from 431-404 BCE, ending the Golden Age of Greece. The Punic Wars (A) between Rome and Carthage occurred from 264-246 BCE, establishing Roman dominance. Hence these both occurred far later than the Trojan War.

55. A: This poem is a sonnet. Specifically, it is the Petrarchan (Italian) sonnet form, composed of an octave (eight lines) and a sestet (six lines), with the transition from former to latter signaling a major change. (The Shakespearean or English sonnet is composed of three quatrains followed by a couplet.) It is not a villanelle (B), which has 19 lines rather than the sonnet's 14, it alternately repeats the first stanza's first and third lines in each subsequent stanza's last line as the refrain, and then repeats the refrain at the end of the last stanza. This poem uses rhyme schemes of ABAB repeated in the octave and ABC repeated in the sestet, and is in iambic pentameter, hence it is not free verse (C). It is not a sestina (D), which dates back to 12th-century Provençal troubadours and has 39 lines rather than 14.

56. B: Yeats' question at the end of the poem best suggests the poignancy of the human condition, which is necessarily incomplete as we do not and cannot have the power or knowledge of the divine. Yeats asks whether, but does not state that, Leda "put on his knowledge with his power" (A). While certainly ancient Greece portrayed humans interacting differently with divinity than modern Western culture does (C), this is not Yeats's point. He uses this mythological event as a device for telescoping sex and history, showing how it generated ("engenders there") forces dominating the Western world, and musing about what Leda might have experienced in the moment. Line 13, "...his knowledge with his power" does not indicate she gained the latter but not the former (D). It asks if she "put on" the two together.

57. C: The Syntactic Cueing System is that set of cues available in the syntax. Syntax is the sentence structure and word order of language. The Phonological (A) Cueing System is that set of cues available in the phonological structure of language. Phonological structure is the language's speech sounds and the letters representing them. The Semantic (B) Cueing System is that set of cues available in the semantics. Semantics are the meaning (and meanings) of words and the morphemes (smallest units of meaning) that comprise words. The Three Cueing Systems model does not include a Pragmatic (C) system. However, it recognizes, as all linguists and reading instructors do, that pragmatic cues involve reader understanding of their reasons for reading and of how text structures operate. (In linguistics, pragmatics is the study of how language is used for social communication.)

58. D: Semantics refers to the meanings of words and language. The semantic system in the Three Cueing Systems model is the set of cues (including words, phrases, sentences, discourse, and complete text) that readers can use to recognize words based on meanings. Pragmatic cues (A) are based on reader purposes for reading and reader understanding of text structure. The phonological system (B) consists of cues related to the phonemic (or sound) structure of language. The syntactic system (C) consists of cues related to the sentence structure and word order of language.

59. C: Phonological cues are based on the speech sounds in words and their alphabetic representations in print. Readers can identify words by knowing sound-to-letter correspondences. Syntactic cues (A) are based on how words are arranged and ordered to create meaningful phrases, clauses and sentences. Semantic cues (B) are based on the

Copyright © Mometrix Media. You have been licensed one copy of this document for personal use only. Any other reproduction or redistribution is strictly prohibited. All rights reserved.

meanings of morphemes and words and how they combine to create additional meanings. Pragmatic cues (D) are based on the readers' purposes for reading and their understanding of how textual structures function in the texts that they read.

60. B: Pragmatics is the study of how language is used socially for communication. In reading instruction, pragmatic cues relate to the reader's purposes for reading and the reader's understanding of the workings of textual structures. Although pragmatic cues are valid and important, the Three Cueing Systems model does not include a pragmatic "system." The three cueing systems named in this theory are the phonological system of sound cues (D), the Semantic system of meaning cues (C), and the Syntactic system of sentence-structure cues (A).

61. D: Reading instructors should teach students to activate their prior knowledge because it will improve their reading comprehension. Before reading choice A, teachers should discuss and model connections with existing knowledge to prepare students by helping them consider what they already know about the subject of the text. While they read option B, students can make better sense of the text by considering how it fits with what they already know. After reading choice C, teachers can lead discussions helping students focus on how the connections they made between the text and their previous knowledge informed their understanding of the text, and on how the text helped them build their foundations of existing knowledge.

62. C: Certain cognitive strategies used by good readers have been identified through research. Teaching children these strategies and helping them apply these until they can do so independently are found to support mastery of reading comprehension. Good readers who use such successful strategies are not necessarily reading teachers, and it is not necessary for students to find different ways (A) to apply them. Such strategies are less likely to be used by beginning students, and always applying them with assistance (B) without ever graduating to independent application is less effective. These strategies are used by all proficient readers, not just published writers. Finally, creativity is important to many kinds of writing (D), but not necessary to understand what one reads.

63. A: The student making this observation is connecting reading of a mythological text (presumably Greek or Roman) s/he reads to the world—in this instance, to human nature—by noting that despite greater powers, the gods' emotional reactions and behaviors are like those of humans. The student statement in choice B reflects a connection of text to text—fiction (a novel) to historical accounts of a period (for example, see Dickens's *A Tale of Two Cities*). The student statement in option C reflects a connection of text to self: the student can relate to the feelings of a character in the text. Because each choice reflects a different one of the three kinds of student connections named, choice D is incorrect.

64. C: Thinking about thinking, or understanding our own cognitive processes, is known as metacognition. Explicitly teaching effective reading comprehension strategies does more than deepen student understanding of reading: it also promotes higher-order, abstract cognitive skill of metacognition. Schemata (A) (plural, singular *schema*) is Piaget's term for mental constructs we form to understand the world. Piaget said we either assimilate new information into an existing schema or alter an existing schema to accommodate the new knowledge. Reading instruction experts may refer to experience or background knowledge as schemata because students undergo this cognitive process when they fit what they read to their existing knowledge/experience. Scaffolding (B), a term coined by Jerome Bruner,

Copyright © Mometrix Media. You have been licensed one copy of this document for personal use only. Any other reproduction or redistribution is strictly prohibited. All rights reserved.

means the temporary support given to students as needed while they learn and is gradually reduced as they become more independent. Reading instruction experts may also describe students' connections of text to prior experience as scaffolding. Metamorphosis (D) is a term meaning a transformation—literally in biology as with caterpillars into butterflies, or figuratively, as in Franz Kafka's *The Metamorphosis,* wherein protagonist Gregor Samsa becomes a cockroach.

65. B: Why the students participate in a reading/learning activity refers to the motivation for the activity. Option A refers to the timing of the reading/learning activity. Choice C refers to the place or physical setting of the learning activity. Option D refers to the way(s) in which the learning activity is defined and executed. All of these activity settings are factors that influence learning differentially according to the different cultural, social, and economic factors involved in each specific situation.

66. A: The process of actively constructing meaning from reading is interactive, in that it involves the text itself, the person reading it, and the setting in which the reading is done: the reader interacts with the text, and the text interacts with the reader by affecting him/her; the context of reading interacts with the text and the reader by affecting them both; and the reader interacts with the reading context as well as with the text. Choice B is a better definition of the *strategic* aspect of the process. Options C and D are better definitions of the *adaptable* aspect of the process.

67. B: Researchers find that learners of both their native language (L1) and a second language (L2) go through all three developmental stages, which means that choices A and C are both incorrect. However, learners of a second language are often urged by teachers and others to skip the Silent Period, whereas young children acquiring their native languages are not similarly expected to speak immediately. L2 learners are not likely to undergo the third stage later (D) but sooner than or at a similar time as L1 learners, due either to having not yet learned all linguistic forms of the L2 or to being unable to access all of the L2's forms as they produce language.

68. C: L2s can be learned in a number of educational contexts, such as being segregated from the L1, formally taught via the medium of the L1, through submersion, or within the language classroom but not used to communicate outside it, among many others. They can also be taught/learned in several natural contexts: as the majority language to members of ethnic minority groups, as the official language of a country where learners speak a different language, or for international communication purposes separate from the L1 or official language. Therefore, it is not accurate that L2s are never learned in natural contexts (B and D). Unlike L2s, L1s are always first acquired in natural contexts, meaning choice A is inaccurate.

69. D: The process of fossilization occurs when some of the incorrect forms a learner of a second language has developed are not corrected over time, but become permanently fixed. (When a learner's L2 contains many such fossilized forms, it is termed an interlanguage.) Vygotsky's Zone of Proximal Development (A), wherein a learner can accomplish tasks with assistance that s/he could not yet achieve independently, applies to the acquisition of both first and second languages. The hypothesis that there is a critical period for learning language (B) has also been applied to both L1 and L2 acquisition. In the same way, proponents of linguistic universals—both the typological universals proposed by Greenberg and the Universal Grammar described by Chomsky—find that in both first- and second-

Copyright © Mometrix Media. You have been licensed one copy of this document for personal use only. Any other reproduction or redistribution is strictly prohibited. All rights reserved.

language learning, marked (language-specific) features do not transfer and are harder to learn, while unmarked (universal across most languages) features conform to general linguistic principles and are easier to learn. Fossilization is the only choice that occurs exclusively in second-language acquisition.

70. C: Omitting articles (for example, *a/an, the, these*) and plural endings (*–s*), which is common among Chinese ESL students, is not because they have not yet learned the English forms (A) or words for these. Nor are these omissions a way to avoid having to choose the correct form among various English irregularities (C). These errors are also not due to the student's not understanding the relationship between the Chinese and English versions of the forms (D). Rather, Chinese does not include articles or plural endings the way English does, so the student has no frame of reference or comparison. Therefore, the student's ESL pattern of absent articles and plurals reflects the nature and rules of the L1, which have transferred to the L2 but are incompatible with it.

71. B: As linguists have long pointed out, dialects are NOT non-standard versions of a language (A). In linguistics, dialects are *differing* varieties of any language, but these may be vernacular (nonstandard) OR standard versions of a language. They are often considered less socially acceptable, especially in educational, occupational and professional settings, than whichever standard version is most accepted. The linguistic features of dialects are not incorrect (C), but simply different. Their use does not indicate poor or incomplete language learning (D).

72. A: The formal version of Standard English is reflected in dictionaries and grammar books and applied in written language. In speech, Standard English is NOT universal (B): it differs in pronunciation between the northern and southern regions of North America and between native English speakers in England, Ireland, Australia, India, and other English-speaking areas. Speech communities use a more flexible variety of *informal* Standard English rather than the Standard English of writing (C). The construct of Standard English actually includes a range of dialects (D) because formal Standard English is used in writing and not speech, which by nature dictates a less formal, more flexible version.

73. C: The Great Vowel shift was a huge shift in the phonemics of English pronunciation that occurred from the 15th to 18th centuries in all places where English was spoken and written. The other answer choices are incorrect ranges for this major change in the English language.

74. B: During the Great Vowel shift, the location of the tongue in the mouth where the long vowels in English were produced eventually shifted to a higher position in the mouth, altering the sounds of their pronunciation. For example, the letter "e," pronounced /e/ (the sound spelled as "-ay" by Modern English speakers) in Chaucer's day (as it is still pronounced in Romance languages), gradually changed to be pronounced /i/ (the sound spelled as "ee" in Modern English). The tongue's movement back (A), down (C), or front (D) in the mouth would produce respectively different phonemes.

75. A: Shakespeare lived from circa 1564-1616 and wrote most of his known plays and poems between 1589 and 1613, or in the late 16th and early 17th centuries. The Great Vowel Shift occurred from the 15th to 18th centuries. Thus, Shakespeare's Elizabethan English fell during this major language change. Geoffrey Chaucer (B) lived from circa 1343-1400 and wrote his known works between roughly 1369 and 1399. Therefore, his Middle English was

Copyright © Mometrix Media. You have been licensed one copy of this document for personal use only. Any other reproduction or redistribution is strictly prohibited. All rights reserved.

the form that existed *before* the Great Vowel Shift took place. Emily Dickinson (C) wrote her poetry during the 19ᵗʰ century, *after* the Great Vowel Shift. The Pearl Poet (D), author of the *Pearl* poem, *Sir Gawain and the Green Knight,* and other works was a contemporary of Chaucer, meaning his works were also written *before* the Great Vowel Shift.

76. B: Linguists generally analyze the Great Vowel Shift as having consisted of eight steps: Step 1 = /i/ and /u/ → /əI/ and /əU/; Step 2 = /e/ and /o/ → /i/ and /u/; Step 3 = /a/ → /æ/; Step 4 = /ɛ/ → /e/, /ɔ/ → /o/; Step 5 = /æ/ → /ɛ/; Step 6 = /e/ → /i/; Step 7 = /ɛ/ → /e/; and Step 8 = / əI/ and / əU/ → /aI/ and /aU/. Step 1 involved downward shifts, Step 3 a forward shift, and Step 8 downward shifts. However, the overall effect of the Great Vowel Shift across all of its steps was an upward shift in the placement of the tongue in the mouth in the pronunciation of all long English vowels.

77. D: The Great Vowel Shift ultimately changed the pronunciation of the long vowels in English completely. Consequently, it has affected orthographic conventions and rules (A), instruction in reading (B), and how easily the modern readers of English texts can comprehend literature written before the GVS (C), as in the works of Chaucer and others. The sources of difficulty (in addition to changes in vocabulary and usage) for modern readers include not only the earlier spellings, but moreover the pronunciations that affected those spellings, as well as rhymes.

78. C: The etymology, or origin, of the English word *debt* is the Latin word *debitum*. It came into English during the Middle English form of the language. Therefore, this word was not originally a Middle English word (A) but a Latin word. Because it came from Latin into Middle English, it did not exist as an Old English word with a voiced *b* (B) as Old English preceded Middle English. The origin of this word was not Greek (D) but Latin. NOTE: Early scribes and printers, described by some as "inkhorn scholars," introduced many silent letters to English spellings to indicate their Latin or Greek roots, as in this case.

79. B: In Old Italian, the word *disastro* meant unfavorable in one's stars. It was commonplace to attribute bad fortune to the influences of the stars in the Medieval and Renaissance eras. The Old Italian word came into English in the late 1500s as "disaster" and was used by Shakespeare (cf. *King Lear)*. The word's Latin root is *astrum*, meaning "star," and the Latin prefix *dis-*, meaning "apart" and signifying negation. *Catastrophe* (A) and *misfortune* (C) are both Modern English meanings of the word "disaster," whereas the "ill-starred" meaning used in Elizabethan times has now become archaic or obsolete. The root means "star," not the aster flower (D).

80. A: The Latin word *sal* meant "salt." According to the famous ancient historian Pliny the Elder, "in Rome, a soldier was paid in salt," a means of preserving food in the days before refrigeration and was thus a very valuable commodity. The Latin term *salarium,* from the root *sal,* originally meant the salt paid to soldiers but eventually became generalized to mean any kind of payment. (The expression "worth your salt" also derives from this origin.) "Salary" may sound similar to "celery" (B), but their roots and meanings are not the same. ("Celery" came to English via French from Italian, which came from Latin, which in turn got the word from a Greek root.) While it eventually meant any kind of payment including money or other kinds, it never originally meant *money* (C). "Earnings" (D) is a Modern English synonym for "salary" rather than the original meaning of its root word.

Copyright © Mometrix Media. You have been licensed one copy of this document for personal use only. Any other reproduction or redistribution is strictly prohibited. All rights reserved.

81. B: The word "brunch" is a blend of "breakfast" and "lunch". Blends of two or more words are known as portmanteau words. (*Portmanteau* is a French word meaning a suitcase.) "Fax" (A) is an example of clipping, or shortening a word, from its original "facsimile." "Babysitter" (C) is an example of compounding, or combining two or more words into one. "Saxophone" (D) is an example of proper noun transfer: A Belgian family that built musical instruments had the last name of Sax, and this wind instrument was named after them. These represent some of the ways that new words have entered—and still do enter—the English language.

82. C: Neologisms (from *neo-* meaning "new"), also known as "creative coinages," are new words sometimes invented by people which then become parts of our vocabulary. The word "quark" was first coined by the great Irish author James Joyce; he used it in his last novel, *Finnegans Wake.* The physicist Murray Gell-Mann then chose this word from Joyce's work to name the model of elementary particles he proposed (also proposed concurrently and independently by physicist George Zweig) in 1964. Blending (A) is another way new words come into our language; for example, "moped" is a blend of the respective first syllables of "motor" and "pedal." Conversion (B), also called functional shift, changes a word's part of speech. For example, the common nouns "network," "microwave," and "fax," along with the proper noun "Google" have all been converted to verbs in modern usage. Onomatopoeia (D) means words that imitate associated sounds, such as "meow" and "click." New words are also created this way.

83. D: This is an example of a compound-complex sentence. A simple (A) sentence contains a subject and a verb and expresses a complete thought. Its subject and/or verb may be compound (e.g., "John and Mary" as subject and "comes and goes" as verb). A complex (B) sentence contains an independent clause and one or more dependent clauses. The independent and dependent clause(s) are joined by a subordinating conjunction or a relative pronoun. A compound (C) sentence contains two independent clauses—two simple sentences—connected by a coordinating conjunction. A compound-complex (also called complex-compound) sentence, as its name implies, combines both compound and complex sentences: it combines more than one independent clause with at least one dependent clause. In the example sentence given, the first two clauses, joined by "however," are independent, and the clause modifying "actual test questions," beginning with "which cover," is a relative, dependent clause.

84. C: A euphemism is an expression used instead of more literal words to make a harsh expression sound softer, to make an impolite description sound more polite, or to make a description less polite (such as saying "bit the dust" instead of "died" in a formal setting). Jargon (A) is the specialized terminology of a specific field or group. This example, however, is NOT medical jargon; a better example might be "expired" or "deceased." Ambiguity (B) means unclear and/or open to multiple interpretations. A better example of ambiguity in this scenario might be, "The surgery did not obtain all of the desired outcomes." This can mean a greater number of things than that the patient died. A connotation (D) is a suggested meaning associated with the literal meaning of a word. For example, "The surgery was abortive" does not state that the patient died, but if the surgery was meant to save the patient's life, the adjective "abortive," meaning unsuccessful or failing to obtain the desired result, could connote that the patient died.

85. B: Typically, after students write something, their teachers may ask them to reflect upon what they wrote, which would mean that this is NOT a prewriting activity. In writing

Copyright © Mometrix Media. You have been licensed one copy of this document for personal use only. Any other reproduction or redistribution is strictly prohibited. All rights reserved.

exercises, teachers will typically ask students to plan (A) what they will write in order to clearly define their main topic and organize their work. Many teachers find it helps students to visualize (C) what they are reading and/or want to write about, and make drawings of what they visualize as preparation for writing. Brainstorming (D) is another common prewriting activity designed to generate multiple ideas from which students can then select to include in their writing.

86. A: After prewriting (planning, visualizing, brainstorming), the correct sequence of steps in the writing process are drafting, in which the writer takes the material generated during prewriting work and making it into sentences and paragraphs; revising, where the writer explores any changes in what one has written that would improve the quality of the writing; editing, in which the writer examines his or her writing for factual and mechanical (grammar, spelling, punctuation) errors and correcting them; and publishing, when the writer finally shares what he or she has written with others who will read it and give feedback.

87. B: Researchers have found that the writing processes both form a hierarchy and are observably recursive in nature. Moreover, they find that when students continually revise their writing, they are able to consider new ideas and to incorporate these ideas into their work. Thus they do not merely correct mechanical errors when revising (A), they also add to the content and quality of their writing. Furthermore, research shows that writers, including students, not only revise their actual writing, during rewrites, they also reconsider their original writing goals rather than always retaining them (C), and they revisit their prewriting plans rather than leaving these unaffected in rewriting (D).

88. C: Researchers have found that children know a great deal more about a given topic than what their writing usually reflects. Therefore, options A and D are incorrect. Furthermore, researchers have concluded from their findings that when children stop writing, they do not do so because they have run out of things they want to write about the topic (B), but rather because they have not yet developed the means to articulate their knowledge adequately. Educational experts find that these research findings inform writing instruction in that the process of continually rewriting helps children to access and articulate more of the knowledge they actually have.

89. D: This description is most typical of the process of peer review. Classmates read Arthur's paper and then they identify values in it, describe it, ask questions about it, and suggest points for revision. These are types of helpful feedback identified by experts on writing and collaborative writing. The other choices, however, are not typically collaborative. For a portfolio assessment (A), the teacher collects finished work products from a student over time, eventually assembling a portfolio of work. This affords a more authentic assessment using richer, more multidimensional, and more visual and tactile products for assessment instead of using only standardized test scores for assessment. Holistic scoring (B) is a method of scoring a piece of writing for overall quality (evaluating general elements such as focus, organization, support, and conventions) rather than being overly concerned with any individual aspect of writing. A scoring rubric (C) is a guide that gives examples of the levels of typical characteristics in a piece of writing that correspond to each available score (for example, scores from 1-5).

90. C: According to the Association of College and Research Libraries, Information Literacy is the set of skills that an individual must have for finding, retrieving, analyzing, and using

Copyright © Mometrix Media. You have been licensed one copy of this document for personal use only. Any other reproduction or redistribution is strictly prohibited. All rights reserved.

information. It is required not just for reading and understanding information (A). Information Literacy does not mean learning and retaining a lot of information (B), or only sharing it with others (D), but rather knowing how to find information one does not already have and how to evaluate that information critically for its quality and apply it judiciously to meet one's purposes.

91. B: The early 21st century has been dubbed the Information Age primarily because, with widespread Internet use and other innovations in electronic communications and publishing, there are more sources of information and greater output of available information than ever before. While some agencies might require more information (A), this is only possible because such information is more readily available now. Professionals in higher education and research find that with this new explosion of information, college students cannot possibly gain enough information literacy by just reading texts and writing research papers, and cannot learn all they need to know in four years (C). This period is also not called the Information Age due to an increased student interest in acquiring information (D), but due to the increased access to information.

92. A: It is a standard of Information Literacy (IL) that students must use their own critical thinking skills to evaluate the quality of the information and its sources before they use it. Another standard is that the student should ascertain how much information s/he needs for his/her purposes first, deciding this after uncovering excessive information is inefficient (B). An additional IL standard is to access necessary information in an efficient and effective way. However, none of these standards include the idea that students will lose incidental learning or broadness of scope by doing so (C). IL standards include the principle that students *should* use the information they find in ways that are effective for attaining their specific purposes (D).

93. B: The MLA (Modern Language Association) system for documenting literary sources defines in-line citations in a paper as combining signal phrases, which usually include the author name and introduce information from a source via a fact, summary, paraphrase, or quotation; parenthetical references following the material cited, frequently at the end of the sentence; and, except for web sources that are unpaginated, page number(s). MLA defines a list of works cited (A) as an alphabetized list found at the end of a research paper that gives the information sources referenced in the paper, including each source's publication information, quotations, summaries, and paraphrases. Guidelines for preparing the list of works cited are provided in the *MLA Handbook*. MLA information notes (C) are an optional addition to the MLA parenthetical documentation system. These notes can be used to add important material without interrupting the paper's flow, and/or to supply comments about sources or make references to multiple sources. They may be endnotes or footnotes. Option D is incorrect.

94. C: On the Internet, it often occurs that the name of the author of an article or book is actually provided but is not obviously visible at first glance. Web sources frequently include the author's name, but on another page of the same site, such as the website's home page, or in a tiny font at the very end of the web page, rather than in a more conspicuous location. In such cases, students doing online research may have to search more thoroughly than usual to find the author's name. Therefore, they should not immediately assume the author is not named (A). Also, many Web sources are sponsored by government agencies or private corporations and do not give individual author names. In these cases, the research paper *should* cite the agency or corporation name as author (B). Finally, it is much more common

Copyright © Mometrix Media. You have been licensed one copy of this document for personal use only. Any other reproduction or redistribution is strictly prohibited. All rights reserved.

for online sources to omit an author's name than it is in print sources. In these cases, it is both permitted and advised by the MLA to cite the article or book title instead (D).

95. D: When online sources you are citing in your research paper are in PDFs and other file formats that have stable pagination, the MLA advises including the page number in the research paper's in-text citation because these numbers are valid and do not change. If a Web source has no pagination, as often happens, the MLA does NOT advise avoiding the citation (A), it advises simply making the citation without a page number because there is not one available. Unlike in PDFs (above), when citing a source from a printout, the MLA advises NOT including page numbers even if you see them because the same page numbers are not always found in all printouts (B). It is not true that in-text citations should never include page numbers (C).

96. D: The MLA guidelines for citing multiple authors of the same work in in-text citations (for both print and online sources) dictate using the first author's name plus "et al" for the other authors when there are four or more authors. If there are two (options A and B) or three (options B and C) authors, the guidelines say to name each author, either in a signal phrase [for example, "Smith and Jones note that... (45)" or "Smith, Jones, and Gray have noted... (45)"] or in a parenthetical reference ["(Smith, Jones, and Gray 45)."].

97. C: Persuasive writing has the purpose of expressing the writer's opinion and/or of convincing the reader of something. A movie review is one example of this writing purpose and type. Other examples include advertisements, editorials, book and music reviews, and literary essays. Narration (A) is a type of writing for telling stories. Description (B) is a type of writing for creating a picture using words that evoke imagery for the reader. Exposition (D) is a type of writing for informing the reader of things and/or explaining things to the reader.

98. B: Persuasive writing tries to convince readers to agree with the author's opinion or position regarding a topic. To convince others, writers must have sufficient knowledge about the topic, logical thinking skills, strong beliefs about the topic, and enough technical skill for making logical points, supporting one's opinions, and swaying the reader's emotions. Expository (A) writing aims to give information and/or explanations. It requires sufficient knowledge, practicality, and the technical skill for writing clarity, but it is not as hard as persuasion because it seeks not to convince the reader of anything, only to inform or explain. Descriptive (C) writing seeks to paint verbal pictures that make the described things real to readers through sensory details. This requires imagination and strong creative writing skills, but is not as difficult as persuading the reader to agree with the author's viewpoint. Narrative (D) writing tells a story and can be the easiest, as storytelling and enjoying stories are natural for most people.

99. A: *The Adventures of Huckleberry Finn* by Mark Twain is a fictional novel. *The Diary of a Young Girl* by Anne Frank is a non-fictional journal. *The Fall of the House of Usher* by Edgar Allan Poe is a fictional short story in the horror genre. Novels, personal narratives like diaries/journals, and short stories, as well as biographies and anecdotes are all types of narrative. Narration tells a story, often (but not always) advances chronologically, and has a beginning, middle, and end. Descriptive writing (B) paints a word picture using sensory imagery to make an event, scene, thing, or person more real to the imagination of the reader. Other than character sketches, picture captions, and some kinds of advertising, most writing is not completely descriptive: narrative works typically include descriptive parts.

Copyright © Mometrix Media. You have been licensed one copy of this document for personal use only. Any other reproduction or redistribution is strictly prohibited. All rights reserved.

Exposition (C) is found in news stories, encyclopedias, research papers, informational essays, and instruction manuals rather than fiction or journals. Persuasion (D) is more characteristic of editorials, reviews, ads, and literary essays than novels, short stories or diaries.

100. B: For any writing assignment, you should first target an audience, perform an audience analysis, and develop an audience profile to determine what you should include in and omit from your writing. Even though the assigning teacher may be the only one to read your writing, you should not assume s/he is your main audience (A) because the teacher may expect you to write for other readers. In addition to first knowing your purpose for writing before beginning, you should also consider what purpose your writing will meet for your readers (C) and how they are likely to use it. Considering what your audience's attitudes toward what you will write and their likely reactions to it is also important to shaping your writing and is NOT overthinking (D).

101. C: The kind of audience for whom you are writing, as well as your purpose for writing, will determine what style, tone, and wording you choose. Knowing who your audience is will enable you to select writing strategies, a style and tone, and specific word choices that will be most understandable and appealing to your readers. Knowing the type of audience will also dictate how much time to spend on research (A). Some readers will expect more supporting evidence, while others will be bored or overwhelmed by it. Similarly, you will want to include more or less information depending on who will be reading what you write (B). And while the structure of your piece does inform how you organize your information, you should also vary your organization according to who will read it (D).

102. D: It is best to begin an essay or paper with a broader, more general introduction to the topic, and move to a more focused and specific point regarding the topic—not vice versa (C)—by the end of the introduction. This point is your thesis statement. Writing experts advise *against* the technique of beginning an essay with a dictionary definition (A) because it has been so overused that it has become ineffective and uninteresting. To engage the reader's interest in your topic, it is best to *begin* with some very attention-getting material rather than leaving it for later (B).

103. C: The first part of the introduction to an essay or paper should be some original, fresh material that will engage the attention of readers enough so they are interested in continuing to read it. Following this should be the transitional portion of the introduction, which gives some pertinent background information about the piece's particular purpose (B). This informs the reader of your reason for focusing on your paper or essay's specific topic. The transitional portion moves the piece to the third part of the introduction: the thesis statement (A), which is a clear expression of the main point you are trying to make in your essay or paper. An optional addition in the introduction is an explanation of how you will defend your thesis, giving readers a general idea of how your essay or paper's various points will be organized. This is sometimes described as a "road map" (D).

104. B: One recommended technique for beginning the introductory part of a paper or essay is to cite a statistic related to your paper/essay's topic that readers are likely to find surprising. This will get the readers' attention, while also giving some information about the topic to be discussed in the rest of the piece. Another effective technique for starting the introduction is to use an interesting quotation that summarizes your position. This adds interest, support, and power; it is not true that you should use only your own words instead

Copyright © Mometrix Media. You have been licensed one copy of this document for personal use only. Any other reproduction or redistribution is strictly prohibited. All rights reserved.

of quoting another (A). It is also not true that opening with a story or anecdote is contrary to the purposes of an essay or paper (C): when you as the writer have some personal interest in your topic, this technique is useful for getting the readers as emotionally engaged in the subject matter as you are. It is not true that asking rhetorical questions will only frustrate readers (D): this is a technique that helps readers imagine being in different situations so they can consider your topic in new ways.

105. A: While students may sometimes regard the conclusion of their essay or paper as simply the last paragraph that includes all the pieces that they could not fit into earlier parts of the piece, this is an inadequate treatment of the conclusion. Because the conclusion is the last thing the audience reads, they are more likely to remember it. Also, the conclusion is an excellent opportunity to reinforce your main point, remind readers of the importance of your topic, and prod readers to consider the effects of the topic in their own lives and/or in the world at large. A good conclusion should restate your original thesis statement (B), pull together and/or summarize the main points you made (C), and make clear(er) your discussion's or argument's context (D).

106. B: Tone is the way in which the writer writes overall to express his or her attitude. Voice is who the reader hears speaking in the writing, the individual way the writer uses to express his or her tone—not vice versa (A). Style (options C and D) is the effect a writer creates through language, mechanics, and attitude or the sound (formal or informal) or impressions (seriousness, levity, grace, fluency) of the writing.

107. C: Diction refers to your overall choice of language for your writing, while vocabulary refers to the specific words in a discipline that you use when writing in or about that discipline—not vice versa (A). Jargon (B) is very specialized terminology used in a discipline that is not readily understood by readers outside of that discipline. It is hence less accessible than the vocabulary of the discipline, and only used in writing intended only for those who are already familiar with it. Diction and vocabulary are elements of writing style (D).

108. D: Knowing your purpose for writing means knowing what you want to achieve with the content of your writing, and knowing this will determine your writing style. Your choice of words and how formal or informal your writing is—your diction—*does* affect your style (A). Diction and tone should be consistent in your writing style, and should reflect vocabulary and writing patterns that suit your writing purpose best. Style is not added later to give writing personality (B). It develops from your purpose for writing, or what you want to accomplish with your writing. Style *is* directly related to your control of the content (C) of your writing.

109. C: The verbs quoted all refer to interpreting information in your own words. This task targets the cognitive objective of comprehension. Tasks targeting the cognitive objective of knowledge recall (A) would ask you to name, label, list, define, repeat, memorize, order, or arrange the information. Tasks targeting the cognitive objective of application (B) would ask you to calculate, solve, practice, operate, sketch, use, prepare, illustrate, or apply the material. Tasks targeting the cognitive objective of evaluation (D) would ask you to judge, appraise, evaluate, conclude, predict, score, or compare the information.

110. B: The verbs quoted all refer to taking pieces or parts of information or knowledge and bringing them together to create a whole, and to building relationships among the parts to

Copyright © Mometrix Media. You have been licensed one copy of this document for personal use only. Any other reproduction or redistribution is strictly prohibited. All rights reserved.

fit new or different circumstances. Analysis (A) is the opposite of synthesis—breaking information down into its component parts and demonstrating the relationships among those parts. An assignment for analysis would ask you to compare, distinguish, test, categorize, examine, contrast, or analyze information. Evaluation (C) is making judgments of information based on given criteria, confirming or supporting certain preferences, and persuading the reader. An assignment targeting evaluation would use words like evaluate, predict, appraise, conclude, score, judge, or compare. Application (D) is using knowledge in new contexts. The assignment would ask you to apply, prepare, practice, use, operate, sketch, calculate, solve, or illustrate.

111. A: Evaluation is the most complex of the thinking/writing strategies listed in these choices because it commonly incorporates the other thinking strategies. Knowledge recall (D) requires showing mastery of information learned. Comprehension (C) requires showing understanding of the information learned. Application (B) requires taking the information learned and using it in new or different circumstances. These processes are not as complex as evaluating (or making critical judgments) the information learned. Analysis, synthesis, and evaluation are more complex than knowledge recall, comprehension, and application. Of analysis, synthesis, and evaluation, evaluation is the most complex.

112. D: Comparing and contrasting, explaining cause and effect relationships, and analyzing are the most commonly used forms of analysis in college-level writing. Supporting an opinion (C) you have stated in your writing is one of the most commonly used forms of *synthesis*, not analysis, in college-level writing.

113. C: Proposing a solution to some problem or situation is one of the most commonly used forms of synthesis strategies in college-level writing. The other most commonly used synthesis writing strategy is stating an opinion and supporting it with evidence. Explaining cause and effect (A) and comparing and contrasting (B) are two of the most commonly used *analysis* (not synthesis) writing strategies. Using persuasion (D) to convince the reader is typically used together with the other strategies named to add credibility and acceptance to the position stated by the writer.

114. B: A white paper, opinion survey, annotated bibliography, and problem solution are all examples of the exploratory discourse aim. So are definitions, diagnoses, marketing analyses, feasibility studies, and literature (*not* literary) reviews. The expressive (A) discourse aim is reflected in things like vision statements, mission statements, proposals, constitutions, and legislative bills. Examples of writing reflecting the informative (C) discourse aim include news and magazine articles, reports, and encyclopedia articles. Examples of writing reflecting the persuasive (D) discourse aim include political speeches; editorials; ad campaigns; and works of artistic, social, or political criticism.

115. A: This sentence is an analogy, which compares similarities between two concepts to establish a relationship. Analogy can enhance comprehension of a new concept via comparison to an older/more familiar concept. Allegory (B) uses symbolism to represent a more abstract concept with a more concrete concept. Examples of literary works which are overall allegories include Dante's poem *Divine Comedy* and the novels *Animal Farm* by George Orwell (1945) and *Lord of the Flies* by William Golding (1954). Allusion (C) is a passing reference to a literary work/place/person/event, wherein the reader must make the connection. For example, saying "Susan loves to help and care for other people so much that her friends call her Mother Teresa" is an allusion to a famous person exemplifying

- 144 -

Copyright © Mometrix Media. You have been licensed one copy of this document for personal use only. Any other reproduction or redistribution is strictly prohibited. All rights reserved.

Susan's personal qualities. Antithesis (D) juxtaposes words/phrases/sentences with opposite meanings, balancing these to add insight. A good example is Neil Armstrong's statement during his and Buzz Aldrin's moon landing: "That's one small step for man, one giant leap for mankind."

116. D: All these choices use the literary device of an extended metaphor, as does the quoted Shakespeare passage wherein Romeo describes Juliet as the sun. In option A, Eliot describes the fog as a cat ("...rubs its back... rubs its muzzle... licked its tongue... Let fall upon its back the soot... curled once about the house, and fell asleep.") Similarly, Carl Sandburg's (1916) poem *Fog* (C) describes the fog that "comes on little cat feet." In option B, Frost uses the extended metaphor of two roads that "diverged in a wood" to describe the journey of life.

117. C: This sentence appeals to the reader's emotions by stating simply that it is dangerous and "really stupid" to use a cell phone while driving; it does not provide any evidence or logic to support the statement. Choice A offers a logical, common-sense argument in that steering one-handed makes driving more dangerous. Choice B refers to statistics of greater accident risk to support the statement that cell phone use while driving is dangerous. Such supporting evidence is an appeal to logic. Choice D cites the fact that many state laws ban cell phone use while driving to support the idea that it is dangerous, and also refers to data on more accidents from doing so. These pieces of supporting evidence also appeal to logic rather than emotion.

118. A: A fallacy of inconsistency exists in a statement that contradicts itself or defeats itself. Saying there are exceptions to all general statements is itself a general statement; therefore, according to the content, this statement must also have an exception, implying there are NOT exceptions to all general statements. Option B is an example of a fallacy of irrelevance: passing or failing is determined by course performance, so asking to pass because parents will be upset if one fails is an irrelevant reason for appealing to a teacher for a passing grade. Choice C is an example of a fallacy of insufficiency: a statement is made with insufficient evidence to support it. A lack of evidence of innocence is not enough to prove one is guilty because there could also be an equal lack of evidence of guilt. Option D is an example of a fallacy of inappropriate presumption: asking someone if s/he has stopped cheating presumes that s/he has cheated in the past. The person being asked this question cannot answer either "yes" or "no" without confirming that s/he has indeed been cheating. If the person being asked has not been cheating, then the person asking the question is making a false assumption.

119. B: A clustering illusion is a cognitive bias of attributing cause and effect and patterns to unrelated or random events. The character described considers the phone's ringing an effect caused by flushing the toilet, when in reality the two are unrelated. The first ring's occurring after he flushed was merely a coincidence; subsequent rings always occur at preset time intervals, and his repeated flushes simply coincided right before each ring. The above-average effect (A) is the cognitive bias of overestimating our own abilities. The confirmation bias (C) is our tendency to focus on information confirming our pre-existing beliefs while overlooking conflicting information. In comparing ourselves with other people, we notice others' errors more and our own errors less. The framing bias (D) is being influenced by how information is framed rather than the facts. For example, whether a

Copyright © Mometrix Media. You have been licensed one copy of this document for personal use only. Any other reproduction or redistribution is strictly prohibited. All rights reserved.

doctor presents the success or failure rate of an operation can influence the patient's decision to undergo it, even if both rates reflect identical data.

120. A: The example statement reflects a stereotype. A stereotype is an assumption or generalization made about everybody in an identified group. Assumptions (C) can be made about many things, not just about the members of a certain group. Generalizations (D) also apply to a great many subjects, not just to the characteristics of a specific group of people. An inference (B) is a conclusion based on available evidence rather than on an overt statement of fact. For example, if Archie said, "That guy there is Asian, so he must be a terrible driver," he would be making an inference based on his stereotype of Asian people. Therefore, stereotype is the most precise definition of the statement example given.

Copyright © Mometrix Media. You have been licensed one copy of this document for personal use only. Any other reproduction or redistribution is strictly prohibited. All rights reserved.

Secret Key #1 - Time is Your Greatest Enemy

Pace Yourself

Wear a watch. At the beginning of the test, check the time (or start a chronometer on your watch to count the minutes), and check the time after every few questions to make sure you are "on schedule."

If you are forced to speed up, do it efficiently. Usually one or more answer choices can be eliminated without too much difficulty. Above all, don't panic. Don't speed up and just begin guessing at random choices. By pacing yourself, and continually monitoring your progress against your watch, you will always know exactly how far ahead or behind you are with your available time. If you find that you are one minute behind on the test, don't skip one question without spending any time on it, just to catch back up. Take 15 fewer seconds on the next four questions, and after four questions you'll have caught back up. Once you catch back up, you can continue working each problem at your normal pace.

Furthermore, don't dwell on the problems that you were rushed on. If a problem was taking up too much time and you made a hurried guess, it must be difficult. The difficult questions are the ones you are most likely to miss anyway, so it isn't a big loss. It is better to end with more time than you need than to run out of time.

Lastly, sometimes it is beneficial to slow down if you are constantly getting ahead of time. You are always more likely to catch a careless mistake by working more slowly than quickly, and among very high-scoring test takers (those who are likely to have lots of time left over), careless errors affect the score more than mastery of material.

Secret Key #2 - Guessing is not Guesswork

You probably know that guessing is a good idea. Unlike other standardized tests, there is no penalty for getting a wrong answer. Even if you have no idea about a question, you still have a 20-25% chance of getting it right.

Most test takers do not understand the impact that proper guessing can have on their score. Unless you score extremely high, guessing will significantly contribute to your final score.

Monkeys Take the Test

What most test takers don't realize is that to insure that 20-25% chance, you have to guess randomly. If you put 20 monkeys in a room to take this test, assuming they answered once per question and behaved themselves, on average they would get 20-25% of the questions correct. Put 20 test takers in the room, and the average will be much lower among guessed questions. Why?
1. The test writers intentionally write deceptive answer choices that "look" right. A test

- 147 -

Copyright © Mometrix Media. You have been licensed one copy of this document for personal use only. Any other reproduction or redistribution is strictly prohibited. All rights reserved.

taker has no idea about a question, so he picks the "best looking" answer, which is often wrong. The monkey has no idea what looks good and what doesn't, so it will consistently be right about 20-25% of the time.

2. Test takers will eliminate answer choices from the guessing pool based on a hunch or intuition. Simple but correct answers often get excluded, leaving a 0% chance of being correct. The monkey has no clue, and often gets lucky with the best choice.

This is why the process of elimination endorsed by most test courses is flawed and detrimental to your performance. Test takers don't guess; they make an ignorant stab in the dark that is usually worse than random.

$5 Challenge

Let me introduce one of the most valuable ideas of this course—the $5 challenge:

You only mark your "best guess" if you are willing to bet $5 on it.
You only eliminate choices from guessing if you are willing to bet $5 on it.

Why $5? Five dollars is an amount of money that is small yet not insignificant, and can really add up fast (20 questions could cost you $100). Likewise, each answer choice on one question of the test will have a small impact on your overall score, but it can really add up to a lot of points in the end.

The process of elimination IS valuable. The following shows your chance of guessing it right:

If you eliminate wrong answer choices until only this many remain:	Chance of getting it correct:
1	100%
2	50%
3	33%

However, if you accidentally eliminate the right answer or go on a hunch for an incorrect answer, your chances drop dramatically—to 0%. By guessing among all the answer choices, you are GUARANTEED to have a shot at the right answer.

That's why the $5 test is so valuable. If you give up the advantage and safety of a pure guess, it had better be worth the risk.

What we still haven't covered is how to be sure that whatever guess you make is truly random. Here's the easiest way:

Always pick the first answer choice among those remaining.

Such a technique means that you have decided, **before you see a single test question**, exactly how you are going to guess, and since the order of choices tells you nothing about which one is correct, this guessing technique is perfectly random.

Copyright © Mometrix Media. You have been licensed one copy of this document for personal use only. Any other reproduction or redistribution is strictly prohibited. All rights reserved.

This section is not meant to scare you away from making educated guesses or eliminating choices; you just need to define when a choice is worth eliminating. The $5 test, along with a pre-defined random guessing strategy, is the best way to make sure you reap all of the benefits of guessing.

Secret Key #3 - Practice Smarter, Not Harder

Many test takers delay the test preparation process because they dread the awful amounts of practice time they think necessary to succeed on the test. We have refined an effective method that will take you only a fraction of the time.

There are a number of "obstacles" in the path to success. Among these are answering questions, finishing in time, and mastering test-taking strategies. All must be executed on the day of the test at peak performance, or your score will suffer. The test is a mental marathon that has a large impact on your future.

Just like a marathon runner, it is important to work your way up to the full challenge. So first you just worry about questions, and then time, and finally strategy:

Success Strategy

1. Find a good source for practice tests.
2. If you are willing to make a larger time investment, consider using more than one study guide. Often the different approaches of multiple authors will help you "get" difficult concepts.
3. Take a practice test with no time constraints, with all study helps, "open book." Take your time with questions and focus on applying strategies.
4. Take a practice test with time constraints, with all guides, "open book."
5. Take a final practice test without open material and with time limits.

If you have time to take more practice tests, just repeat step 5. By gradually exposing yourself to the full rigors of the test environment, you will condition your mind to the stress of test day and maximize your success.

Secret Key #4 - Prepare, Don't Procrastinate

Let me state an obvious fact: if you take the test three times, you will probably get three different scores. This is due to the way you feel on test day, the level of preparedness you have, and the version of the test you see. Despite the test writers' claims to the contrary, some versions of the test WILL be easier for you than others.

Since your future depends so much on your score, you should maximize your chances of success. In order to maximize the likelihood of success, you've got to prepare in advance.

Copyright © Mometrix Media. You have been licensed one copy of this document for personal use only. Any other reproduction or redistribution is strictly prohibited. All rights reserved.

This means taking practice tests and spending time learning the information and test taking strategies you will need to succeed.

Never go take the actual test as a "practice" test, expecting that you can just take it again if you need to. Take all the practice tests you can on your own, but when you go to take the official test, be prepared, be focused, and do your best the first time!

Secret Key #5 - Test Yourself

Everyone knows that time is money. There is no need to spend too much of your time or too little of your time preparing for the test. You should only spend as much of your precious time preparing as is necessary for you to get the score you need.

Once you have taken a practice test under real conditions of time constraints, then you will know if you are ready for the test or not.

If you have scored extremely high the first time that you take the practice test, then there is not much point in spending countless hours studying. You are already there.

Benchmark your abilities by retaking practice tests and seeing how much you have improved. Once you consistently score high enough to guarantee success, then you are ready.

If you have scored well below where you need, then knuckle down and begin studying in earnest. Check your improvement regularly through the use of practice tests under real conditions. Above all, don't worry, panic, or give up. The key is perseverance!

Then, when you go to take the test, remain confident and remember how well you did on the practice tests. If you can score high enough on a practice test, then you can do the same on the real thing.

General Strategies

The most important thing you can do is to ignore your fears and jump into the test immediately. Do not be overwhelmed by any strange-sounding terms. You have to jump into the test like jumping into a pool—all at once is the easiest way.

Make Predictions

As you read and understand the question, try to guess what the answer will be. Remember that several of the answer choices are wrong, and once you begin reading them, your mind will immediately become cluttered with answer choices designed to throw you off. Your mind is typically the most focused immediately after you have read the question and digested its contents. If you can, try to predict what the correct answer will be. You may be surprised at what you can predict.

Copyright © Mometrix Media. You have been licensed one copy of this document for personal use only. Any other reproduction or redistribution is strictly prohibited. All rights reserved.

Quickly scan the choices and see if your prediction is in the listed answer choices. If it is, then you can be quite confident that you have the right answer. It still won't hurt to check the other answer choices, but most of the time, you've got it!

Answer the Question

It may seem obvious to only pick answer choices that answer the question, but the test writers can create some excellent answer choices that are wrong. Don't pick an answer just because it sounds right, or you believe it to be true. It MUST answer the question. Once you've made your selection, always go back and check it against the question and make sure that you didn't misread the question and that the answer choice does answer the question posed.

Benchmark

After you read the first answer choice, decide if you think it sounds correct or not. If it doesn't, move on to the next answer choice. If it does, mentally mark that answer choice. This doesn't mean that you've definitely selected it as your answer choice, it just means that it's the best you've seen thus far. Go ahead and read the next choice. If the next choice is worse than the one you've already selected, keep going to the next answer choice. If the next choice is better than the choice you've already selected, mentally mark the new answer choice as your best guess.

The first answer choice that you select becomes your standard. Every other answer choice must be benchmarked against that standard. That choice is correct until proven otherwise by another answer choice beating it out. Once you've decided that no other answer choice seems as good, do one final check to ensure that your answer choice answers the question posed.

Valid Information

Don't discount any of the information provided in the question. Every piece of information may be necessary to determine the correct answer. None of the information in the question is there to throw you off (while the answer choices will certainly have information to throw you off). If two seemingly unrelated topics are discussed, don't ignore either. You can be confident there is a relationship, or it wouldn't be included in the question, and you are probably going to have to determine what is that relationship to find the answer.

Avoid "Fact Traps"

Don't get distracted by a choice that is factually true. Your search is for the answer that answers the question. Stay focused and don't fall for an answer that is true but irrelevant. Always go back to the question and make sure you're choosing an answer that actually answers the question and is not just a true statement. An answer can be factually correct, but it MUST answer the question asked. Additionally, two answers can both be seemingly correct, so be sure to read all of the answer choices, and make sure that you get the one that BEST answers the question.

Milk the Question

Some of the questions may throw you completely off. They might deal with a subject you have not been exposed to, or one that you haven't reviewed in years. While your lack of knowledge about the subject will be a hindrance, the question itself can give you many clues that will help you find the correct answer. Read the question carefully and look for clues. Watch particularly for adjectives and nouns describing difficult terms or words that you

Copyright © Mometrix Media. You have been licensed one copy of this document for personal use only. Any other reproduction or redistribution is strictly prohibited. All rights reserved.

don't recognize. Regardless of whether you completely understand a word or not, replacing it with a synonym, either provided or one you more familiar with, may help you to understand what the questions are asking. Rather than wracking your mind about specific detailed information concerning a difficult term or word, try to use mental substitutes that are easier to understand.

The Trap of Familiarity

Don't just choose a word because you recognize it. On difficult questions, you may not recognize a number of words in the answer choices. The test writers don't put "make-believe" words on the test, so don't think that just because you only recognize all the words in one answer choice that that answer choice must be correct. If you only recognize words in one answer choice, then focus on that one. Is it correct? Try your best to determine if it is correct. If it is, that's great. If not, eliminate it. Each word and answer choice you eliminate increases your chances of getting the question correct, even if you then have to guess among the unfamiliar choices.

Eliminate Answers

Eliminate choices as soon as you realize they are wrong. But be careful! Make sure you consider all of the possible answer choices. Just because one appears right, doesn't mean that the next one won't be even better! The test writers will usually put more than one good answer choice for every question, so read all of them. Don't worry if you are stuck between two that seem right. By getting down to just two remaining possible choices, your odds are now 50/50. Rather than wasting too much time, play the odds. You are guessing, but guessing wisely because you've been able to knock out some of the answer choices that you know are wrong. If you are eliminating choices and realize that the last answer choice you are left with is also obviously wrong, don't panic. Start over and consider each choice again. There may easily be something that you missed the first time and will realize on the second pass.

Tough Questions

If you are stumped on a problem or it appears too hard or too difficult, don't waste time. Move on! Remember though, if you can quickly check for obviously incorrect answer choices, your chances of guessing correctly are greatly improved. Before you completely give up, at least try to knock out a couple of possible answers. Eliminate what you can and then guess at the remaining answer choices before moving on.

Brainstorm

If you get stuck on a difficult question, spend a few seconds quickly brainstorming. Run through the complete list of possible answer choices. Look at each choice and ask yourself, "Could this answer the question satisfactorily?" Go through each answer choice and consider it independently of the others. By systematically going through all possibilities, you may find something that you would otherwise overlook. Remember though that when you get stuck, it's important to try to keep moving.

Read Carefully

Understand the problem. Read the question and answer choices carefully. Don't miss the question because you misread the terms. You have plenty of time to read each question thoroughly and make sure you understand what is being asked. Yet a happy medium must be attained, so don't waste too much time. You must read carefully, but efficiently.

Copyright © Mometrix Media. You have been licensed one copy of this document for personal use only. Any other reproduction or redistribution is strictly prohibited. All rights reserved.

Face Value

When in doubt, use common sense. Always accept the situation in the problem at face value. Don't read too much into it. These problems will not require you to make huge leaps of logic. The test writers aren't trying to throw you off with a cheap trick. If you have to go beyond creativity and make a leap of logic in order to have an answer choice answer the question, then you should look at the other answer choices. Don't overcomplicate the problem by creating theoretical relationships or explanations that will warp time or space. These are normal problems rooted in reality. It's just that the applicable relationship or explanation may not be readily apparent and you have to figure things out. Use your common sense to interpret anything that isn't clear.

Prefixes

If you're having trouble with a word in the question or answer choices, try dissecting it. Take advantage of every clue that the word might include. Prefixes and suffixes can be a huge help. Usually they allow you to determine a basic meaning. Pre- means before, post- means after, pro - is positive, de- is negative. From these prefixes and suffixes, you can get an idea of the general meaning of the word and try to put it into context. Beware though of any traps. Just because con- is the opposite of pro-, doesn't necessarily mean congress is the opposite of progress!

Hedge Phrases

Watch out for critical hedge phrases, led off with words such as "likely," "may," "can," "sometimes," "often," "almost," "mostly," "usually," "generally," "rarely," and "sometimes." Question writers insert these hedge phrases to cover every possibility. Often an answer choice will be wrong simply because it leaves no room for exception. Unless the situation calls for them, avoid answer choices that have definitive words like "exactly," and "always."

Switchback Words

Stay alert for "switchbacks." These are the words and phrases frequently used to alert you to shifts in thought. The most common switchback word is "but." Others include "although," "however," "nevertheless," "on the other hand," "even though," "while," "in spite of," "despite," and "regardless of."

New Information

Correct answer choices will rarely have completely new information included. Answer choices typically are straightforward reflections of the material asked about and will directly relate to the question. If a new piece of information is included in an answer choice that doesn't even seem to relate to the topic being asked about, then that answer choice is likely incorrect. All of the information needed to answer the question is usually provided for you in the question. You should not have to make guesses that are unsupported or choose answer choices that require unknown information that cannot be reasoned from what is given.

Time Management

On technical questions, don't get lost on the technical terms. Don't spend too much time on any one question. If you don't know what a term means, then odds are you aren't going to get much further since you don't have a dictionary. You should be able to immediately recognize whether or not you know a term. If you don't, work with the other clues that you have—the other answer choices and terms provided—but don't waste too much time trying

Copyright © Mometrix Media. You have been licensed one copy of this document for personal use only. Any other reproduction or redistribution is strictly prohibited. All rights reserved.

to figure out a difficult term that you don't know.

Contextual Clues

Look for contextual clues. An answer can be right but not the correct answer. The contextual clues will help you find the answer that is most right and is correct. Understand the context in which a phrase or statement is made. This will help you make important distinctions.

Don't Panic

Panicking will not answer any questions for you; therefore, it isn't helpful. When you first see the question, if your mind goes blank, take a deep breath. Force yourself to mechanically go through the steps of solving the problem using the strategies you've learned.

Pace Yourself

Don't get clock fever. It's easy to be overwhelmed when you're looking at a page full of questions, your mind is full of random thoughts and feeling confused, and the clock is ticking down faster than you would like. Calm down and maintain the pace that you have set for yourself. As long as you are on track by monitoring your pace, you are guaranteed to have enough time for yourself. When you get to the last few minutes of the test, it may seem like you won't have enough time left, but if you only have as many questions as you should have left at that point, then you're right on track!

Answer Selection

The best way to pick an answer choice is to eliminate all of those that are wrong, until only one is left and confirm that is the correct answer. Sometimes though, an answer choice may immediately look right. Be careful! Take a second to make sure that the other choices are not equally obvious. Don't make a hasty mistake. There are only two times that you should stop before checking other answers. First is when you are positive that the answer choice you have selected is correct. Second is when time is almost out and you have to make a quick guess!

Check Your Work

Since you will probably not know every term listed and the answer to every question, it is important that you get credit for the ones that you do know. Don't miss any questions through careless mistakes. If at all possible, try to take a second to look back over your answer selection and make sure you've selected the correct answer choice and haven't made a costly careless mistake (such as marking an answer choice that you didn't mean to mark). The time it takes for this quick double check should more than pay for itself in caught mistakes.

Beware of Directly Quoted Answers

Sometimes an answer choice will repeat word for word a portion of the question or reference section. However, beware of such exact duplication. It may be a trap! More than likely, the correct choice will paraphrase or summarize a point, rather than being exactly the same wording.

Copyright © Mometrix Media. You have been licensed one copy of this document for personal use only. Any other reproduction or redistribution is strictly prohibited. All rights reserved.

Slang

Scientific sounding answers are better than slang ones. An answer choice that begins "To compare the outcomes…" is much more likely to be correct than one that begins "Because some people insisted…"

Extreme Statements

Avoid wild answers that throw out highly controversial ideas that are proclaimed as established fact. An answer choice that states the "process should used in certain situations, if…" is much more likely to be correct than one that states the "process should be discontinued completely." The first is a calm rational statement and doesn't even make a definitive, uncompromising stance, using a hedge word "if" to provide wiggle room, whereas the second choice is a radical idea and far more extreme.

Answer Choice Families

When you have two or more answer choices that are direct opposites or parallels, one of them is usually the correct answer. For instance, if one answer choice states "x increases" and another answer choice states "x decreases" or "y increases," then those two or three answer choices are very similar in construction and fall into the same family of answer choices. A family of answer choices consists of two or three answer choices, very similar in construction, but often with directly opposite meanings. Usually the correct answer choice will be in that family of answer choices. The "odd man out" or answer choice that doesn't seem to fit the parallel construction of the other answer choices is more likely to be incorrect.

Copyright © Mometrix Media. You have been licensed one copy of this document for personal use only. Any other reproduction or redistribution is strictly prohibited. All rights reserved.

Special Report: How to Overcome Test Anxiety

The very nature of tests caters to some level of anxiety, nervousness, or tension, just as we feel for any important event that occurs in our lives. A little bit of anxiety or nervousness can be a good thing. It helps us with motivation, and makes achievement just that much sweeter. However, too much anxiety can be a problem, especially if it hinders our ability to function and perform.

"Test anxiety," is the term that refers to the emotional reactions that some test-takers experience when faced with a test or exam. Having a fear of testing and exams is based upon a rational fear, since the test-taker's performance can shape the course of an academic career. Nevertheless, experiencing excessive fear of examinations will only interfere with the test-taker's ability to perform and chance to be successful.

There are a large variety of causes that can contribute to the development and sensation of test anxiety. These include, but are not limited to, lack of preparation and worrying about issues surrounding the test.

Lack of Preparation

Lack of preparation can be identified by the following behaviors or situations:

Not scheduling enough time to study, and therefore cramming the night before the test or exam
Managing time poorly, to create the sensation that there is not enough time to do everything
Failing to organize the text information in advance, so that the study material consists of the entire text and not simply the pertinent information
Poor overall studying habits

Worrying, on the other hand, can be related to both the test taker, or many other factors around him/her that will be affected by the results of the test. These include worrying about:

Previous performances on similar exams, or exams in general
How friends and other students are achieving
The negative consequences that will result from a poor grade or failure

There are three primary elements to test anxiety. Physical components, which involve the same typical bodily reactions as those to acute anxiety (to be discussed below). Emotional factors have to do with fear or panic. Mental or cognitive issues concerning attention spans and memory abilities.

Copyright © Mometrix Media. You have been licensed one copy of this document for personal use only. Any other reproduction or redistribution is strictly prohibited. All rights reserved.

Physical Signals

There are many different symptoms of test anxiety, and these are not limited to mental and emotional strain. Frequently there are a range of physical signals that will let a test taker know that he/she is suffering from test anxiety. These bodily changes can include the following:

Perspiring
Sweaty palms
Wet, trembling hands
Nausea
Dry mouth
A knot in the stomach
Headache
Faintness
Muscle tension
Aching shoulders, back and neck
Rapid heart beat
Feeling too hot/cold

To recognize the sensation of test anxiety, a test-taker should monitor him/herself for the following sensations:

The physical distress symptoms as listed above
Emotional sensitivity, expressing emotional feelings such as the need to cry or laugh too much, or a sensation of anger or helplessness
A decreased ability to think, causing the test-taker to blank out or have racing thoughts that are hard to organize or control.

Though most students will feel some level of anxiety when faced with a test or exam, the majority can cope with that anxiety and maintain it at a manageable level. However, those who cannot are faced with a very real and very serious condition, which can and should be controlled for the immeasurable benefit of this sufferer.

Naturally, these sensations lead to negative results for the testing experience. The most common effects of test anxiety have to do with nervousness and mental blocking.

Nervousness

Nervousness can appear in several different levels:

The test-taker's difficulty, or even inability to read and understand the questions on the test
The difficulty or inability to organize thoughts to a coherent form
The difficulty or inability to recall key words and concepts relating to the testing questions (especially essays)
The receipt of poor grades on a test, though the test material was well known by the test taker

Copyright © Mometrix Media. You have been licensed one copy of this document for personal use only. Any other reproduction or redistribution is strictly prohibited. All rights reserved.

Conversely, a person may also experience mental blocking, which involves:

Blanking out on test questions
Only remembering the correct answers to the questions when the test has already finished.

Fortunately for test anxiety sufferers, beating these feelings, to a large degree, has to do with proper preparation. When a test taker has a feeling of preparedness, then anxiety will be dramatically lessened.

The first step to resolving anxiety issues is to distinguish which of the two types of anxiety are being suffered. If the anxiety is a direct result of a lack of preparation, this should be considered a normal reaction, and the anxiety level (as opposed to the test results) shouldn't be anything to worry about. However, if, when adequately prepared, the test-taker still panics, blanks out, or seems to overreact, this is not a fully rational reaction. While this can be considered normal too, there are many ways to combat and overcome these effects.

Remember that anxiety cannot be entirely eliminated, however, there are ways to minimize it, to make the anxiety easier to manage. Preparation is one of the best ways to minimize test anxiety. Therefore the following techniques are wise in order to best fight off any anxiety that may want to build.

To begin with, try to avoid cramming before a test, whenever it is possible. By trying to memorize an entire term's worth of information in one day, you'll be shocking your system, and not giving yourself a very good chance to absorb the information. This is an easy path to anxiety, so for those who suffer from test anxiety, cramming should not even be considered an option.

Instead of cramming, work throughout the semester to combine all of the material which is presented throughout the semester, and work on it gradually as the course goes by, making sure to master the main concepts first, leaving minor details for a week or so before the test.

To study for the upcoming exam, be sure to pose questions that may be on the examination, to gauge the ability to answer them by integrating the ideas from your texts, notes and lectures, as well as any supplementary readings.

If it is truly impossible to cover all of the information that was covered in that particular term, concentrate on the most important portions, that can be covered very well. Learn these concepts as best as possible, so that when the test comes, a goal can be made to use these concepts as presentations of your knowledge.

In addition to study habits, changes in attitude are critical to beating a struggle with test anxiety. In fact, an improvement of the perspective over the entire test-taking experience can actually help a test taker to enjoy studying and therefore improve the overall experience. Be certain not to overemphasize the significance of the grade - know that the result of the test is neither a reflection of self worth, nor is it a measure of intelligence; one grade will not predict a person's future success.

Copyright © Mometrix Media. You have been licensed one copy of this document for personal use only. Any other reproduction or redistribution is strictly prohibited. All rights reserved.

To improve an overall testing outlook, the following steps should be tried:

Keeping in mind that the most reasonable expectation for taking a test is to expect to try to demonstrate as much of what you know as you possibly can.
Reminding ourselves that a test is only one test; this is not the only one, and there will be others.
The thought of thinking of oneself in an irrational, all-or-nothing term should be avoided at all costs.
A reward should be designated for after the test, so there's something to look forward to. Whether it be going to a movie, going out to eat, or simply visiting friends, schedule it in advance, and do it no matter what result is expected on the exam.

Test-takers should also keep in mind that the basics are some of the most important things, even beyond anti-anxiety techniques and studying. Never neglect the basic social, emotional and biological needs, in order to try to absorb information. In order to best achieve, these three factors must be held as just as important as the studying itself.

Study Steps

Remember the following important steps for studying:

Maintain healthy nutrition and exercise habits. Continue both your recreational activities and social pass times. These both contribute to your physical and emotional well being.
Be certain to get a good amount of sleep, especially the night before the test, because when you're overtired you are not able to perform to the best of your best ability.
Keep the studying pace to a moderate level by taking breaks when they are needed, and varying the work whenever possible, to keep the mind fresh instead of getting bored.
When enough studying has been done that all the material that can be learned has been learned, and the test taker is prepared for the test, stop studying and do something relaxing such as listening to music, watching a movie, or taking a warm bubble bath.

There are also many other techniques to minimize the uneasiness or apprehension that is experienced along with test anxiety before, during, or even after the examination. In fact, there are a great deal of things that can be done to stop anxiety from interfering with lifestyle and performance. Again, remember that anxiety will not be eliminated entirely, and it shouldn't be. Otherwise that "up" feeling for exams would not exist, and most of us depend on that sensation to perform better than usual. However, this anxiety has to be at a level that is manageable.

Of course, as we have just discussed, being prepared for the exam is half the battle right away. Attending all classes, finding out what knowledge will be expected on the exam, and knowing the exam schedules are easy steps to lowering anxiety. Keeping up with work will remove the need to cram, and efficient study habits will eliminate wasted time. Studying should be done in an ideal location for concentration, so that it is simple to become interested in the material and give it complete attention. A method such as SQ3R (Survey, Question, Read, Recite, Review) is a wonderful key to follow to make sure that the study habits are as effective as possible, especially in the case of learning from a

Copyright © Mometrix Media. You have been licensed one copy of this document for personal use only. Any other reproduction or redistribution is strictly prohibited. All rights reserved.

textbook. Flashcards are great techniques for memorization. Learning to take good notes will mean that notes will be full of useful information, so that less sifting will need to be done to seek out what is pertinent for studying. Reviewing notes after class and then again on occasion will keep the information fresh in the mind. From notes that have been taken summary sheets and outlines can be made for simpler reviewing.

A study group can also be a very motivational and helpful place to study, as there will be a sharing of ideas, all of the minds can work together, to make sure that everyone understands, and the studying will be made more interesting because it will be a social occasion.

Basically, though, as long as the test-taker remains organized and self confident, with efficient study habits, less time will need to be spent studying, and higher grades will be achieved.

To become self confident, there are many useful steps. The first of these is "self talk." It has been shown through extensive research, that self-talk for students who suffer from test anxiety, should be well monitored, in order to make sure that it contributes to self confidence as opposed to sinking the student. Frequently the self talk of test-anxious students is negative or self-defeating, thinking that everyone else is smarter and faster, that they always mess up, and that if they don't do well, they'll fail the entire course. It is important to decreasing anxiety that awareness is made of self talk. Try writing any negative self thoughts and then disputing them with a positive statement instead. Begin self-encouragement as though it was a friend speaking. Repeat positive statements to help reprogram the mind to believing in successes instead of failures.

Helpful Techniques

Other extremely helpful techniques include:

Self-visualization of doing well and reaching goals
While aiming for an "A" level of understanding, don't try to "overprotect" by setting your expectations lower. This will only convince the mind to stop studying in order to meet the lower expectations.
Don't make comparisons with the results or habits of other students. These are individual factors, and different things work for different people, causing different results.
Strive to become an expert in learning what works well, and what can be done in order to improve. Consider collecting this data in a journal.
Create rewards for after studying instead of doing things before studying that will only turn into avoidance behaviors.
Make a practice of relaxing - by using methods such as progressive relaxation, self-hypnosis, guided imagery, etc - in order to make relaxation an automatic sensation.
Work on creating a state of relaxed concentration so that concentrating will take on the focus of the mind, so that none will be wasted on worrying.
Take good care of the physical self by eating well and getting enough sleep.
Plan in time for exercise and stick to this plan.

- 160 -

Copyright © Mometrix Media. You have been licensed one copy of this document for personal use only. Any other reproduction or redistribution is strictly prohibited. All rights reserved.

Beyond these techniques, there are other methods to be used before, during and after the test that will help the test-taker perform well in addition to overcoming anxiety.

Before the exam comes the academic preparation. This involves establishing a study schedule and beginning at least one week before the actual date of the test. By doing this, the anxiety of not having enough time to study for the test will be automatically eliminated. Moreover, this will make the studying a much more effective experience, ensuring that the learning will be an easier process. This relieves much undue pressure on the test-taker.

Summary sheets, note cards, and flash cards with the main concepts and examples of these main concepts should be prepared in advance of the actual studying time. A topic should never be eliminated from this process. By omitting a topic because it isn't expected to be on the test is only setting up the test-taker for anxiety should it actually appear on the exam. Utilize the course syllabus for laying out the topics that should be studied. Carefully go over the notes that were made in class, paying special attention to any of the issues that the professor took special care to emphasize while lecturing in class. In the textbooks, use the chapter review, or if possible, the chapter tests, to begin your review.

It may even be possible to ask the instructor what information will be covered on the exam, or what the format of the exam will be (for example, multiple choice, essay, free form, true-false). Additionally, see if it is possible to find out how many questions will be on the test. If a review sheet or sample test has been offered by the professor, make good use of it, above anything else, for the preparation for the test. Another great resource for getting to know the examination is reviewing tests from previous semesters. Use these tests to review, and aim to achieve a 100% score on each of the possible topics. With a few exceptions, the goal that you set for yourself is the highest one that you will reach.

Take all of the questions that were assigned as homework, and rework them to any other possible course material. The more problems reworked, the more skill and confidence will form as a result. When forming the solution to a problem, write out each of the steps. Don't simply do head work. By doing as many steps on paper as possible, much clarification and therefore confidence will be formed. Do this with as many homework problems as possible, before checking the answers. By checking the answer after each problem, a reinforcement will exist, that will not be on the exam. Study situations should be as exam-like as possible, to prime the test-taker's system for the experience. By waiting to check the answers at the end, a psychological advantage will be formed, to decrease the stress factor.

Another fantastic reason for not cramming is the avoidance of confusion in concepts, especially when it comes to mathematics. 8-10 hours of study will become one hundred percent more effective if it is spread out over a week or at least several days, instead of doing it all in one sitting. Recognize that the human brain requires time in order to assimilate new material, so frequent breaks and a span of study time over several days will be much more beneficial.

Additionally, don't study right up until the point of the exam. Studying should stop a minimum of one hour before the exam begins. This allows the brain to rest and put

Copyright © Mometrix Media. You have been licensed one copy of this document for personal use only. Any other reproduction or redistribution is strictly prohibited. All rights reserved.

things in their proper order. This will also provide the time to become as relaxed as possible when going into the examination room. The test-taker will also have time to eat well and eat sensibly. Know that the brain needs food as much as the rest of the body. With enough food and enough sleep, as well as a relaxed attitude, the body and the mind are primed for success.

Avoid any anxious classmates who are talking about the exam. These students only spread anxiety, and are not worth sharing the anxious sentimentalities.

Before the test also involves creating a positive attitude, so mental preparation should also be a point of concentration. There are many keys to creating a positive attitude. Should fears become rushing in, make a visualization of taking the exam, doing well, and seeing an A written on the paper. Write out a list of affirmations that will bring a feeling of confidence, such as "I am doing well in my English class," "I studied well and know my material," "I enjoy this class." Even if the affirmations aren't believed at first, it sends a positive message to the subconscious which will result in an alteration of the overall belief system, which is the system that creates reality.

If a sensation of panic begins, work with the fear and imagine the very worst! Work through the entire scenario of not passing the test, failing the entire course, and dropping out of school, followed by not getting a job, and pushing a shopping cart through the dark alley where you'll live. This will place things into perspective! Then, practice deep breathing and create a visualization of the opposite situation - achieving an "A" on the exam, passing the entire course, receiving the degree at a graduation ceremony.

On the day of the test, there are many things to be done to ensure the best results, as well as the most calm outlook. The following stages are suggested in order to maximize test-taking potential:

Begin the examination day with a moderate breakfast, and avoid any coffee or beverages with caffeine if the test taker is prone to jitters. Even people who are used to managing caffeine can feel jittery or light-headed when it is taken on a test day.
Attempt to do something that is relaxing before the examination begins. As last minute cramming clouds the mastering of overall concepts, it is better to use this time to create a calming outlook.
Be certain to arrive at the test location well in advance, in order to provide time to select a location that is away from doors, windows and other distractions, as well as giving enough time to relax before the test begins.
Keep away from anxiety generating classmates who will upset the sensation of stability and relaxation that is being attempted before the exam.
Should the waiting period before the exam begins cause anxiety, create a self-distraction by reading a light magazine or something else that is relaxing and simple.

During the exam itself, read the entire exam from beginning to end, and find out how much time should be allotted to each individual problem. Once writing the exam, should more time be taken for a problem, it should be abandoned, in order to begin another problem. If there is time at the end, the unfinished problem can always be returned to and completed.

Copyright © Mometrix Media. You have been licensed one copy of this document for personal use only. Any other reproduction or redistribution is strictly prohibited. All rights reserved.

Read the instructions very carefully - twice - so that unpleasant surprises won't follow during or after the exam has ended.

When writing the exam, pretend that the situation is actually simply the completion of homework within a library, or at home. This will assist in forming a relaxed atmosphere, and will allow the brain extra focus for the complex thinking function.

Begin the exam with all of the questions with which the most confidence is felt. This will build the confidence level regarding the entire exam and will begin a quality momentum. This will also create encouragement for trying the problems where uncertainty resides.

Going with the "gut instinct" is always the way to go when solving a problem. Second guessing should be avoided at all costs. Have confidence in the ability to do well.

For essay questions, create an outline in advance that will keep the mind organized and make certain that all of the points are remembered. For multiple choice, read every answer, even if the correct one has been spotted - a better one may exist.

Continue at a pace that is reasonable and not rushed, in order to be able to work carefully. Provide enough time to go over the answers at the end, to check for small errors that can be corrected.

Should a feeling of panic begin, breathe deeply, and think of the feeling of the body releasing sand through its pores. Visualize a calm, peaceful place, and include all of the sights, sounds and sensations of this image. Continue the deep breathing, and take a few minutes to continue this with closed eyes. When all is well again, return to the test.

If a "blanking" occurs for a certain question, skip it and move on to the next question. There will be time to return to the other question later. Get everything done that can be done, first, to guarantee all the grades that can be compiled, and to build all of the confidence possible. Then return to the weaker questions to build the marks from there.

Remember, one's own reality can be created, so as long as the belief is there, success will follow. And remember: anxiety can happen later, right now, there's an exam to be written!

After the examination is complete, whether there is a feeling for a good grade or a bad grade, don't dwell on the exam, and be certain to follow through on the reward that was promised...and enjoy it! Don't dwell on any mistakes that have been made, as there is nothing that can be done at this point anyway.

Additionally, don't begin to study for the next test right away. Do something relaxing for a while, and let the mind relax and prepare itself to begin absorbing information again.

From the results of the exam - both the grade and the entire experience, be certain to learn from what has gone on. Perfect studying habits and work some more on confidence in order to make the next examination experience even better than the last one.

Copyright © Mometrix Media. You have been licensed one copy of this document for personal use only. Any other reproduction or redistribution is strictly prohibited. All rights reserved.

Learn to avoid places where openings occurred for laziness, procrastination and day dreaming.

Use the time between this exam and the next one to better learn to relax, even learning to relax on cue, so that any anxiety can be controlled during the next exam. Learn how to relax the body. Slouch in your chair if that helps. Tighten and then relax all of the different muscle groups, one group at a time, beginning with the feet and then working all the way up to the neck and face. This will ultimately relax the muscles more than they were to begin with. Learn how to breathe deeply and comfortably, and focus on this breathing going in and out as a relaxing thought. With every exhale, repeat the word "relax."

As common as test anxiety is, it is very possible to overcome it. Make yourself one of the test-takers who overcome this frustrating hindrance.

Copyright © Mometrix Media. You have been licensed one copy of this document for personal use only. Any other reproduction or redistribution is strictly prohibited. All rights reserved.

Additional Bonus Material

Due to our efforts to try to keep this book to a manageable length, we've created a link that will give you access to all of your additional bonus material.

Please visit http://www.mometrix.com/bonus948/mtelenglish to access the information.

Copyright © Mometrix Media. You have been licensed one copy of this document for personal use only. Any other reproduction or redistribution is strictly prohibited. All rights reserved.